M000287670

Often, the most profound staten[...] response, probing the very core [...] renewed perspective in our lives. *Doing What Jesus Did* (DWJD) is a book that strikes within us a call to examine the essential values of our purpose and stirs a flame for the rededication of our lives to fill up with the magnificent character of Christ! Out of our renewed commitment to *Doing What Jesus Did*, I know that the world will receive a fresh dose of authentic love, as we willingly and consciously become living testimonies of Christ and His Kingdom. This wonderful book by John and Sonja Decker calls us to practice what we preach!

—GLENN C. BURRIS, JR.
PRESIDENT, THE FOURSQUARE CHURCH

Someone has well said, "If we have all Word and no Spirit, we dry up; if we have all Spirit and no Word, we flare up; but if we have both the Word and the Spirit, we grow up!" While I'm grateful for my upbringing in an evangelical tradition that highly valued the Word of God, that same tradition left me with unanswered questions about the place and the power of the Holy Spirit in today's Church. Gratefully, John and Sonja Decker have helped bridge the gap by providing a powerful tool that brings together the power of the Word and the Spirit. Today, at the church I lead, not only are we enjoying the study of what Jesus taught but we are learning to do what Jesus did (and I might add, regularly seeing tangible evidence of the Spirit's power in the process). DWJD has transformed our church and it can transform yours!

—CAL RYCHENER
NORTHWOODS COMMUNITY CHURCH

The church has been given a tremendous gift in the resource, *Doing What Jesus Did*. John and Sonja Decker not only provide Biblical understanding of what it means to do the works of Jesus today but also model it in their lives. They give themselves to mentoring and training thousands so that what they have written becomes praxis in the lives of Christians to make a difference in the world.

—TAMMY DUNAHOO
GENERAL SUPERVISOR, VICE PRESIDENT U.S. OPERATIONS
THE FOURSQUARE CHURCH

As the lead pastor of a local church who has been leveraging *Doing What Jesus Did* consistently for over 10 years, I do not know of a better, more thoughtful, New Testament-oriented book to equip those in my congregation for substantive ministry in our church and community. It gives practical guidelines for how to live in our world like Jesus would with purpose and power.

—STEVE MICKEL
LEAD PASTOR, WESTSIDE CHURCH
BEND, OREGON

Rarely have I read a book like this one—one that so ignited my passions in two ways: One, to love Jesus more deeply, and two, to minister His life, love, and power more dynamically. As you take it in hand, it may appear to be a handbook of principles of New Testament life, but it's actually more of a catapult to move forward in living it—that is, to live out that full-dimensioned *life* Christ came to multiply *through us*, not only bring to us!

—JACK W. HAYFORD
FORMER PRESIDENT, THE FOURSQUARE CHURCH
CHANCELLOR, THE KING'S COLLEGE AND SEMINARY
FOUNDING PASTOR, THE CHURCH ON THE WAY

Doing What Jesus Did is one of the most practical tools I have ever seen for equipping the saints. John and Sonja are anointed teachers who have shared their knowledge and insight with Christian leaders in city churches, rural congregations, and in meeting places in many foreign countries. Their wisdom is intensely practical and translates across all ethnic and social barriers. I highly recommend this book to men and women who want to base their ministry on a foundation that is scripturally solid and enduring.

—CLIFF HANES
FORMER VICE PRESIDENT
THE FOURSQUARE CHURCH
LOS ANGELES, CALIFORNIA

This is a great read! John and Sonja Decker understand what people need to know and understand about the kingdom of God to be ministering people who can serve in the life-flow of Jesus Christ. In my opinion, every leader in today's church needs to read this book.

—JIM HAYFORD SR.
PASTOR EMERITUS, EASTSIDE FOURSQUARE CHURCH
BOTHELL, WASHINGTON

What a treasure chest of practical guidelines and stories! Certainly twenty-first century Christianity is too much about theory and too little about practice. Theoretical, philosophical, doctrinal Christianity was meant to be a launching pad for powerful, personal, experiential Christianity. I hope every believer gets to discover for himself/herself the rich treasures in *Doing What Jesus Did*.

—KEN JOHNSON
SENIOR PASTOR, WESTSIDE CHURCH
BEND, OREGON

Doing What Jesus Did is a captivating book. It is biblical and balanced, simple and sound, informative and inspiring, practical and proven—an extremely valuable tool to equip the saints for the work of ministry in doing what Jesus did. John and Sonja Decker not only talk about "doing the stuff," they do it and show others how to do it—the works of Jesus, including miracles.

After more than thirty years of "doing the stuff" around the world, the Deckers are experienced practitioners and gifted trainers in leading others into supernatural ministry, both in the marketplace and the meeting place. They have discovered how to multiply ministry through the "training of trainers" who learn six essential and reproducible ministry strategies Jesus Himself modeled and taught His disciples—winning the lost, empowering for ministry, healing the sick, hearing God's voice, knowing the Spirit's leading, and casting out demons.

Doing What Jesus Did is the best way to communicate and demonstrate the gospel in all the world as a witness to all nations as we anticipate the end of this age and the return of our Savior in power and great glory.

—JOHN L. AMSTUTZ
MISSIONS TRAINER AND CONSULTANT
FOURSQUARE MISSIONS INTERNATIONAL, FRESNO, CALIFORNIA

This is certainly the most detailed, practical, how-to manual on spiritual warfare I have ever seen. It is well organized, and the use of ministry anecdotes to illustrate the scriptural principles is unique. The dispensational and traditional evangelical readers who reject the use of the charismatic gifts in the contemporary church will, of course, resist it. Written from the classical Pentecostal position, this book avoids the rigid formulas of the word of faith position while affirming the sovereignty of God as the Holy Spirit works. Emphasizing the role of spiritual discernment in the prophetic word, the Deckers show how the Christian can work in the power and leadership of the Spirit to lead others to minister through the spiritual gifts.

The manual maintains an Orthodox Trinitarian position and emphasizes that the ministry of and the baptism in the Holy Spirit are founded upon the incarnational and personal work of Christ in the atonement of the cross and Resurrection. While not all evangelicals will agree with this strong charismatic emphasis in ministry, it is clear that the present cultural situation in the world is so deeply involved in spiritual activity that the church needs to respond through spiritual means in order to be effective in evangelism and discipleship today. The Deckers have presented a thoughtful and practical training manual for preparing Christians for effective spiritual ministry.

—R. Larry Shelton, Th.D.
Richard B. Parker Professor of Theology
George Fox Evangelical Seminary
Portland, Oregon

DOING WHAT JESUS DID

DOING
WHAT
JESUS
DID

JOHN AND SONJA DECKER

CREATION
HOUSE

DOING WHAT JESUS DID by John and Sonja Decker
Published by Creation House
A Charisma Media Company
600 Rinehart Road
Lake Mary, Florida 32746
www.charismamedia.com

This book or parts thereof may not be reproduced in any form, stored in a retrieval system, or transmitted in any form by any means—electronic, mechanical, photocopy, recording, or otherwise—without prior written permission of the publisher, except as provided by United States of America copyright law.

Unless otherwise noted, all Scripture quotations are from the Holy Bible, New International Version. Copyright © 1973, 1978, 1984, International Bible Society. Used by permission.

Scripture quotations marked nkjv are from the New King James Version of the Bible. Copyright © 1979, 1980, 1982 by Thomas Nelson, Inc., publishers. Used by permission.

Scripture quotations marked NASB are from the New American Standard Bible. Copyright © 1960, 1962, 1963, 1968, 1971, 1972, 1973, 1975, 1977, 1995 by The Lockman Foundation. Used by permission.

Previously published by Christ's Ambassadors International, Bend, Oregon, copyright © 2003, 2005, ISBN 0-9728621-0-2.

Design Director: Justin Evans
Cover design by Nathan Morgan

Copyright © 2015 by Foursquare Media
All rights reserved.

Visit the author's website: www.ministrytraining.org

Library of Congress Cataloging-in-Publication Data: 2014956276
International Standard Book Number: 978-1-62998-414-8
E-book International Standard Book Number: 978-1-62998- 415-5

While the author has made every effort to provide accurate telephone numbers and Internet addresses at the time of publication, neither the publisher nor the author assumes any responsibility for errors or for changes that occur after publication.

First edition

15 16 17 18 19 — 987654321
Printed in Canada

ACKNOWLEDGMENTS

THANKS...

- To our gracious God who has called all Christians to be like His Son, Jesus Christ, and to do the things He did.

- To the International Church of the Foursquare Gospel, our wonderful church family where people are loved, accepted, and forgiven. We, with you, are contending for our supernatural heritage.

- To Pastor Jack Hayford, former president of the International Foursquare Churches and chancellor of The King's College and Seminary, who has personally inspired and encouraged us over the years.

- To Jim Hayford Sr., pastor emeritus of Eastside Foursquare Church, Bothell, Washington, who has been a loving pastor and wise counselor over the years.

- To Dr. John Amstutz, missions trainer and consultant, Foursquare Missions International, who encouraged us to write The Ambassador Series curriculum and this book. He took time to read every word of the manuscripts and to give us invaluable input.

- To R. Larry Shelton, Th.D., Richard B. Parker Professor of Theology, George Fox Evangelical Seminary, Portland, Oregon, who has assured us that our theology and conclusions are sound and has encouraged us along the way.

- To Greg and Karen Fry, our dear friends and co-laborers, who spent many hours of their busy schedules proofreading the manuscript and helping us laugh along the way. We treasure your friendship.

CONTENTS

PREFACE

THIS BOOK IS an invitation to all Christians to learn how to move into the supernatural realm in which Jesus said we could enter. It means learning six essential ministry strategies that Jesus prescribed for effective discipleship. He said we would have to do what He did to get the same results that He got. We invite believers worldwide to join an expanding army of courageous ministers who are daring to believe for miraculous results. We are encouraging Christians to learn how to accomplish a series of personal ministry strategies that will help usher in the final ingathering of souls and Jesus Christ's Second Coming. We will address the following six ministry skills:

- Leading people to Christ
- Leading Christians into the Holy Spirit baptism
- Learning how to heal the sick
- Hearing from God
- Healing the sick by revelation
- Dealing with demons

This book is intended to help Christians do what Jesus said they could do, including the miracles. We have framed our principles, insights, and recommendations around a large number of Scripture passages. After every Scripture reference, there are suggestions of how to put God's Word into practice. These are intended to help us do what Jesus wants us to do. The authors have italicized some words and phrases to emphasize key points that should be examined carefully.

> But be doers of the word, and not hearers only, deceiving your-
> selves. For if anyone is a hearer of the word and not a doer, he is
> like a man observing his natural face in a mirror; for he observes

himself, goes away, and immediately forgets what kind of man he was. But he who looks into the perfect law of liberty and continues in it, and is not a forgetful hearer but a doer of the work, this one will be blessed in what he does.

—JAMES 1:22–25, NKJV

The mission of all Christians should be to put into practice what Scripture tells them to do. This scripture says we will be blessed if we do what God's Word says. Our mission in this book is to encourage believers to not only hear the Word, but to do it.

—JOHN AND SONJA DECKER
BEND, OREGON

FOREWORD

RARELY HAVE I read a book like this one—one that so ignited my passions in two ways: One, to love Jesus more deeply, and two, to minister His life, love, and power more dynamically. As you take it in hand, it may appear to be a handbook of principles of New Testament life, but it's actually more of a catapult to move forward in living it—that is, to live out that full-dimensioned *life* Christ came to multiply *through us*, not only bring to us!

There are three things that make this book a must-read for anyone who takes God's love-gift in Christ seriously. It touches the *core*, the *heart*, and the *purpose* of the Savior's plan for His own—His plan to spread what *He* did through people He enables to do the same things. In short, here is a book targeting a replication of the reality of Jesus Christ in your own soul, through your own hands, and with your own voice. It's about the Word becoming flesh—not only in the Person of God's Son over twenty centuries ago, but in the daily life of His new-birthed sons and daughters in the twenty-first century.

At the *core*, the gospel is about *full salvation*—a saving power that begins with that gift of forgiveness and eternal life—an overflowing of saving power that was released through Jesus' death on the cross, which we unashamedly exalt (see Rom. 1:16). It's a power that transforms the personality, flows health into the human body, begets wholeness in the mind and emotions, and ignites a power to become everything any one of us were originally "meant to be." This power makes it possible to do what Jesus did (see John 14:12).

At the *heart* of the gospel is a river of love—a stream that finds its source in heaven and unleashes a torrent of the real stuff love is actually about—giving, serving, caring, supporting, uplifting, and abiding in a constancy of commitment to others. It's the love that not only was spoken from the cross, giving life and forgiveness, but the love that is "poured out...into our hearts by the Holy Spirit, whom he has given us" (Rom. 5:5). This love breathes into us the *compulsion* to do what Jesus did (2 Cor. 5:14).

Finally, the *purpose* in the gospel is that every person alive might know how great the almighty God is, how alive His Son Jesus Christ is, and how personal His dear Holy Spirit is. God wants us to *know* Him—not as an abstract or theological idea, but as a living, freeing, healing redeemer who is ready to meet us wherever we are and to answer whatever we need of His love and power. He does this through people He fills with Himself, giving them power to be "evidence for the case"—that is, witnesses who not only talk about Jesus, but who multiply what Jesus did!

At the bottom line, this is what discipleship is really about. It begins with God's Word, but it isn't completed until we learn how to do His Son's works. Welcome to a textbook for real disciples, and welcome to a meeting with two faith stimulators, John and Sonja Decker. They are trustworthy leaders, proven faithful servants, gifted teachers, and anointed communicators who make genuine, vibrant, Spirit-filled living so practical that you will find yourself wanting to do something about your love for Christ. That "something" is to do what He did in the daily affairs or your ordinary daily living; in the challenges of your complex circumstances; in the realities of your home, family, and workplace; and through the grace and power of the One who has come to live in you.

His name is Jesus. The two people who wrote this book are going to help you love Him more than ever as you discover His ability to enable you to represent Him in ways beyond which you've ever thought possible.

"Unto him that is able to do exceeding abundantly above all that we ask or think" (Eph. 3:20, KJV).

—JACK W. HAYFORD, FORMER PRESIDENT
INTERNATIONAL FOURSQUARE CHURCHES
CHANCELLOR, THE KING'S COLLEGE AND SEMINARY
FOUNDING PASTOR, THE CHURCH ON THE WAY

Introduction

WHO'S DOING IT?

NITIATING A CONVERSATION about Jesus to pre-Christians is intimidating for many Christians. They do not want to be rejected or embarrassed. It's easier to say, "Let the pastor do it. That's what we pay him for."

When we first led people to Christ, we experienced all the initial emotions of witnessing: fear of failure, stumbling over Scripture, and wishing we had better prepared our thoughts. But it is amazing how quickly the Holy Spirit took over. The conversations continued in a supernatural way. Afterward, joy and excitement flooded our hearts.

From those moments on, we were hooked on doing what Jesus did. The more we shared about the Lord and prayed for people, the more the Lord manifested Himself. We started praying for the sick, and God healed them! Our first attempts were pathetic. But we soon discovered that God could use amateurs who were willing to pray for people and see what God would do.

Many who read this book have never done these things because they lack confidence. That is the main reason we wrote this book. With some practical training, today's Christians can become effective witnesses for Christ. They are then prepared to fulfill their part of the Great Commission. It is our conviction that these last instructions given by Jesus Christ, recorded below, are for every person claiming to be His follower:

> Go therefore and make disciples of all the nations, baptizing them
> in the name of the Father and of the Son and of the Holy Spirit,
> teaching them to observe all things that I have commanded you;
> and lo, I am with you always, even to the end of the age.
> —MATTHEW 28:19–20, NKJV

As we enter the end of the age, all Christians have been commissioned to go and make disciples. After we have learned the things

Jesus commanded, we are to do them and teach others what we have learned. Many Christians believe that commissioning was just for the early apostles. However, we are part of the "disciples of all the nations." We are a part of "them" that have been discipled since Jesus gave this command. He sent out the first generation of disciples to make more disciples. This has been going on since the first century and has continued with little interruption.

More disciples have been made in the last 100 years than in the previous 1,900 years. As we prepare for the final harvest, every believer can fully participate and help usher in the Second Coming of Jesus Christ.

It continues to happen

Did Jesus truly intend for us to do the same things He did and get the same results? Various Bible passages support this claim: Matthew 10:1, 7–8; Luke 9:1–2, 6; and especially John 14:11–14.

> Believe me when I say that I am in the Father and the Father is in me; or at least believe on the evidence of *the miracles* themselves. I tell you the truth, anyone who has faith in me will do what I have been doing. He will do even greater things than these, because I am going to the Father. And I will do whatever you ask in my name, so that the Son may bring glory to the Father. You may ask me for anything in my name, and I will do it.
> —JOHN 14:11–14, EMPHASIS ADDED

Did Jesus really mean it? Is this promise for today? Some professors, teachers and pastors teach that this scripture applies to the early apostles and to a time long ago. But we believe that this promise is for all His disciples! And that includes us!

Go where it is happening

Participating in authentic demonstrations of the Holy Spirit's power is the best remedy for unbelief. The reason miracles are more evident in developing countries is simple: Christians there are more aware of the supernatural. Many have no other option than to believe for healing. John 14:11–14 is real to them and it comes to life when preached among them. They expect miracles whenever they hear the full gospel preached in their towns and villages.

Our doctor friend went to Thailand

Believers desperately need to be discipled and mentored in this type of ministry. At our Ministry Training Institutes (MTIs), we teach a series of ministry skills. After thorough teaching and extensive practicing of the skills, students are ready to minister wherever they go. The following chapters outline these six ministry skills.

One of our students, Dr. Carl Berner, a surgeon, asked to go with us on a trip to Thailand. He believed the accounts of the miraculous healings and of people being set free from demonic spirits, but he had never seen it firsthand. Dr. Berner and his wife, a surgical nurse, accompanied us, and they saw miraculous healings happen through their own hands.

The demon manifested

At a healing meeting in Chiang Mai, Dr. Berner pleaded with John to go see what was happening to a woman on the other side of the room. The woman was on the floor and in full demonic manifestation. John, of course, knew that only by the Holy Spirit's revelation gift of discerning of spirits.

Dr. Berner told John that the woman's two caregivers had brought her forward for prayer for her bad heart. When the team began to pray for her, the woman collapsed and seemed unconscious. Her caregivers thought she was having a heart attack. Dr. Berner immediately took her pulse and found it was steady and strong. From what he had learned in class, he suspected it was a demonic spirit, and that was why he asked John to assess the situation.

She had a grotesque look on her face

This woman's deliverance was like many others we have seen. John had the caregivers help the woman stand. Her eyes were rolling around, and she could not focus. She had a grotesque look on her face and was moaning. John followed Jesus' example as recorded in the Gospels and addressed the evil demonic spirit: "You spirit of infirmity, I command you to come out of this woman in the name of Jesus!" The spirit was expelled, and the woman literally came to herself and had a beautiful smile on her face. She was set free and healed. Dr. Berner had witnessed a spiritual deliverance up close and personal.

We must experience it

Jesus Himself gave the authority by which we do these things. His promise was to all who have faith in Him (John 14:12). That includes every Christian. There is no higher name or authority in the universe than the name of the Lord Jesus Christ, and whatever we ask in His name will be done. He said He would place His stamp of authority on those things we do for the benefit of others when we do them in His name. We want believers to experience the life-changing presence of God working through them as they do what Jesus did.

THE MAIN PREMISE OF THIS BOOK

Jesus came to Earth as a man

We know that Adam and Eve and all mankind were stripped of the authority they originally had because of willful disobedience. Satan became the god of this world. However, God's plan of redemption was that His Son, Jesus Christ, would come to Earth and be born of a virgin. Jesus was God in the flesh. Jesus, the last Adam, was all God and all man.

> So it is written: "The first man Adam became a living being"; *the last Adam*, a life-giving spirit.
> —1 CORINTHIANS 15:45, EMPHASIS ADDED

> For what the law was powerless to do in that it was weakened by the sinful nature, God did by sending his own Son *in the likeness of sinful man* to be a sin offering.
> —ROMANS 8:3, EMPHASIS ADDED

> For we do not have a high priest who is unable to sympathize with our weaknesses, but we have one *who has been tempted in every way*, just as we are—yet was without sin.
> —HEBREWS 4:15, EMPHASIS ADDED

> Your attitude should be the same as that of Christ Jesus: Who, being in very nature God, did not consider equality with God something to be grasped, but made himself nothing, taking the very nature of a servant, *being made in human likeness. And*

being found in appearance as a man, he humbled himself and became obedient to death—even death on a cross!

—PHILIPPIANS 2:5–8, EMPHASIS ADDED

Jesus did everything on Earth as a man filled with the mighty power of the Holy Spirit. Therefore, those who follow Him and are filled with the same Holy Spirit, are able to do what He did. In human terms, He is our perfect human example, the Author and Perfecter of our faith.

Jesus did everything as a man

There are no recorded miracles in the first 30 years of Jesus' life. He began ministry after He was baptized in the Holy Spirit, and He did everything as a man filled with the Holy Spirit. He ministered on Earth as God had created the first Adam to do. Only by being human could He become our Savior. He had to defeat Satan as a man obeying the Father in heaven by relying upon the power of the Holy Spirit. Thus, He took back the authority that Satan stole from the first Adam.

Jesus delegated His authority to believers

Jesus died, was resurrected to eternal life, and was exalted into heaven, thus completing the plan of redemption. He told His followers to go into all the world. He said we could now do what He did because His authority has been given to us, and He is with us. He told us to use His name and do what He did.

> Then Jesus came to them and said, "All authority in heaven and on earth has been given to me. Therefore go and make disciples of all nations, baptizing them in the name of the Father and of the Son and of the Holy Spirit, and teaching them to obey everything I have commanded you. And surely I am with you always, to the very end of the age."
>
> —MATTHEW 28:18–20

And God placed all things under his feet and appointed him to
be head over everything for the church, which is his body, the
fullness of him who fills everything in every way.

                                        —EPHESIANS 1:22–23

Now it is up to us, the church

Ephesians chapter 1 says that Jesus did everything for the benefit of
His body, the church. The church is to fulfill the Great Commission
by doing the same things Jesus did. He empowered us with the Holy
Spirit so that we can go into the entire world and make disciples by
doing the same things He did. The balance of this book illustrates a
series of ministry skills needed to help facilitate and fulfill the Great
Commission.

How did Jesus do it?

Before we go any further, we want to establish how Jesus ministered
to people:

Then Jesus answered and said to them, "Most assuredly, I say
to you, the Son can do nothing of Himself, but what He sees
the Father do; for whatever He does, the Son also does in like
manner. For the Father loves the Son, and shows Him all things
that He Himself does; and He will show Him greater works than
these, that you may marvel."

                                        —JOHN 5:19–20, NKJV

When we learn how to hear from God by
seeing what He wants done, we will be operating in the miraculous realm, similar to how
Jesus did. We are convinced that Jesus accomplished a perfect ministry of healing and
setting people free because He did everything by revelation.

John 5:19–20 states that Jesus only did what He saw the Father
doing. That is how Jesus operated perfectly in all that He did during
His earthly ministry. He did everything as the Father directed, and
that is how believers today must minister to people.

What did Jesus see?

The word *sees* (*blepo*) in verse 19, is a very common but extremely important word the Gospel writer used to convey a continuous or repeated action in which Jesus engaged Himself with the Father. John was an eyewitness of how Jesus interacted with the Father on a daily basis. He also witnessed the results of this perfect kind of obedience.

All the words that He preached about the kingdom, all the healings, all the actions, and all the miracles resulted from Jesus' seeing and hearing from the Father. Jesus never acted independently apart from the Father's will and purpose. The Book of John emphasizes that Jesus Christ's work was to do the will of the Father—not as a slave, but as a Son. He was totally obedient to the divine purposes of the Father's complete revelation and will for mankind.

The total mandate and will of the Father was present in Christ from the beginning of time. John 5:19–20 strongly suggests that the will of the Father was implemented on a moment-by-moment basis through Jesus Christ. His words and actions were for the direct benefit of His followers to remember and record. As the Father revealed what He desired, Jesus obeyed. His actions, words, and deeds were in direct response to the Father's revelation.

Can we see the same things?

Jesus is the Author and Finisher of our faith. When our faith is based on the promises from His Word and coupled with divine revelation from the Holy Spirit, we begin to function just like Jesus did. Jesus Christ modeled the use of the word of wisdom, word of knowledge, and discerning of spirits. The Father continuously revealed to Jesus what He wanted to accomplish; as Jesus saw what the Father wanted, He obeyed.

Jesus Christ showed His followers how to operate in the three gifts of revelation that Paul discussed in 1 Corinthians:

> But the manifestation of the Spirit is given to each one for the profit of all: for to one is given the word of wisdom through the Spirit, to another the word of knowledge through the same Spirit, to another faith by the same Spirit, to another gifts of healings by the same Spirit, to another the working of miracles, to another prophecy, to another discerning of spirits, to another different

kinds of tongues, to another the interpretation of tongues. But one and the same Spirit works all these things, distributing to each one individually as He wills.

—1 CORINTHIANS 12:7–11, NKJV

The revelations of the Holy Spirit came in the form of words of wisdom, knowledge, and the discerning of spirits. Since we have the same gifts with us today, it is safe to say that we can see the same kinds of things that Jesus saw with the Father. There will be no new revelations concerning the plan of salvation, redemption, kingdom principles, or the written Word. But the Holy Spirit will reveal a host of specifics to us when we submit to His leadership and obey Him. To be effective in today's marketplace, we must learn to minister in love, relying on the prompting and revelation of the Holy Spirit. Then we will be doing ministry just like Jesus did!

Doing what Jesus did requires that we learn to obey what the Holy Spirit reveals. We must learn to hear God's voice, and we must learn to obey what He is revealing. A thorough discussion of operating by revelation knowledge will be given in chapters 5 and 6. God has a plan and purpose for every single believer. That plan is revealed in the Word of God and accentuated by occasional words directly from the Holy Spirit.

THE FOUNDATION FOR DOING WHAT JESUS DID

The key that produces supernatural ministry

Using John 14:11–14, we will base our approach to ministry squarely on what Jesus said we could and should do. He said we could do what He did. He did not give us any specifics other than His reference to miracles. And He said we can do the same. When we couple John 5:19–20 with John 14:11–14, we begin to grasp how this can be accomplished.

> Believe me when I say that I am in the Father and the Father is in me; or at least believe on the evidence of the miracles themselves.
>
> —JOHN 14:11

> For us to do what Jesus did requires that we
> believe and act on the promise that we can
> do what He did. If He said we could, then
> we can! This obviously involves a process
> of learning how to minister like Jesus did
> with reliance on the Holy Spirit and what He
> reveals.

The things Jesus said we can do

If we dare to believe we can do the same works Jesus did, then let's take a look at some of the things He did. It seems that He clearly wanted His followers to function in a series of ministry skills until His return. These ministry skills function for the benefit of anyone coming to the Lord for help, including pre-Christians. When we function in healing and setting people free, this boldly demonstrates that Jesus Christ is Lord and is very much alive. This creates a prime opportunity for winning the lost to Him.

> He called his twelve disciples to him and gave them authority to drive out evil spirits and to heal every disease and sickness…As you go, preach this message: "The kingdom of heaven is near." Heal the sick, raise the dead, cleanse those who have leprosy, drive out demons. Freely you have received, freely give.
> —MATTHEW 10:1, 7–8

> When you enter a town and are welcomed, eat what is set before you. Heal the sick who are there and tell them, "The kingdom of God is near you."…I have given you authority to trample on snakes and scorpions and to overcome all the power of the enemy; nothing will harm you. However, do not rejoice that the spirits submit to you, but rejoice that your names are written in heaven.
> —LUKE 10:8–9, 19–20

> Then Jesus came to them and said, "All authority in heaven and on earth has been given to me. Therefore go and make disciples of all nations, baptizing them in the name of the Father and of the Son and of the Holy Spirit, and teaching them to obey

everything I have commanded you. And surely I am with you always, to the very end of the age."

—MATTHEW 28:18–20

On one occasion, while he was eating with them, he gave them this command: "Do not leave Jerusalem, but wait for the gift my Father promised, which you have heard me speak about. For John baptized with water, but in a few days you will be baptized with the Holy Spirit…But you will receive power when the Holy Spirit comes on you; and you will be my witnesses in Jerusalem, and in all Judea and Samaria, and to the ends of the earth."

—ACTS 1:4–5, 8

The preceding scriptures are powerful promises. They include many of the things Jesus did and promised that we could do also.

Here is a list of things Jesus said we can do:

- Drive out evil spirits.
- Heal every disease and sickness.
- Preach the full gospel of the kingdom.
- Raise the dead.
- Cleanse those who have leprosy.
- Command spirits to submit to us.
- Make disciples of all nations.
- Teach new disciples to obey everything Jesus commanded.
- Be baptized with the Holy Spirit.
- Receive the power of the Holy Spirit.
- Be His witness to the ends of the Earth.

Can we do all of these things?

Yes! Jesus meant what He said. We may not accomplish the entire list; we may only experience a few of these things. We need to pay whatever price there is and start wherever we are. It may take some time, training, and a change of attitude, but it will be worth it. That is what this book is all about. We will focus on six things Jesus said we should do. We will call them "ministry skills." They are as follows:

- Leading people to Christ
- Leading Christians into the Holy Spirit baptism
- Learning how to heal the sick
- Hearing from God
- Healing the sick by revelation
- Dealing with demons

The first step—salvation

We begin our strategies for the harvest in chapter 1 by discussing how to lead people to Christ. This is the first and most important mandate from our Lord Jesus Christ. He said, "Go and make disciples" (Matt. 28:19).

Leading people into salvation through the sacrificial blood of Jesus Christ cannot be understood with the rational mind. It can only be understood and experienced through the supernatural work of the Holy Spirit. The following is an attempt to explain the mystery of salvation through Jesus Christ.

When we confess our sins (true repentance) and accept the Lord Jesus Christ into our lives, a mystical and spiritual impartation takes place (Luke 13:5). The term "born again" best describes this event (John 3:3). Our spirits are touched, quickened by the Holy Spirit of God, and we receive God's life into our being. We are translated from the kingdom of darkness into His glorious kingdom of light (Col. 1:13). Then we begin to understand what the Bible says. We begin to receive revelation about spiritual realities.

By faith we are brought mysteriously into relationship with the triune Godhead. We are describing the interpersonal relationship with Jesus Christ as Savior, our heavenly Father, and His Holy Spirit. It is our relationship with Christ that forms the basis for our salvation. God's Word tells us there is no other name whereby we are saved (Acts 4:12), and that no one can come to the Father except through Him (John 14:6). This relationship is the basis for all spiritual growth.

By responding to God's offer of the gift of salvation, we enter into a covenant relationship with Him. This new covenant was sealed with His own blood and body, in contrast to the old covenant that was sealed with the blood of animals. It is this tangible interpersonal relationship of Jesus Christ in us, the hope of glory, that fuels our convictions and our desire to obey God's commands. It is the living presence of the Holy Spirit within and upon us that permeates our thoughts and influences our daily actions.

LET'S PRACTICE

James 1:22 says to do what we have heard (read).

Consider doing what is recommended in this chapter by referring to the "Let's Practice" in Appendix B, page 251.

Do the ministry skill assignment titled, "Share What You Believe About Miracles."

LEADING PEOPLE TO CHRIST

In this chapter you will learn how to share your faith in a natural way by simply telling a thoughtful story of how you accepted Jesus Christ as your Savior and the change He has made in your life.

ANY OF US remember when we first became Christians. We wanted to tell everyone what happened to us. We were so excited that we did not care if we were politically correct. All we could talk about was God. We allowed the Holy Spirit freedom to use us as witnesses. The Lord placed a new urgency in our hearts to proclaim what God was doing. We were free of condemnation and guilt. We had been forgiven. We were on our way to heaven. It was all so wonderful we had to tell somebody! Ministry Skill One was already manifesting without our even thinking about it. We were obeying the "go" commanded in Matthew 28 because we had become the "new creation" described in 2 Corinthians 5.

> Then Jesus came to them and said, "All authority in heaven and on earth has been given to me. Therefore *go and make disciples* of all nations, baptizing them in the name of the Father and of the Son and of the Holy Spirit, and teaching them to obey everything I have commanded you. And surely I am with you always, to the very end of the age."
> —MATTHEW 28:18–20, EMPHASIS ADDED

> Therefore, if anyone is in Christ, *he is a new creation;* the old has gone, the new has come! All this is from God, who reconciled us to himself through Christ and gave us the ministry of reconciliation: that God was reconciling the world to himself in Christ, not counting men's sins against them. And he has committed to us the message of reconciliation. We are therefore Christ's

ambassadors, as though God were making his appeal through us. We implore you on Christ's behalf: Be reconciled to God.

—2 CORINTHIANS 5:17–20, EMPHASIS ADDED

Jesus meant for His followers to reach out and make disciples wherever they could. All Christians have been given a ministry—reconciling their families, friends, and neighbors to Christ. We have been commissioned as ambassadors of reconciliation.

Every Christian is commissioned

Every Christian has been commissioned to participate in the Great Commission as a witness for Christ. The part each of us plays depends on how God has gifted us. We are all gifted differently. A small percentage of Christians has a strong gift and desire for evangelism. The balance of the body of Christ does not. But, this does not excuse any believer from becoming an effective witness. Jesus commissioned every one of His followers to go and make disciples. This means they must find a way to participate in the ministry of reconciliation. We must not ignore our responsibility to fulfill what God has given every believer to do.

Just tell what happened to you

The first lesson of our six-volume curriculum, The Ambassador Series, encourages student ministers to learn to lead others into salvation. We devote six to twelve weeks to enable each person to master a personal testimony that can be used to accomplish this first and most basic ministry skill. With a little encouragement and a few guidelines, any willing disciple will be ready to respond to those who ask why we do what we do.

But in your hearts set apart Christ as Lord. Always be prepared to give an answer to everyone who asks you to give the reason for the hope that you have. But do this with gentleness and respect.

—1 PETER 3:15

- When anyone asks us to give the reason for the hope we have in Christ, we must have a ready response.
- Our response should include a personal testimony of what Christ has done to give us this glorious hope.
- We should know how to end our witness with questions that will lead someone into salvation through Jesus Christ.

How the world will be evangelized

True evangelism that produces lasting disciples is done on a one-on-one basis. That means that Christians must be trained to share their faith with pre-Christians and lead them into a personal encounter with the living Christ. They must learn to include the new converts in their church activities. They will need to go to new believers classes offered for new people (if there is one) and invite them to their home groups. In other words, they must accept some personal responsibility for seeing that new believers are assimilated into the life of the church.

Not too long ago, a woman in our church came to me (Sonja) before church. She works with women who come out of jails and prisons, and she asked me to pray that the woman she had brought to church would accept the Lord. The woman was living a lesbian lifestyle. We are part of a church that is so committed to the lost that we can feel safe to invite people who are not only lost but also negatively predisposed toward Christians. That particular day, our pastor was talking about how our church should not be a social hall for Christians, but a rescue station for the lost and hurting; he stated that we must treat them with the love and respect they deserve.

I saw my friend the next Wednesday, and she said her guest had loved the church and the message and was joining a Bible study. Not too long after that, the woman gave her heart to the Lord and gave up her lesbian lifestyle.

That is how the world will be won. People must realize they have a responsibility to share the Good News with others, and they must be committed to helping others become fully-devoted disciples who will also reach others.

When we speak in churches on marketplace ministry, I (Sonja) often ask the congregation what would happen if each one led just one person to Christ and helped that person get plugged into the church during the coming year. The obvious answer, of course, is that the church would double in size. And if we discipled our new people to do the same, we would double again the following year. How simple!

WHY ARE WE NOT DOING IT?

We will not take time to review the 100 reasons most churches in the West are not involved in effective evangelism. They just are not. Does this mean it is OK to ignore Christ's command to go and make new disciples? We think not. Most pastors will tell you they have a desire to see evangelism take place in their churches. But they are searching for ways to incorporate it into the weekly routine of services. We want to salute those pastors who are still brave enough to end their messages by inviting people to receive Jesus Christ as their Savior.

Could it be we need a new paradigm? It would be nice if the majority of those who call themselves Christian had the knowledge and confidence to witness for Christ and could lead their friends and neighbors to Him. What a radical concept. According to 2 Peter, the Lord is patiently waiting for us to lead others to repentance.

> The Lord is not slow in keeping his promise, as some understand slowness. He is patient with you, not wanting anyone to perish, but everyone to come to repentance.
> —2 PETER 3:9

- Since the Lord wants everyone to come to repentance, we should have a personal plan in mind to respond to those who ask us about our faith in Christ.
- Everyone we meet is a candidate to become a Christian. People need someone who will share the Good News with them.
- If every Christian were prepared to give a marketplace testimony with an invitation to receive Christ, the world could be won to Christ in a short period of time.

The most introverted person in the class

We were doing a workshop in California for a large group of pastors and leaders. One of the men was an extreme introvert. When he found out he would have to give a five-to-seven-minute marketplace testimony in front of the class, his face turned ashen! He told us he just could not do the practicum assignment. He had never been able to do such a thing, and he was not about to start now. We told him we could understand his anxiety, but that it would be good for him. He could tell we were not about to make an exception. He then asked if he could be the last person to share. We did agree to that.

When it came his time to share with the class, he was literally shaking with fright. With the carefully-written-out testimony in his hands, he began to speak. We were sure he was planning to read it, but a wonderful thing happened. When he opened his mouth and spoke just a few words, the anointing of the Holy Spirit came upon him, and he was powerful! Those who knew him were amazed. When he finished, the class erupted in thunderous applause. His story of how he came to Christ was exciting and interesting. He even closed his testimony with the all-important invitation: "Now that is how I came to know Jesus Christ as my Savior. Would you like to have Him forgive all your sins, give you a clear conscience, and come into your life?" We all responded with a resounding "Yes!"

The Holy Spirit tapped him on the shoulder

This story does not end there. The man went to work on Monday, and encountered a fellow employee who was having a rough time and for whom he had been praying. The coworker said that things had gotten so bad over the weekend that he had even picked up a Bible and begun reading it. The man stated, "It was as if the Holy Spirit tapped me on the shoulder and said 'That's your cue.' I shared my testimony that I had written out, practiced, and timed for hours before I gave it in class. I asked him the question, and guess what? He said yes, and I led him in the sinner's prayer I have heard a hundred times at church. Can you believe it? I led someone to the Lord! I would never, never have believed I could do such a thing! Thank you! Thank you! Thank you for making me take that step of faith. I will never be the same!"

It happened to me

I (John) vividly remember the events of early 1973. If the Campus Crusade for Christ leaders had not given witnessing tools to an engineering student named Dave, this book would not have been written. I might still be lost in my sin, unforgiven, and on my way to hell.

Nineteen-year-old Dave was quiet and somewhat reserved. His parents attended the same church I did. He presented a booklet to me entitled, "The Four Spiritual Laws." My church did not preach that you must be born again, but, the booklet said you must. Dave presented me with the same booklet every other Sunday. Confused and quite irritated, I told him I did not appreciate his approach and to take his religion somewhere else. Each week Dave would smile, say hello, and, with booklet in hand, he would ask if I had any questions about what it said. Finally, to get him to go away, I consented to listen to a tape he gave me.

For the first time in my life, I heard the rest of the gospel. God not only loved me but He also had a plan for my life. If I allowed Jesus Christ to forgive me of my sin and asked Him to take control of my life, He would show me the plans that God had for me and would give me eternal life. All this from a thirty-minute cassette tape by a minister named Josh McDowell. The Holy Spirit was drawing me to Christ.

> No one can come to Me unless the Father who sent Me draws him; and I will raise him up on the last day.
> —John 6:44, nasb

- The Father uses Christians to spread the gospel in ways that draw the lost to Him.
- Your testimony, a tract, or a CD can be used to "preach" the gospel to those who do not know Christ.
- Faith to receive Christ comes by hearing the Word.

It happened in my living room

The churches in my city launched a region-wide outreach program called "Key '73." Our church responded by arranging a series of home gatherings. I offered my home for one of the Sunday nights. Dave and some of his friends showed up and began talking about how great it was to have a personal relationship with God and how He was directing their lives. They even talked about how they were absolutely sure where they would spend eternity. At the end of the evening they began to take prayer requests. When they asked me if they could pray for any of my concerns, I nervously indicated that I needed a few weeks to think over this "God stuff."

They prayed out loud

Dave and his friends prayed things such as, "Thank You, Jesus, for being right here. Thank You, God, for seeing into John's heart. You know everything he is thinking right now. Help him to accept You as his Lord and Savior." All the prayers were soft, personal, and non-condemning.

When it was my turn to pray, all I could do was cry. I said, "God, I quit. I'm so sorry. I didn't believe You arose from the dead. But, You did. You are alive. Take my life. Do what You have to do to me. Amen." I wept from way down deep inside me. I could not stop crying. Dave and everyone else came over and hugged me and welcomed me into the kingdom. They said that I had just been born again.

Dave had led me to Christ. The Holy Spirit had used him to introduce me to Christ in a way that made me want to accept Him as my personal Lord and Savior. That is called effective marketplace witnessing.

IT NEEDS TO BE SIMPLE

The gospel is simple. We make it hard, but Jesus' messages were very simple. He used language that everyone knew. The Holy Spirit revealed the true message behind His stories. Only those to whom God gave understanding knew what He was saying. Religious people did not. The hardest people to witness to today are those who think they know God but do not have a personal relationship with Him. The best strategy is to keep the process simple. It should be so simple that any believer can quickly learn how to become an effective witness. God does not need argumentative, self-styled theologians. He wants ordinary believers who can give personal testimonies that touch the hearts of their friends and coworkers.

Tell it like it is

A short, personal testimony of what God has done for you speaks more clearly than ten Bible verses fired off in rapid succession. Pre-Christians do not want to hear a sanctimonious correction from your wealth of scriptural knowledge. They want to hear about how God repaired your relationship with your spouse. Or how He helped you rise above dysfunction and led you into wholeness. They want to hear how God healed you from an incurable disease. They want to hear how God works in a personal way. They will listen to things they can relate to and understand.

Dave only used one scripture when he first began talking to me. I will never forget it. He used John 14:6 by saying, "John, I found out that there is only one sure way to God. I used to believe there were many ways to God. I found out that Jesus is the only true way to God."

> Jesus answered, "I am the way and the truth and the life. No one comes to the Father except through me."
> —John 14:6

Using this scripture mixed into your testimony is a powerful way to proclaim an eternal truth that will lead others to Christ.

Then Dave said, "John, I had to go through Jesus to get to the Father! That sure made it simple when I discovered that." Then he would let me think about it. I was always nervous when he brought up the subject of a personal God. But, he always calmed my fears by personalizing the gospel to his own life. He used his testimony to preach the gospel to me. Dave did not think he was preaching; he was just telling me what happened to him.

The best preaching is your own story

The best way to preach is to tell the story of how you came to know Jesus Christ. Most people will listen to you, even family members. They already know you are peculiar. They want to know how you got that way. The trick is to know *when* to tell them. The Holy Spirit operates best when we share with sincerity and a loving attitude. We believe God will provide multiple opportunities for witnessing if we pray for them. The best way to get over embarrassment or fear is to ask the Holy Spirit to provide opportunities for sharing. Then, when He does, we can be confident that, since He started it, He will help us finish it. He is always there to help us say the right things.

Marketplace believers are ministers

Marketplace believers are equipped to share the Good News of the Lord Jesus Christ whenever there is an opportunity. We all have different "marketplaces"—where we work, where we shop, our neighborhoods. When we share anything about God, we are ministering. Since the Bible does not make a distinction between clergy and laymen, that makes all Christians ministers. In this book we will use marketplace believers and marketplace ministers interchangeably.

Jesus was the consummate marketplace minister. As always, He is our perfect example. Jesus was out and about—walking from one place to another. When He encountered a funeral procession of a widow's only son, His heart went out to her, and He raised her son from the dead (see Luke 7:11–17).

Matthew 8 and 9 tell us that Jesus healed a man with leprosy, healed the centurion's servant, set demon-possessed men free, healed a paralytic, gave life back to a dead girl, healed a woman who had been bleeding for twelve years, and healed two blind men and a mute. After all of that profound ministry, chapter 9 ends with the following passage, stating that the workers are few:

Jesus went through all the towns and villages, teaching in their synagogues, preaching the good news of the kingdom and healing every disease and sickness. When he saw the crowds, he had compassion on them, because they were harassed and helpless, like sheep without a shepherd. Then he said to his disciples, "The harvest is plentiful but the workers are few. Ask the Lord of the harvest, therefore, to send out workers into his harvest field."

—MATTHEW 9:35–38

We are to be those workers!

Matthew 10 records Jesus' calling of the twelve disciples to Him and giving them authority to drive out evil spirits and to heal every disease and sickness. Jesus showed us what He wants us to do as we go about our lives. We can do it! That is what we are talking about in this book.

The marketplace

As stated previously, we define marketplace as anywhere outside our home where we interact with people. This includes where we work, where we play, our neighborhoods, and other places we frequent. The ministry of reconciliation is played out wherever people are in touch with one another. This can be in your front yard, at your neighbor's barbecue, or in the grocery store.

MARKETPLACE TESTIMONIES

Hold that plane

We were returning from a ministry trip, and our plane was late arriving in Portland, Oregon. As we ran to catch our connecting flight from Portland to Bend, Oregon, where we live, we noticed the gate was closed. When we inquired, the agent told us to run to the gate and that she would call them. The plane was a prop commuter, the motors were running, and the door was closed. However, the door opened, and the next thing we knew, two irritated stand-by passengers disembarked and we were told we could board the plane.

As we moved down the aisle, I (Sonja) asked the Lord just what this was all about. Then I saw a young girl, perhaps twelve or thirteen who was traveling alone, sitting in the seat next to where I was to sit. She was dressed in leather and had lots of body piercing. I struck up a conversation over cookies that I pulled out of my bag. Ten minutes into the flight, I asked her what she believed about God. She thought for a moment and then said, "I think He is good." I met her where she was and told her she was exactly right. I then asked her if she knew that He loved her. The conversation moved along to the point that I felt led to ask her if she would like to know this God through His Son, Jesus Christ, so if something ever happened to her she would spend forever with this loving God. Then she told me how she had almost drowned the previous summer and how terrified she had been at the time.

Praying with her

When I asked if she would like to pray and ask Jesus into her heart and to have Him forgive everything she had ever done that was wrong, she bowed her head and folded her hands just like a little child. I led her in the sinner's prayer just moments before we landed. I gave her the name of a good church in her town and suggested she visit it on Sunday. I put her name on my prayer list, and I pray for her often.

We believe the Lord will give us these opportunities if we are simply willing to be used, even if He has to detain an airplane to get us to the appointment! When we remain sensitive to opportunities for ministry, the Lord always opens fresh avenues for kingdom business. Our daily prayer could be, "Lord, I'm open for business today. Let me know when You want me to do something." Being open for business means being available to help others. Needs are everywhere. When Jesus has a lot of "gift givers" working in the marketplace, it is easy for Him to give His gifts away to meet those needs. But He needs willing disciples through whom He can work. That is where we come in. That is what Paul did in Acts 16.

> On the Sabbath we went outside the city gate to the river, where we expected to find a place of prayer. We sat down and began to speak to the women who had gathered there. One of those listening was a woman named Lydia, a dealer in purple cloth from the city of Thyatira, who was a worshiper of God. The Lord opened her heart

to respond to Paul's message. When she and the members of her
household were baptized, she invited us to her home.

—ACTS 16:13–15

- Wherever people gather can be a place of
  witness.
- Our message must be relevant to those gathered, being sensitive to whoever may be
  listening.
- Lydia was a dealer in purple cloth. It appears
  she and her household were the only ones
  who responded to Paul's testimony about
  Jesus.
- We, too, can be that kind of marketplace
  minister.

We have been given the ministry of reconciling a lost and dying
world to Christ. It is a joint ministry as we work with the Holy Spirit.
He gifts us to fulfill His mission. His mission is our ministry. He
has a "business of blessing" going on, and we are the delivery team.
Wherever a need surfaces, a delivery person is there with a gift to bless
and satisfy the need.

What if my mother is in hell?

Barb came to our neighborhood Bible study as a seeker. She was
skeptical of Christianity and its exclusive claim of salvation. But we
welcomed her honest inquiries and lovingly answered her questions
as best we could. After a few months, she said the only thing that was
preventing her from accepting Christ as her personal Savior was the
fact that her mother had died not knowing God, and that meant she
would never have a chance to see her again. We asked the Lord for
wisdom, and we were led to share the following with her:

- You cannot know for sure what was in your mother's
  heart. We look on the outside, but God looks at the heart.

- In His foreknowledge, God knows everyone who is going
  to accept His gift of salvation.

- If your mother were going to accept salvation, she somehow did so before her death. If not, she could have lived 50 more years and it would not have made a difference.

- What assurance do you have now of seeing your mother after death?

- God is totally just and merciful; therefore, you can trust Him in the matter.

This simple explanation answered her heart's cry, and she accepted the Lord Jesus Christ as her Savior. The transformation was remarkable. She was able to put the matter of her mother's eternal state in the hands of the just and compassionate God she had come to know through a simple neighborhood Bible study.

Open for business

One afternoon, I (John) was in a hurry to buy a witnessing Bible. Only one other person was in the Bible bookstore except for the clerk. I had some sales appointments within the hour, so I had little time to browse. I became a bit irritated when the other person kept asking me which version of the Bible he should buy. But the Holy Spirit nudged me and said, "Ask him if he knows Me." My first thought was that I did not have the time. Then I remembered that I had prayed that morning to be open for kingdom business. I promised the Lord I would do whatever He told me.

Divine appointment

I asked the man, "How well do you know the Author of that Bible?" He asked me what I meant, and I said, "If you died today, would you be with Jesus Christ?" When he said that he did not know, I asked him if he would like to be sure. He said yes. Then I heard the Lord say, "Kneel with him." I led the man to Jesus Christ through a simple prayer, on our knees, in the middle of a bookstore. I had him tell the clerk what happened, and then I invited him to church as we were paying for our new Bibles. I made it to my appointments with time to spare. Being open for business does not mean carrying a big black Bible under your arm. It means being sensitive to needs people have wherever you go.

The neighbor came to speak to me

One day, I (John) was puttering around the yard when my pre-Christian neighbor walked across the street to let me know his family was going on vacation. I offered to watch over their home and property even though we did not know each other very well. The neighbor was very appreciative and gave me instructions in case of an emergency. Later they were open to our invitation to attend a special musical outreach event at our church, and we became very good friends. Their need pointed to one of God's gifts. They needed the gift of helps. We released it, and they became open to the gospel. We engaged in marketplace ministry as God's fellow workers.

> As God's fellow workers we urge you not to receive God's grace in vain. For he says, "In the time of my favor I heard you, and in the day of salvation I helped you." I tell you, now is the time of God's favor, now is the day of salvation.
>
> —2 CORINTHIANS 6:1–2

God is always ready to save people. We should always be ready as His instruments to usher others into salvation.

When is the best time?

Little signs can let us know when an opportunity is right for witnessing. Here are a few:

- The conversation naturally turns to a spiritual subject.

- You hear a reference to God or Jesus that is not biblically based.

- Someone expresses a kind of problem from which God previously rescued you (destructive habits, substance abuse, family problems, sin, etc.).

- Someone tells you about experiencing a life threatening medical problem, and you know someone (or yourself) who prayed and experienced healing.

- Someone brings up a subject that you heard about in a sermon or recently read about in a Christian book.

- The Holy Spirit says for you to witness.

The signs listed above can be defined as conversational cues. These are a few from a hundred possibilities.

Cues from the Holy Spirit

One of the easiest ways to refocus a conversation on the gospel is to wait for a cue from the person with whom you are talking. Learn to wait until the cues happen naturally; they should never be forced. Many of the cues are obviously inspired by the Holy Spirit. If you suddenly change the conversation to Jesus Christ for no reason, a pre-Christian can become defensive. When that occurs, it is very difficult for the person to hear your story.

Sonja has become a master at capitalizing on conversational cues in the marketplace. She is very adept at redirecting the conversation to the things of the Lord. One day Sonja's secretary asked her if she had seen the New Age channeler on TV the previous night. As it turned out, Sonja had watched the program. She seized the opportunity to talk about the supernatural power of God as contrasted with the supernatural power of Satan. She stressed that, when the supernatural power of God is manifesting through a Christian, the person is in control of his or her faculties. In the case of the channeler, by her own admission, she was possessed by an entity that spoke through her. The secretary was amazed that the supernatural power of Satan enslaves people. On the other hand, the supernatural power of God is used to heal people or set them free.

Sonja was eventually able to lead her secretary to the Lord. The story does not end there. Her secretary later invited the receptionist to a meeting where Sonja was speaking. When Sonja gave the invitation for those who wanted to accept the Lord, the receptionist was the first to give her life to Christ.

Two people were born again because Sonja had responded to a cue from a legitimate question about spiritual things. But she did it with gentleness and respect in a nonthreatening way. I believe that is what Peter was telling us to do.

But in your hearts set apart Christ as Lord. Always be prepared to give an answer to everyone who asks you to give the reason for the hope that you have. But do this with gentleness and respect.

—1 PETER 3:15

- When we respond in a natural, non-threatening way, people will remain curious about our life in Christ.
- Gentleness and respect for people's feelings and having the understanding of spiritual things will open many opportunities to lead others to Christ.

What if they are ready now?

Once in a while you may meet someone who is so ready to receive Christ that you just know it. If this happens, we recommend having two questions firmly in mind. During John's years with the Christian Broadcasting Network, these two questions were the pivotal difference between someone's receiving Christ or not. They are yes or no questions, and they work so well that we recommend them to anyone wanting a way to "cinch" the witness and have the person commit his or her life to Christ. It works like this:

Ask: "If you died today, would you be with Jesus?"

Their response may be, "I hope so," or, "I don't know," or, "I don't think so."

Then ask: "Would you like to know for sure?"

If the answer is yes, then you lead the person in the following prayer:

Jesus, I want to be with You when I die. Forgive me of everything I've done wrong. Come into my life. I repent of my sin. Become my Lord and my God. Amen.

Short and to the point

In a fellowship gathering at church, we were introduced to a pre-Christian who indicated that he was "checking out God." When a pre-Christian brings up God, it is a cue from the Holy Spirit. I (John) simply said, "May I ask you a question?" He said that would be fine, so I said, "If you died tonight, would you be with Jesus Christ?" When he said that he really couldn't answer that, I asked him if he would like to be sure, and I invited him to pray with me. I put my hand on his shoulder, bowed my head and began a simple prayer of repentance and asking the Lord to forgive him. He followed along with me word for word.

After we concluded the prayer, I asked him again, "If you died right now, would you be with Jesus?" He looked me in the eye, and with a big grin he said, "I believe I would!" I gave him a firm handshake and told him he would never be the same.

Later, our friends who had introduced us to the young man told us that they were amazed at how easily we led him to salvation. We thanked them for preparing the way by praying for him. We were being marketplace ministers and just made sure the man had a life-changing encounter with Jesus Christ.

Is your hope showing?

Pre-Christians know who we are. It is reflected in our actions and our conversation. Jesus said they would know us by the love we show each other. We do not have to preach to our coworkers. They already know what kind of people we are by how we treat them. People are watching how we treat others at the office, at school, on the job, and at home. That is why Paul encouraged us to allow the fruit of the Spirit to flow through us. Then our actions will speak boldly of a person who has hope beyond the ordinary. When others see the fruit in action, a brilliant hope will radiate that only comes from a genuine follower of Jesus Christ.

Hope opens the door

Peter is right. We have a kind of hope that causes people to ask about it. First Peter 3:15 tells us what to do with the hope that we have. Hope opens the door for witnessing. People are drawn to those who have genuine hope—hope that they can solve personal problems; hope that they can overcome adverse societal pressures; and hope that they can believe in a God that leads them into personal restoration and peace. If we give evidence of that kind of hope, people will eventually ask us about how they can get it, too.

Little neighborhood cherubs

At one time we lived in a beautiful new condo in a mostly adult complex. On Saturdays, I (Sonja) baked cookies, and the aroma wafted through the air. One such day our doorbell rang, and I opened it to find a beautiful little six-year-old girl who told me that her name was Gwendolyn. She said, "I just wanted to thank you for making that wonderful smell." I smiled at the gorgeous little cherub with the dark, long, natural curls. I told her my name and told her that I would love to share the cookies with her if her mother said it was OK. She hastily turned to go ask her mother. She returned momentarily, and I invited her in for cookies and milk.

We soon became fast friends, and every week she showed up with new friends she had met that week. Before too long it was apparent that none of the seven children were Christians; nor did they go to church. They shared their lives with me each week, and it was heartbreaking to hear about some of their stories. Gwendolyn once told me that her mommy and her mommy's boyfriend had a big fight and he had moved out. But, not to worry, a new boyfriend had moved in the next day!

At Christmastime I shared the Christmas story with the children, and they loved it, and Gwendolyn asked if I would tell them a story each week. I said I would be happy to if their parents said it was OK. I spoke with all the parents and told them I would just use the children's illustrated Bible, which I showed to them. They all agreed, and we began learning about Jesus. One-by-one, I led each of those children—aged five to eleven—into a personal relationship with Jesus.

After a few months, Alan and Michelle's parents stopped me in the parking lot and thanked me for spending time with their children. They were amazed at the changes in them. I explained it was because they had come to know the Lord Jesus Christ in a personal way and He always brought positive change. They smiled and thanked me again.

By June, every one of those seven children had moved away. It was as if that had been a God-ordained year in their lives when He could reach down into the middle of dysfunctional situations and capture their hearts.

To be effective marketplace ministers, we sometimes have to be nontraditional. The seven children's parents were not receptive to taking or even sending their children to church, but coming to our home in the neighborhood was fine. I often think about and pray for those little ones the Lord entrusted to me at that time.

MASTERING YOUR MARKETPLACE TESTIMONY

Have you ever been at a loss for words when the subject of God came up? Most believers get tongue-tied when they find themselves in the middle of a witnessing opportunity. One of our students at MTI remarked, "I knew I was supposed to share my faith. But I felt so ill-equipped. I thought if I did, I would screw it up so badly that the person might never come to the Lord." She said that her time at MTI had given her confidence to share her story. To her utter amazement, the people she shared with wanted to accept Jesus Christ as their Lord and Savior.

She had mastered her marketplace testimony. Mastering your testimony simply means telling a series of little stories about when Jesus Christ showed up in your life and how He made a difference. Everyone's story is different, and that is what makes them so effective. Pre-Christians are always curious about what makes Christians tick. They may seem skeptical and even hostile at times, but they will seldom stop you in the middle of your story. If they do, the Holy Spirit may be telling you to save the story for another time.

The Bible According To You

It has been said that the only Bible pre-Christians see is you. Are they reading you the way you want them to? Jesus said, "A new command I give you: Love one another" (John 13:34). When we share how the grace of God has transformed us from who we were then to who we are now, people listen. Our stories reveal the incredible God of love who bestows grace, forgiveness, and restoration upon a broken and fractured race of people. Our stories release a fresh message of hope; they show the way out of the dead end of sin and debauchery. It is the Bible according to you. Pre-Christians don't just need to hear it—they want to hear it.

A STORY THAT LEADS PEOPLE TO CHRIST

The recipe for a good story

Mastering your marketplace testimony requires an understanding of why it is so powerful to pre-Christians. Choosing parts of your personal history with Jesus Christ that will have high impact with others requires thought. Those you share with will always welcome effective stories that penetrate their personal hurts and needs. The recipe for a good testimony will include these elements:

- A short story of who you were and what you were experiencing before coming to Christ

- The personal factors that finally caused you to look to God for help

- The personal details surrounding the actual surrender and submission to God's will

- A short story of who you have become and what you are now experiencing as a result of turning to God for help

- An encouragement to those listening that they can experience the same results by submitting to Jesus Christ

Keep it simple

These components may seem too simple. They can be said in less than five minutes. Many will argue that you must use many scriptures to be effective. This may be true in some instances, but there will be ample opportunities to interject your favorite Bible passage as you tell your story. Avoid using phrases such as "the Bible says...," or "verse 9 of chapter 10 of Romans says...." Pre-Christians do not believe the Bible has any relevance to their lives. Simply paraphrase the truth from the Bible and insert it into your story. They will not know you are quoting the Bible. The Holy Spirit will use it to penetrate deep into their hearts and cause them to want to know Christ. Here are five things that make a powerful testimony:

1. Tell who you were.

   Americans are used to hearing their friends talk about

themselves in a negative way. It is part of our culture to stress the negative. We usually refer to the next intersection as having a red light, not green. Polls often refer to the 25 percent that disagreed rather than the 75 percent that agreed. The six o'clock news seldom reports on the good things that happened during the day. All we hear and see are fires, plane crashes, rape victims, murders, wars, and all categories of violence.

Beginning your story with how messed up you used to be is a good way to get a pre-Christian's attention. They can relate to that. They have been there or may be experiencing the same circumstances. Everyone has periods in their lives when things do not work out. The negatives permeate our society. Bad things happen to good people. Even Christians are not shielded from accidents, abuse, and persecutions. We live in a fallen and decaying world, and bad things happen to everyone.

Incorporating the circumstances of your life prior to when you submitted to Christ should not be done with any hint of bragging or longing for what is past. Nor should you dwell on the gory details. The information should be presented as facts that describe what you were experiencing and what kind of person you were before encountering Jesus Christ. This sets the stage for the next phase of your story.

People who accepted the Lord as children, as Sonja did, may begin their testimonies with significant events in their lives that caused them to turn to God wholeheartedly. Perhaps it was a difficult marriage, bad health, death of a child, or an accident.

2. Explain what caused you to look to God.

Most people can relate to times when they ran out of ideas on how to fix their problems. It is vital to tell about those personal events and factors where you knew you were at a crossroads. You could stress the options of continuing as you were and where that would have led. You could also mention what your friends and family suggested that you do. You could refer to specific people in your testimony that gave you input that eventually caused you to look to God for the answer. At this point in your story it is vital that you describe how you were feeling at the time.

3. Describe what happened when you surrendered.

Pre-Christians need to hear the specifics of how to surrender to Jesus Christ. Your story must include the personal details surrounding your submission to God. This opens the door for your listeners to know how to submit to Jesus Christ. Take time to describe how you felt, what words you said to God and the emotions you experienced. This has high impact on those who hear your story. Do not lightly skip over this part. It is the pivotal point that causes another to either want to do what you did or dismiss the whole idea. Allow it to be a clear description of your conversion and surrender to God's will for your life. By repeating the prayer you said to the Lord, you are showing pre-Christians how to pray. It shows them how they can receive salvation like you did. You do not have to be dramatic. Just explain how it happened.

4. Tell what is happening now.

Your story should conclude with what happened as a result of submitting yourself to God. This part should be very positive. We are all in the process of becoming more like Jesus, but no one has arrived. However, we are better than when we first began. So tell a short story of who you are becoming and some of the good things that have happened since you made your decision to follow Christ. Relate what you are now experiencing as a result of turning to God. Tell how it has made a difference in your personal life, your work, or your relationship with others. Pre-Christians need to hear the personal benefits of giving their lives to Jesus Christ in very personal terms. This will help them decide to surrender to the Lord.

5. Give your listeners an opportunity to decide.

Always end your story with an encouragement for your listeners to do what you did. If you were sincere, truthful, and talking from the heart, your listeners will want to do something about what you said. If they need to get saved, ask them! If they need to rededicate their lives to God, ask them! If they need to repent of their sin and get right with the Lord, ask them! By now the Holy Spirit is lovingly drawing them to Jesus. God has just used you to preach the gospel in a way they can understand and grasp. Always end your story with a loving invitation for your listeners to submit their lives and situation to Jesus Christ. God will give you the right words to say.

Always end your witness with a simple invitation. Keep the prayer simple. It can be long or short, depending on the situation. The main thing is addressing the prayer to Jesus Christ and including repentance and forgiveness. Helping people with what to pray relieves them of the embarrassment of not knowing what to say. Remember, they may only know what to say by what you have told them in your story. Make it as easy as you can for them to surrender to God. Eyes open, eyes closed, standing, sitting, kneeling, hands clasped, hands at their side—it makes no difference. Just do whatever seems most appropriate and natural. At this point, God is in charge. Allow people space to have an authentic encounter with the Lord Jesus Christ.

"He did all this for me, and He will do it for you, too. Would you like to ask Jesus Christ to come into your life now? I will help you do it. Say these words with me to God: 'Jesus Christ, come into my life. I repent of all my sin. Forgive me for what I've said and done. I receive You as my Savior and Lord. Thank You for forgiving me. Amen.'"

Follow up

It is critical for the person who just received Christ to immediately be told what to do next. This primary responsibility falls with the person who was most instrumental in the person's coming to the Lord. That could be you, the person who prayed the prayer with them, the evangelist who gave the altar call, or the pastor who gave the invitation. New babies in the Lord should not be allowed to leave God's altar of repentance without being told what to do next. Give new believers the following next steps:

- Get baptized in water to bury the old life.

- Get baptized in the Holy Spirit for power to resist sin and be an effective witness.

- Get a Bible, and begin reading the New Testament daily.

- Get into a weekly Bible discipleship class for new believers, and hang around those who have been walking with the Lord for a long time.

- Get into to a Spirit-filled, Bible-believing church every time the doors are open.

LEADING PEOPLE BACK TO CHRIST

Coming to Christ is one thing; staying with Christ your whole life is another. There is a tendency for us to wander away, some further than others. Jesus illustrated this in Matthew 18:

> What do you think? If a man owns a hundred sheep, and one of them wanders away, will he not leave the ninety-nine on the hills and go to look for the one that wandered off? And if he finds it, I tell you the truth, he is happier about that one sheep than about the ninety-nine that did not wander off.
> —Matthew 18:12–13

> Jesus' teaching clearly shows the value of the person who has wandered away. He goes to look for that person—sometimes through those of us who are willing to be used in that way.

Seek those who are lost

Over the years, I (Sonja) have been privileged to be used by the Lord to help people find their way back to Him. Following is an account of one such instance.

Why?

I worked in a large office building that headquartered several companies. As I went up and down the elevators to and from my office, I occasionally saw a very attractive young woman get off on the floor below mine. I felt the Holy Spirit prompting me to befriend her, but she was extremely aloof.

One day I asked her if she would like to have lunch someday. She abruptly blurted out, "Why?" I was caught off guard by her response but recovered enough to say that I would just like to get to know her. Again, she responded with, "Why?" It was one of the most unusual responses I had ever had to a simple luncheon invitation. Again, I said I would just like to get acquainted. She reluctantly said, "Well, I guess I could. How about Friday?" We agreed to meet in the lobby at noon, and, with that, she scampered away like a frightened rabbit.

I was very perplexed

I was certain the Lord was leading me to reach out to this young woman, but I admitted to Him that I was very perplexed. Friday came, and we walked across the street to a hotel dining room. I had picked it because it had an atmosphere that was conducive for conversation. I did a monologue for about twenty minutes. The young woman simply would not engage in conversation.

Toward the end of our luncheon, she seemed to relax a bit. As we walked back to work, she finally disclosed the reason for her mysterious behavior. She said, "You really did just want to get acquainted, didn't you?" I responded affirmatively and then asked her what she thought I wanted.

I broke into hilarious laughter

She sheepishly related that she heard I was a strong Christian, and she was backslidden. She was certain God had told me to get her aside and rebuke her and tell her she was headed straight for hell! I broke into hilarious laughter—and she laughed as well. That dirty liar, the deceiver, had once more been exposed!

That luncheon was the beginning of a lifelong friendship, not just with me but with all of my family—my husband, parents, and grand-parents. The young woman began to attend my Saturday morning prayer meeting. I cannot remember the exact circumstances of when she came back to the Lord; it just happened over time. She is a very spiritual woman who is used mightily by the Lord.

People need someone to genuinely care about them

Over the years I have led numerous hairdressers, neighbors, coworkers, and even church attendees back into relationship with Jesus. People simply needed someone to care about them and share just how much God loves them and is waiting for them to return. More often than not, I share the story of the ninety-nine sheep the shepherd left in order to seek the lost one. Somehow, that, more than anything, convinces them of God's personal love and concern for them. Of course, the prodigal son story in Luke 15:11–31 is a great reference if they are having a "pigpen" experience.

This is how it works

Perhaps you are thinking, "Sure, Sonja, that's easy for you, but that is not my gift. I can't just extend myself to strangers that way. You see, I'm an introvert." Well I would respond by telling you that every Christian, yes *every* Christian, including you, can be used this way!

This is how it works: You discover how the Lord has gifted you. Perhaps it is mercy, encouragement, helps, service, hospitality, or any number of other gifts. We provide a gift assessment and teach on thirty gifts and talents of the Holy Spirit in our *Ambassador Series*. You simply tell the Lord you are willing to be used. He then takes you at your word and sets up an opportunity where you give your gifts away.

Eventually, someone will comment or ask you why you did a particular thing or why you are the way you are. That is your cue to simply say that you are a Christian and you enjoy helping others. You might even say that you were not always this way, but Jesus has changed you. Do not overpower people, even if they act interested. Leave them wanting more and feeling safe. Too often people show a little interest, and we, in our zeal, scare them or turn them off. If people are ready, they will keep coming around until they get back into relationship with the Lord. You can do it.

We may need more confidence

If we lack confidence to be an effective minister in the marketplace, we should check how much the Holy Spirit has been allowed to work through us. Perhaps we need more of His power. The best way to gain more confidence is to ask God for more power to be an effective witness. When we ask Jesus for more power to witness, He will likely lead us to the Holy Spirit baptism. This spiritual baptism of power is the next step to becoming an effective marketplace minister. This is the next ministry skill that we will learn about and master in chapter 2.

LET'S PRACTICE

James 1:22 says to do what we have heard (read).

Consider doing what is recommended in this chapter by referring to the "Let's Practice" in Appendix B, page 253.

Do the ministry skill assignment titled, "Leading People to Christ."

LEADING CHRISTIANS INTO THE HOLY SPIRIT BAPTISM

Jesus promised believers a wonderful spiritual experience, "the gift of the Holy Spirit." Believers receive power to become His witnesses and to do the works that He did. Once we have had this marvelous encounter with the Holy Spirit, we can then lead other Christians into the same experience.

THE HOLY SPIRIT baptism is a wonderful, biblical, empowering experience that is often the Christian's introduction to the super-natural power and realm of God. It certainly was mine (Sonja)! Raised in an evangelical church where Daddy was a deacon and Mother sang in the choir, I came to faith in Jesus Christ so early I do not even remember exactly when. I had no trouble relating to God, the heavenly Father, due in large part to my wonderful relationship with my earthly father. Jesus Christ, my Savior, my elder brother, was easily believed. I knew my sins were forgiven and that, if I died, I would go to heaven. But the Holy Spirit was some nebulous "It"! I did not know He was a Person who could be known personally. However, that was all going to change.

Twentieth-century visitation

During the twentieth century, the Holy Spirit of God, through a profound and life-changing supernatural experience, visited millions of Christians worldwide. These believers were longing for a closer and more intimate relationship with God, and many were earnestly praying and seeking Him. In some cases the people were in desperate circumstances, even fearing for their very lives. Others were safe, affluent, and possessed every material comfort a person could desire; yet they, too, were empty and devoid of spiritual reality. They lived in

almost every country on the face of the earth and represented almost
every ethnic group.

Hungry hearts

It was as if the Holy Spirit swept over the face of the earth seeking
those hungry hearts, and, when He found them, He came upon them
and they were transformed. There were no socioeconomic, ethnic,
gender, or denominational barriers. I personally know of heads of
state and U.N. ambassadors, as well as ditch-diggers and farmers who
have had this common experience.

We know from the Bible and historical fact that God has deter-
mined seasons and events that express His sovereign will and fulfill
His eternal purposes. One such event was this outpouring of His Holy
Spirit at this appointed time.

In his book, *The Holiness-Pentecostal Tradition*, Vinson Synan discussed the stunning growth of the Pentecostal tradition at the end of
the twentieth century. He says:

> This could well be the major story of Christianity in the twen-
> tieth century. If what Peter Wagner says is true, "In all of
> human history, no other non-political, non-militaristic, volun-
> tary human movement has grown as rapidly as the Pentecostal-
> charismatic movement in the last twenty-five years," then
> Pentecostalism indeed deserves to be seen as a major Christian
> tradition alongside the Roman Catholic, Orthodox, and
> Reformation Protestant traditions.[1]

Back in the first century A.D., John the Baptist named the experience by telling his contemporary believers that they were going to be
baptized with the Holy Spirit.

> And this was his [John's] message: "After me will come one more
> powerful than I, the thongs of whose sandals I am not worthy to
> stoop down and untie. I baptize you with water, but he will bap-
> tize you with the Holy Spirit."
>   —MARK 1:7–8

> Jesus Christ is the One who baptizes with the Holy Spirit. All believers need to ask Jesus for the gift of the Holy Spirit.

SONJA'S INTRODUCTION TO THE SUPERNATURAL POWER OF GOD

When I was 27 years old, I came to a point in my life where I began to cry out to God. I told Him that there had to be more to Him than I had experienced. I did not have enough power for myself, much less enough to help someone else. In my desperation, God met me in a most wonderful manner.

Cousin Fay was miraculously healed

At that time, I had an older cousin who was dying from congestive heart failure and was confined to bed. We were expecting to hear of her death any day. Instead, Grammy Hatcher informed me one day that my cousin had been miraculously healed. I was stunned, so I called Cousin Fay and invited her to my home to tell me what had happened. Honestly, she sounded like a different woman!

She came for a visit, and I was amazed to hear what had happened to her. As she lay in bed crying out to God to help her, suddenly her bedroom filled with the presence of God. She sat up and began to speak in a language she had never learned. She prayed and prayed in this new language so loudly that her husband came to look in on her. She said her church actually taught against this experience and she did not know anything about it. But her husband had been to a Pentecostal church when he was younger, and he knew what it was. He just smiled at her, closed the door, and left her with her Lord. The next day she was up and about, called her doctor for an appointment, and was not surprised to learn that her critically high blood pressure was normal and her heart was beating as it should! By the way, she lived another 25 years in good health.

Something stirred in me

As I listened to my cousin, something stirred in me—a hunger for a relationship with God that would cause the supernatural to be evident in my life. Before Fay left that day, we knelt together and she prayed in English and then in the beautiful heavenly language the Lord had given her. I could not deny the wonderful miracle-healing that had happened in her life, yet I had serious reservations about the "speaking in tongues."

Everyone in the family was talking about what had happened to Cousin Fay. My mother had an old book entitled *The Gift of the Holy Spirit*, by John Stiles. As I read the book, I turned to the scriptures in my Bible to make sure what I was reading was actually in my own Bible! Sure enough, they were there; I had just never read them with understanding before.

My church also taught against this experience

My church did not teach about the supernatural working of the Holy Spirit. In fact, the church taught against it and warned me to stay away from such nonsense. Yet, as I read this book, I came to see that the Holy Spirit is a Person of the triune Godhead, just as the Father and the Son are, and that I could have a personal relationship with Him. Further, I learned that I could know the Holy Spirit in a greater dimension as Teacher, Counselor, Comforter, and the One who would give me the ability to be an effective witness. Those were the very things my heart longed for.

As previously mentioned, I did not have enough power for myself to live the Christian life, much less enough to help someone else. I had never led another person into a relationship with Jesus Christ. The most daring thing I remember doing was inviting two girlfriends to visit my church, and they only came because of the cute boy that was in my youth group. Talk about being powerless! I actually got embarrassed if a Christian began talking about Jesus in front of pre-Christians. I would think, "Why don't they shut up? Can't they see they are embarrassing that person?" Later I came to realize that I would rather embarrass people than let them go to hell!

Jesus baptized me with the Holy Spirit

After I finished reading the book about the Holy Spirit, one Friday evening while home alone, I knelt beside my bed and prayed a very simple prayer that went something like this:

> Lord Jesus, I understand that You are the One who baptizes with the Holy Spirit. I also understand that this is a free gift just like salvation, and it is mine for the asking. In receiving this gift I will come to know the Holy Spirit as Counselor, Teacher, and Comforter and that He will give me the power to become an effective witness for You—something to give to others. I also would like to be able to pray more effectively, so I ask You for the ability to pray in languages I do not know. Thank you. By faith, right now, I receive your free gift and the next words I speak will not be English.

I took a deep breath, and began to speak nonsensical syllables that soon joined together into a fluent language. I prayed for a few minutes and then got up and walked down the hallway to the living room. On the way, I stopped at a mirror and looked at myself as I prayed. All of a sudden, I was halfway irritated as I said aloud, "Why, this is so easy, I could have done this as a child if only someone had told me!"

Would you do it over the telephone?

I called Grammy Hatcher and told her I thought I had been baptized with the Holy Spirit. She rather cautiously asked me what made me think that, and I told her that I asked Jesus for this gift and that I could speak in a language I had not learned. She asked me if I would do that over the telephone so she could hear me. Totally uninhibited, I began to speak in a beautiful language. She became very excited, and I then learned that she had experienced the same thing when she was 16 years old. She had not talked to me about it because she knew my church taught against it. As a child, I heard her singing little songs in another language. At that point, it all made sense to me!

Are you taking super-vitamins?

I did not go around telling others about this wonderful experience, but within weeks my friends at church began asking what had happened to me. It was as if I were glowing with this new Presence. One friend asked if I was taking super-vitamins! I told them one by one about the wonderful, life-changing experience with the Lord. I told them that I would be happy to tell them about it some time. As I shared with them, they indicated their desire for this gift. We would pray, sometimes quietly sitting in a restaurant, and they would also receive. Because of the way I received, it was easy to lead them into the same simple, yet marvelous, experience.

My transformation

The transformation in my life was immediate and powerful. I went from someone who was embarrassed to share my faith with others to someone who looked for opportunities to share. The Holy Spirit then became my Teacher. He led me to read the Bible through time and again. I learned to use all of the Bible study aids, even an interlinear Greek-English New Testament. I also came into relationship with the Holy Spirit as Counselor and Comforter. He became the Friend who always exalted the Lord Jesus Christ.

In my studies I discovered that my friends and I were experiencing exactly the same things the apostles and disciples of Jesus experienced when they were baptized with the Holy Spirit. We will take a look at those experiences in a moment. But first I will give a brief teaching that has enabled me to share this controversial experience with literally thousands of believers.

THE HOLY SPIRIT BAPTISM WITH; WITHIN; UPON

The purpose of the Holy Spirit baptism is to be clothed with more power from heaven so we can be effective witnesses for Jesus Christ. Prior to asking for forgiveness and receiving the Lord as our Savior, we had the Holy Spirit *with* us, drawing us to Christ. We received the Holy Spirit *in* us when we first believed, repented, and received Jesus Christ as Lord of our life. At that time, we were born again by the Holy Spirit. The baptism of the Holy Spirit is in addition to, and separate from, the initial new birth experience. The baptism of the Holy Spirit occurs when the Holy Spirit comes *upon* a believer who asks Jesus Christ for this gift of the Holy Spirit that was promised by the Father.

The following scriptures clearly reveal this distinction of having the Holy Spirit with, within, and upon us:

> And I will ask the Father, and he will give you another Counselor
> to be with you forever—the Spirit of truth. The world cannot

accept him, because it neither sees him nor knows him. But you know him, for he lives *with* you and will be *in* you.

—JOHN 14:16–17, EMPHASIS ADDED

When they arrived, they prayed for them that they might receive the Holy Spirit, because the Holy Spirit had not yet come *upon* any of them; they had simply been baptized into the name of the Lord Jesus. Then Peter and John placed their hands on them, and they received the Holy Spirit.

—ACTS 8:15–17, EMPHASIS ADDED

While Peter was still speaking these words, the Holy Spirit came *on* all who heard the message. The circumcised believers who had come with Peter were astonished that the gift of the Holy Spirit had been poured out even *on* the Gentiles. For they heard them speaking in tongues and praising God.

—ACTS 10:44–46, EMPHASIS ADDED

On hearing this, they were baptized into the name of the Lord Jesus. When Paul placed his hands on them, the Holy Spirit came *on* them, and they spoke in tongues and prophesied.

—ACTS 19:5–6, EMPHASIS ADDED

- We see that the Holy Spirit is with us, drawing us to the Savior prior to our salvation.
- When we came to the point of surrender and asked Jesus Christ to forgive us of our sins and to come into our lives, the Holy Spirit came within us, quickened our spirits, and made us alive unto God. We were born of the Spirit, born from above. We became God's son or daughter. If we died, we would go to heaven.
- However, Scripture very clearly demonstrates that there is a subsequent experience with the Holy Spirit where He comes upon us and baptizes us with power. That is what millions of believers have personally experienced.

THE HOLY SPIRIT IN THE BOOK OF ACTS

We are now going to take a little sojourn through the first twelve chapters of the book of Acts and see for ourselves how the Holy Spirit came upon the apostles, disciples, Jews, Gentiles, men, and women. We should be having the very same life-changing, supernatural encounters they had in the first century A.D.

We will see what the Father, the Lord Jesus Christ, John the Baptist, and the apostles Peter and Paul had to say about this life-changing gift. Keep the following words in mind as you read: *with, within, upon, on, gift, filled, power, and baptized with the Holy Spirit*. It is exciting to observe the activity of the Holy Spirit in the birth of the New Testament church.

The Father's promise

> I am going to send you what my Father has promised; but stay in the city until you have been clothed with *power* from on high.
>
> —LUKE 24:49

> Jesus said that the Father promises we will be clothed with power. The Holy Spirit baptism is for power to witness.

Jesus instructed His disciples to wait for the Father's promise. They had no idea what to expect, but they waited. On the day of Pentecost the promise came.

Jesus, the One who baptizes with the Holy Spirit

We begin with John the Baptist's message as recorded in the first chapter of the Gospel of Mark:

> And this was his message: "After me will come one more powerful than I, the thongs of whose sandals I am not worthy to stoop down and untie. I baptize you with water, but he will baptize you with the Holy Spirit."
>
> —MARK 1:7–8

> In this passage, John distinguished between the water baptism he was administering and the baptizing with the Holy Spirit that Jesus would do.

Jesus instructed His disciples to wait for the gift

The following verses record a command Jesus gave His followers:

> On one occasion, while he was eating with them, he gave them this command: "Do not leave Jerusalem, but wait for the gift my Father promised, which you have heard me speak about. For John baptized with water, but in a few days you will be baptized with the Holy Spirit."
>
> —ACTS 1:4–5

> Jesus gave us a command, not a suggestion, to wait for the gift of the Holy Spirit. We should be baptized in the Holy Spirit so that we can become effective witnesses.

Jesus said His disciples would receive power:

> But you will receive power when the Holy Spirit comes on you; and you will be my witnesses in Jerusalem, and in all Judea and Samaria, and to the ends of the earth.
>
> —ACTS 1:8

> Jesus said that the purpose for the Holy Spirit baptism is for power to be an effective witness.

Jesus' word comes to pass on Pentecost

We know these scriptures were fulfilled as documented in Acts chapter 2. The Holy Spirit came on Pentecost:

> When the day of Pentecost came, they were all together in one place. Suddenly a sound like the blowing of a violent wind came from heaven and filled the whole house where they were sitting. They

saw what seemed to be tongues of fire that separated and came to rest on each of them. All of them were filled with the Holy Spirit and began to speak in other tongues as the Spirit enabled them.

—Acts 2:1–4

> The Holy Spirit came just as the Father and Jesus had promised. These believers caused quite a commotion with this supernatural empowering that enabled them to speak in languages they had not learned. We can do the same.

The disciples were declaring the wonders of God, and the God-fearing Jews from every nation under heaven were bewildered and inquired of them what this meant. A large crowd gathered. Peter stood up, raised his voice, and addressed them with an anointed, masterful message. He referenced the prophet Joel:

In the last days, God says, I will pour out my Spirit on all people. Your sons and daughters will prophesy, your young men will see visions, your old men will dream dreams. Even on my servants, both men and women, I will pour out my Spirit in those days, and they will prophesy.

—Acts 2:17–18

The latter part of Acts 2 records the people's response to Peter's sermon:

When the people heard this, they were cut to the heart and said to Peter and the other apostles, "Brothers, what shall we do?" Peter replied, "Repent and be baptized, every one of you, in the name of Jesus Christ for the forgiveness of your sins. And you will receive the *gift of the Holy Spirit*. The promise is for you and your children and for all who are far off—for all whom the Lord our God will call." With many other words he warned them; and he pleaded with them, "Save yourselves from this corrupt generation." Those who accepted his message were baptized, and about three thousand were added to their number that day.

—Acts 2:37–41, emphasis added

> The Holy Spirit is upon us so that we may continue the task of reconciling the world to God through Jesus Christ.

This promise is for us today

I am so glad the Holy Spirit had Peter's words recorded so we could know for certain that this promise is for us today. We can see with certainty that the gift of the Holy Spirit we receive is the same gift the first believers received—and with the same results. My friends and I knew Jesus Christ as Savior, but we were absolutely powerless. All that changed when we received the gift of the Holy Spirit and began to experience the supernatural things of God. We had found the dimension that had been missing in our lives.

NEW TESTAMENT CHURCH BIRTHED IN THE SUPERNATURAL

The New Testament church was birthed in the marvelous, supernatural outpouring of the promised Holy Spirit. Tremendous healings, deliverances, and miracles began to take place, and God was adding believers to the church every day.

The crippled beggar healed

The Book of Acts is chockfull of demonstrations of the dynamic of the power of the Holy Spirit. Chapter 3 records that Peter healed the crippled beggar; when a crowd gathered, he preached another message urging people to repent and turn to the resurrected Jesus Christ for the forgiveness of sins. Many who heard the message believed, and the number of men grew to about five thousand. What had happened to Peter who, prior to being baptized in the Holy Spirit, was in hiding for fear of the Jewish leaders?

By what power?

Peter and John were put in jail overnight. The next day the rulers, elders, and teachers of the law met in Jerusalem. They had Peter and John brought before them and began to question them: "By what power or what name did you do this?" (Acts 4:7).

It is the name of Jesus Christ of Nazareth

Peter, *filled with the Holy Spirit*, again preached yet another time. He said, "It is by the name of Jesus Christ of Nazareth, whom you crucified but whom God raised from the dead, that this man stands before you healed. Salvation is found in no one else, for there is no other name under heaven given to men by which we must be saved" (Acts 4:10, 12).

> When they saw the courage of Peter and John and realized that they were unschooled, ordinary men, they were astonished and they took note that these men had been with Jesus. But since they could see the man who had been healed standing there with them, there was nothing they could say.
>
> —Acts 4:13–14

> When we experience miracles as we minister, the skeptics have nothing they can say. It is the power of the Holy Spirit that captivates pre-Christians.

This notable miracle could not be denied, so the leaders threatened Peter and John and told them not to speak any longer in that name. They did not punish Peter and John, however, because all Jerusalem knew of the miracle that had been performed and everyone was praising God that the 40-year-old man was able to walk (Acts 4:16, 21-22).

Astounding power

The power that was unleashed through the Holy Spirit baptism was astounding! The unschooled fishermen from Galilee who had been with Jesus were turning their world upside down. It is the same today. Uneducated and educated alike who come into personal relationship with Jesus Christ and are baptized with His Holy Spirit also turn their worlds upside down! This has happened through the centuries with countless millions of people, and it is happening today around the world.

I began to see the miraculous manifest

I (Sonja) personally had this power come into my life. I began to study about the supernatural healing recorded in the book of Acts, and faith for healing began to rise up within me. As I ventured out to pray for people, I began to see the miraculous manifest through my own hands.

Corporate executive healed

One time a corporate executive with whom I worked was scheduled to give an important presentation. He asked me to pray for him because he had such a bad migraine headache that he could hardly see. Another executive overheard the conversation and asked if he could observe how this worked. I told him that would be fine and suggested that the three of us walk away from the group as though we were having a discussion. As we did, I simply reached up, put my hand on the executive's head and commanded the pain to leave in the name of Jesus. The man was instantly healed, and the other man was astounded. He said that he had heard of that type of healing, but he had never before observed such a thing. I then explained about the desire of the Lord to heal and the power of the Holy Spirit, being extremely careful to give the credit and glory to the Lord Jesus Christ. Through that experience, I was given numerous opportunities to pray for the sick in a very natural way that demonstrated God's goodness. The executive I prayed for soon became a Christian.

Place of prayer shaken

Peter and John returned to the believers who were gathered and reported all that happened to them. Then all the believers raised their voices together in prayer to God. After they prayed, the place where they were meeting was shaken. They were all filled with the Holy Spirit and spoke the Word of God boldly (see Acts 4:23–24, 31).

Has the place where you pray ever been shaken? It is our firm conviction that God wants to do the same things today that He did in the first century. We have had experiences in pre-service prayer times that were so powerful that the power emitting from those assembled would almost knock people to their knees.

Revelation gifts began to operate

As we move on to chapter 5 in Acts, we see the revelation gifts of the Holy Spirit being manifested through the apostles in a frightening and awesome way. Ananias and Sapphira, a married couple, lied to the apostles about a gift they gave to the church; both were struck dead because they dared to "test the Spirit of the Lord" (vv. 1-9). Because of that, great fear seized the whole church and all who heard about these events.

Apostles heal many

> The apostles performed many miraculous signs and wonders among the people. And all the believers used to meet together in Solomon's Colonnade. No one else dared join them, even though they were highly regarded by the people. Nevertheless, more and more men and women believed in the Lord and were added to their number. As a result, people brought the sick into the streets and laid them on beds and mats so that at least Peter's shadow might fall on some of them as he passed by. Crowds gathered also from the towns around Jerusalem, bringing their sick and those tormented by evil spirits, and all of them were healed.
>
> —Acts 5:12–16

> New Testament believers were doing what Jesus did and with the same results! This remains true today. Believers filled with the Holy Spirit are healing the sick.

The encounter the apostles had with the Holy Spirit on the day of Pentecost had obviously transformed them into powerful servants of the living Christ!

It is still true today

We have experienced this same power manifested through us for preaching, healing, and deliverances. Specific examples are given in later chapters of this book.

Angels open prison doors

The apostles were jailed for causing such an uproar in Jerusalem. An angel freed them, and yet another opportunity occurred for Peter and the other apostles to preach about Jesus. The Sanhedrin had them flogged, again ordered them not to speak in the name of Jesus, and let them go. They left rejoicing because they had been counted worthy of suffering disgrace for the name (Acts 5:18–19, 40–41).

Stephen martyred

Now Stephen, a man full of God's grace and power, did great wonders and miraculous signs among the people. The men who opposed him could not stand up against his wisdom or the Spirit by whom he spoke. However, they conspired against Stephen with false accusations and had him brought before the Sanhedrin. After he preached a wonderful and convicting message, they dragged him out of Jerusalem and stoned him to death. Saul of Taurus was watching and giving approval of his death (Acts 6,7).

THE CHURCH PERSECUTED AND SCATTERED

On the day Stephen was martyred, a great persecution broke out against the church at Jerusalem, and all except the apostles were scattered through Judea and Samaria.

Philip in Samaria

> Those who had been scattered preached the word wherever they went. Philip went down to a city in Samaria and proclaimed the Christ there. When the crowds heard Philip and saw the miraculous signs he did, they all paid close attention to what he said. With shrieks, evil spirits came out of many, and many paralytics and cripples were healed. So there was great joy in that city.
>
> —ACTS 8:4–8

> When we allow the Holy Spirit to minister through us, He will cause evil spirits to come out, healings to manifest, and miraculous signs to happen.

Simon the sorcerer

> Now for some time a man named Simon had practiced sorcery in the city and amazed all the people of Samaria. He boasted that he was someone great, and all the people, both high and low,

gave him their attention and exclaimed, "This man is the divine power known as the Great Power." They followed him because he had amazed them for a long time with his magic. But when they believed Philip as he preached the good news of the kingdom of God and the name of Jesus Christ, they were baptized, both men and women. Simon himself believed and was baptized. And he followed Philip everywhere, astonished by the great signs and miracles he saw.

—Acts 8:9–13

> As we obey the leading of the Holy Spirit, we will experience the same things that happened to Philip. We must be full of the Holy Spirit for "great signs and miracles" to manifest.

Apostles visit Samaria

When the apostles in Jerusalem heard that Samaria had accepted the word of God, they sent Peter and John to them. When they arrived, they prayed for them that they might receive the Holy Spirit, because the Holy Spirit had not yet come *upon* any of them; they had simply been baptized into the name of the Lord Jesus. Then Peter and John placed their hands on them, and they *received the Holy Spirit*. When Simon saw that the Spirit was given at the laying on of the apostles' hands, he offered them money and said, "Give me also this ability so that everyone on whom I lay my hands may receive the Holy Spirit."

—Acts 8:14–19, emphasis added

> Laying on of hands is a scriptural pattern for those already baptized in the Holy Spirit to minister this experience to others.
> The people who were being baptized in the Holy Spirit were believers who had already been baptized in water.

Holy Spirit baptism is for the converted

This is an excellent example of the subsequent work of the Holy Spirit *after* repentance, salvation, and water baptism. We know Philip would never have baptized people who were not born again by the Holy Spirit through faith in the Lord Jesus Christ. But, "...the Holy Spirit had not yet come upon any of them; they had simply been baptized into the name of the Lord Jesus" (Acts 8:16). When Peter and John placed their hands on them, they received the Holy Spirit. Simon the sorcerer "saw that the Spirit was given at the laying on of the apostles' hands." He even offered them money if they would give him that ability. Of course he was sternly rebuked (Acts 8:18–23).

Aeneas and Dorcas

Peter was traveling about the country empowered by the Holy Spirit and doing the miraculous. Two notable miracles, the healing of Aeneas and the raising of Dorcas from the dead, resulted in many people coming to the Lord in Lydda, Sharon, and Joppa.

> As Peter traveled about the country, he went to visit the saints in Lydda. There he found a man named Aeneas, a paralytic who had been bedridden for eight years. "Aeneas," Peter said to him, "Jesus Christ heals you. Get up and take care of your mat." Immediately Aeneas got up. All those who lived in Lydda and Sharon saw him and turned to the Lord.
> —Acts 9:32–35

> Holy Spirit-baptized believers should be available to heal the sick wherever they go. In this passage, the Lord used healing to quickly evangelize the communities of Lydda and Sharon.

It happened to us in Thailand

We must remember that one of the main purposes of the miraculous is to draw pre-Christians to the saving knowledge of the Lord Jesus Christ. We experienced this in a refugee camp in northern Thailand. Our hosts were Christians, and almost the entire camp had become Christians. The children were well behaved, and we could sense the peace of the Lord. The camp was clean and orderly.

Our host had arranged for us to visit another camp that was totally pre-Christian. What a contrast! The children were like little savages, clawing at us as they were begging. Several of the women approached the men in our group to see if they were interested in sex for money.

We boldly declared that our God would heal the sick

John was led to have the music played loudly to draw a crowd. He then preached a simple message about the God we serve and how powerful He is. Next, he boldly declared that God loved them and would heal those who were sick. A man who was obviously well-known came forward. He had suffered with terrible back pain for quite some time. After prayer, he was healed; his healing caused quite a stir among the hundred or so people watching. Afterward, John gave an altar call for salvation, and people responded. This was unheard of since the camps usually responded only when the tribal chief indicated that it was the thing to do. However, some responded for salvation because of what they had observed. The chief invited our host to come back the next week because he wanted to explore Christianity further.

Cornelius called for Peter in Acts 10

A Gentile man named Cornelius, a centurion in the Roman army, lived in Caesarea. He and all his family were devout and God-fearing. Cornelius gave generously to those in need and prayed to God regularly. One day an angel of God spoke to him and told him to send men to Joppa to bring back a man named Simon who was called Peter. The angel even told him the exact home where Peter was staying.

The next day as the messengers were approaching the city, Peter was given a vision about not calling anything impure that God has made clean. The Spirit told Peter that three men were coming, and he was to go with them to Caesarea. The next day he went with the men to Cornelius' home, where he preached a powerful message about Jesus of Nazareth (Acts 10:1-43).

The Holy Spirit came on the Gentiles

> While Peter was still speaking these words, the Holy Spirit came *on* all who heard the message. The circumcised believers who had come with Peter were astonished that the *gift* of the *Holy Spirit* had been poured out even *on* the Gentiles. For they heard them

speaking in tongues and praising God. Then Peter said, "Can anyone keep these people from being baptized with water? They have received the Holy Spirit just as we have." So he ordered that they be baptized in the name of Jesus Christ. Then they asked Peter to stay with them for a few days.

—ACTS 10:44–48, EMPHASIS ADDED

> Speaking in tongues (spiritual language) and praising God is a definite pattern in Scripture that accompanies the Holy Spirit baptism. The same should be expected whenever the Holy Spirit comes upon those who believe.

Peter explained his actions

The apostles and the brothers throughout Judea heard that the Gentiles also had received the word of God. So when Peter went up to Jerusalem, the circumcised believers criticized him and said, "You went into the house of uncircumcised men and ate with them." Peter began and explained everything to them precisely as it had happened.

—ACTS 11:1–4

As I began to speak, the Holy Spirit came on them as he had come on us at the beginning. Then I remembered what the Lord had said: 'John baptized with water, but you will be baptized with the Holy Spirit.' So if God gave them the same gift as he gave us, who believed in the Lord Jesus Christ, who was I to think that I could oppose God?" When they heard this, they had no further objections and praised God, saying, "So then, God has granted even the Gentiles repentance unto life.

—ACTS 11:15–18

> The Holy Spirit baptism convinced Peter, the apostles, and other Jewish believers that Gentiles were acceptable to God.

It is for today

The Holy Spirit was poured out on Gentile men and women. It was fulfilling Acts 2:38–39 where Peter said, "the gift of the Holy Spirit" was for them and their "children and for all who are far off—for all whom the Lord our God will call." This clearly demonstrates that this wonderful gift is also for us today as we are "all who are far off—for all whom the Lord our God will call."

Saul's conversion and ministry

After Saul's encounter with the living Christ on the road to Damascus, and after Ananias obeyed the Lord's instructions to pray for him and baptize him, Saul immediately began to preach in the synagogues that Jesus is the Son of God (Acts 9).

Some years later, Paul was on a missionary journey that took him to Ephesus. There he found some disciples and asked them If they had received the Holy Spirit:

> While Apollos was at Corinth, Paul took the road through the interior and arrived at Ephesus. There he found some disciples and asked them, "Did you receive the Holy Spirit when you believed?" They answered, "No, we have not even heard that there is a Holy Spirit." So Paul asked, "Then what baptism did you receive?" "John's baptism," they replied. Paul said, "John's baptism was a baptism of repentance. He told the people to believe in the one coming after him, that is, in Jesus." On hearing this, they were baptized into the name of the Lord Jesus. When Paul placed his hands on them, the Holy Spirit came on them, and they spoke in tongues and prophesied. There were about twelve men in all.
>
> —ACTS 19:1–7

Here is recorded another instance years after Pentecost, where the same pattern is followed. Once believers have the proper understanding for receiving the Holy Spirit, hands are laid on them; they receive the gift of the Holy Spirit, and then release a spiritual language or prophesy.

Paul prayed in tongues

It is clear that the baptism of the Holy Spirit was a foundational truth and experience in the New Testament church. The apostle Paul obviously enjoyed that experience himself because he told the Corinthians later that he prayed in tongues more than all of them (1 Cor. 14:18).

Sonja experienced the same things they did

The apostles had been with the Lord for three and a half years. He had personally mentored them. After His resurrection, but before His ascension, He had breathed on them, and they had been born again (John 20:22). Yet they were ineffective and full of fear.

Jesus instructed the apostles to wait for the promise of the Father, for the gift of the Holy Spirit, to be endued with power from on high. On the Day of Pentecost, the Holy Spirit came upon them in such a powerful and supernatural way that they were never the same. They evangelized the then-known world, and most were martyred for their faith. What transformed them? It was the Holy Spirit of God who baptized and clothed them with His power. That is exactly what happened to me (Sonja). I received the same Holy Spirit empowerment, and I have never been the same!

WHAT HAPPENS WHEN WE ASK?

Jesus Christ gives the Holy Spirit to those who ask

> For everyone who asks, receives; and he who seeks, finds; and to him who knocks, it will be opened. Now suppose one of you fathers is asked by his son for a fish; he will not give him a snake instead of a fish, will he? Or if he is asked for an egg, he will not give him a scorpion, will he? If you then, being evil, know how to give good gifts to your children, how much more will your heavenly Father give the Holy Spirit to those who ask Him?
>
> —LUKE 11:10–13, NASB, EMPHASIS ADDED

We receive the gift of the Holy Spirit the moment we ask, just like when we asked for salvation.

How to ask

If you have not had the experience before and would like to receive the gift of the Holy Spirit, you can pray this simple prayer:

Jesus, baptize me in the Holy Spirit. Fill me with Your power so I can be a better witness for You. Thank You, Lord. I have received. Help me now to release my spiritual language. Amen.

Expect the Holy Spirit to come upon you and give you faith to speak words that are foreign to you. He gives the words; you do the speaking.

BIBLICAL REASONS FOR SPEAKING IN TONGUES

I would like every one of you to speak in tongues, but I would rather have you prophesy. He who prophesies is greater than one who speaks in tongues, unless he interprets, so that the church may be edified.

—1 CORINTHIANS 14:5

> Paul encouraged everyone to speak in tongues and to prophesy.

He who speaks in a tongue edifies himself, but he who prophesies edifies the church.

—1 CORINTHIANS 14:4

But you, dear friends, build yourselves up in your most holy faith and pray in the Holy Spirit.

—JUDE 20

> Praying and worshiping in tongues edifies the believer spiritually and builds up the inner spirit.

For if I pray in a tongue, my spirit prays, but my mind is unfruitful. So what shall I do? I will pray with my spirit, but I will also pray with my mind; I will sing with my spirit, but I will also sing with my mind.

—1 Corinthians 14:14–15

> Praying and worshiping in tongues allows us to enter the realm of the supernatural. We are communicating with the Lord in the natural and supernatural dimensions.

What then shall we say, brothers? When you come together, everyone has a hymn, or a word of instruction, a revelation, a tongue or an interpretation. All of these must be done for the strengthening of the church.

—1 Corinthians 14:26

> Praying in tongues allows us to hear words of instruction from the Holy Spirit, receive revelation from Him, and may give us the interpretation of what the Holy Spirit is saying.

HOW IMPORTANT IS SPEAKING IN TONGUES?

You probably know by now that we feel that the Holy Spirit baptism and speaking in tongues are essential if we are going to do what Jesus did. The core issue is about power—supernatural power, dynamite power—given by the Holy Spirit. The vehicle God has chosen for the imparting of this power is the Holy Spirit baptism. The accompanying supernatural occurrence of speaking in tongues is His idea, not ours.

Who would say, "No thanks, Jesus"?

How important is speaking in tongues? Jesus promised the gift of the Holy Spirit to believers so that they can be effective and empowered witnesses. They can be used in supernatural gifts to minister to others. How would you respond if Jesus were to ask you if you wanted that gift? No one in his or her right mind would say, "No thanks, Jesus. I'm satisfied with things just the way they are."

They need additional prayer

One of the reasons we contend for those who have not released their spiritual languages is that it is most often their initiation into the supernatural realm of God. We have observed this over and over. People have prayed and asked for the gift of the Holy Spirit, but have not released their language. Because they asked, the Holy Spirit has come *upon* them; they know something happened, but they know there is more.

Everyone who asks receives

Luke's Gospel states that "everyone who asks receives." It goes on to say that the heavenly Father gives the Holy Spirit to those who ask Him (Luke 11:10,13). However, if people do not release their spiritual language right at that moment, often a barrier is erected, and they need additional ministry. When we give people a clear, biblical teaching and pray against the barriers, almost 100 percent receive their language. When that happens, they begin to move in the supernatural dimensions of God.

Pastor Jim Hayford's story

We do not have space to record all the instances of people we know who have had the experience we just described. But we do want to include the story of our friend, Jim Hayford Sr., pastor emeritus of Eastside Foursquare Church in Bothell, Washington. He related the following testimony regarding his receiving the baptism of the Holy Spirit:

> When I was 15 years old, I visited my brother, Jack, and his wife, Anna, in Indiana where they pastored a small church. That summer, I attended two Foursquare summer camps my brother was directing. An emphasis was made on the ministry of the Holy Spirit. That summer with my brother was my first personal experience with Pentecostal teaching or practice. Believe me when I say it was quite an eye-opener!
>
> It was at the closing of a morning class on the baptism of the Holy Spirit in the big sawdust-floored tabernacle at Spencer Lake, Wisconsin, that I felt compelled to respond to the invitation to "receive the baptism." I know that my young heart was convinced that I needed more of the power of God in my life, so I went forward for prayer. A number of well-meaning people prayed with

me that morning for a considerable period of time, hoping that I would speak in tongues and give them "evidence" of my Holy Spirit baptism.

I remember walking out of that auditorium with two distinct and equally strong impressions. First, I knew God had met me in a profound way that I could not explain—and I knew I was "different" because of it. Second, I was conscious of the fact that I had somehow disappointed my prayer partners because I had not spoken in tongues. Regardless of my feelings or impressions, I am convinced that I rode away from that youth camp the next day having experienced the promise of the Lord Jesus that "from his innermost being will flow rivers of living water" (John 7:38, NASB).

That following year of my life involved an entirely new dimension of boldness in my Christian testimony. I remember that the Bible came alive to me. I found myself regularly reading it with true interest and spiritual hunger, rather than just as required by my parents. My leadership ability became apparent at my church and was recognized by adults and kids alike.

I attribute this remarkable surge of spiritual and personal growth in my life to what happened to me at that altar in Wisconsin the summer before. I believe—even though I did not speak in tongues that historic morning—that I most definitely was baptized in the Holy Spirit. The release of spiritual strength and witness in my life was the direct result and "evidence," if you please, of that experience.

A seed of doubt was most definitely planted in my young mind and developing theological construct after walking away from the altar without a prayer language. I did question (to myself) if I was "Spirit-filled." I sometimes did wonder if I had somehow "flunked" a God-test by not speaking in tongues as prompted. What could I do? I remember praying and asking the Lord to "give me the gift of tongues in His way and in His time." I was open.

Fourteen months later, I sat in the back row of the Foursquare church in Corning, California, where a friend of our family pastored. That summer day, I first spoke in tongues. Much to my own surprise I found myself speaking quietly in a language I had not learned while I sat all alone and was actually focusing my prayers at the time on a small group of young people who were at the front of the church being prayed for by the pastor about some other issue. Hot tears ran down my face as I acknowledged that the Lord had indeed answered my prayers about receiving the gift of tongues. This expression of God's grace has been part of my life every day since.

Years later as a pastor and student of Scripture, I would learn that the baptism of the Holy Spirit and the gifts of the Holy Spirit are not to be confused with one another. While the gift of tongues is obviously important to every believer as indicated by its sovereign occurrence at Pentecost, this gift is not synonymous with a person's baptism. They can be concurrent, or they can be separate. I believe that all gifts flow out of the baptism experience, some sooner than later.

I thank God for the development of the gifts of the Holy Spirit, beginning with the gift of tongues that occurred a full year after my Holy Spirit baptism. Many other spiritual gifts have developed over the years into a useful and edifying part of my life and ministry. I hope this testimony will be encouraging and helpful to others like me who have struggled with the issue of not speaking in tongues "when they were supposed to."

Relationship with the Holy Spirit

Our personal relationship with the Holy Spirit is the key issue. Are we in intimate communion with Him? It is through this personal interchange with Him that His gifts begin to flow through us. Gifts without relationship, love, and biblical foundation can be deceiving.

The gift is given when we ask in faith

We know that classical Pentecostal theology states that you are not baptized in the Holy Spirit until you speak in tongues. However, we believe that the gift is given when we ask in faith believing—just like salvation. Then we can speak in a spiritual language if we understand that we can and if we want to. Because ministers do not always give a thorough scriptural basis for receiving, people may misunderstand and end up with a less-than-satisfactory experience.

That is scary to me

When people come to us to pray for them to receive this gift, we ask them if they thoroughly understand what they are asking for. On numerous occasions, when asked if they want to release their spiritual language when the Holy Spirit comes upon them, they have responded, "Oh, no! I don't want to do that. That's scary to me." We then open Scripture to them and make sure they fully understand the supernatural nature of the experience. Once they see it in the Bible, they can make an informed decision. If we had prayed before interviewing them, we would have been trying to lead them where they did not want to go. Many people have had unpleasant experiences because of expectations put upon them by uninformed or insensitive ministers.

We respect your opinions

We know many Pentecostals will disagree with our thesis that believers are baptized in the Holy Spirit when they ask in faith for the gift. If believers are unable to release their spiritual languages at that very moment, they often do as soon as they get alone and quiet before the Lord. Or they may need further instructions and encouragement before they break the barrier and begin speaking. We will never argue about this subject. We respect others' opinions and respectfully ask they would do the same.

BEING CONTINUALLY FILLED WITH THE SPIRIT

After we are baptized with the Holy Spirit, we are admonished to be *filled* with the Holy Spirit. This experience produces power to live an effective Christian life characterized by joy:

> Do not get drunk on wine, which leads to debauchery. Instead, be *filled* with the Spirit. Speak to one another with psalms, hymns and spiritual songs. Sing and make music in your heart to the Lord.
> —EPHESIANS 5:18–19, EMPHASIS ADDED

We are baptized in the Holy Spirit once. We are then to be filled with the Holy Spirit on a daily basis.

This is not a one-time experience. Rather, it is one we should consciously contend for on a daily basis. One of the primary ways to stay filled is to pray in your spiritual language (tongues). Other ways include daily reading, studying, meditating on the Bible, journaling, fellowshiping with believers, and participating in a small group with other Christians.

Singing spiritual songs

As stated in Ephesians 5:19, when we are filled with the Spirit we can sing spiritual songs. These often come in the form of unpremeditated worship in our spiritual language. We may sing the Spirit-inspired words to a known melody or a brand new one—depending on how the Holy Spirit leads us. This adds a beautiful and supernatural dimension to our worship.

MISUNDERSTANDINGS

The baptism with the Holy Spirit has been a point of confusion within the body of Christ—primarily because of a lack of proper teaching. Millions of believers worldwide in all Christian denominations have experienced Holy Spirit baptism, yet some still deny the authenticity of that experience. The following facts can help clarify some areas of misunderstanding:

- Holy Spirit baptism is not necessarily a sign of spirituality; it is a gift for believers, no matter how young they are in the Lord. A brand new believer can have this experience. Some immature believers have implied to other Christians they were more spiritual because they spoke in tongues. That is completely inaccurate. Many very spiritual Christians have not had this experience. If believers desire more of the Holy Spirit in their lives, this gift is for them. They already have salvation, but this experience is about supernatural power to more effectively live the Christian life and better understand the supernatural realm.

- Holy Spirit baptism is not speaking in tongues only. As wonderful as that experience is, it is only a small part of the total experience. The experience is about supernatural power, edification, and many other dimensions of the Holy Spirit. It is often believers' introduction to the supernatural power of God, and it provides insight into the supernatural power of Satan as well.

- Holy Spirit baptism is about our personal relationship with our Lord Jesus Christ and the Holy Spirit. It is out of this relationship that the gifts and power of the Holy Spirit are released for the benefit of others.

- Very few Christians are comfortable dealing with demonized people if they have not been baptized with the Holy Spirit. To set these people free, believers must operate in the supernatural gifts of discerning of spirits, words of wisdom, and words of knowledge.

- The primary reason for speaking in tongues is to allow the Holy Spirit to pray through us according to the perfect will of God. After we have prayed with our understanding, we often feel inadequate. Sometimes we do not even know how to pray. It is at those times that the Holy Spirit enables us to pray in an unknown language. Something happens in the spiritual dimension because the very Spirit of God has interceded on our behalf!

- The experience of being baptized with the Holy Spirit and praying in tongues (which is for all believers) is not the same as the gifts of "speaking in different kinds of tongues" and "interpretation of tongues" that are discussed by Paul in 1 Corinthians 12:7–11. The speaking in tongues that all believers can experience is a devotional prayer dimension that Paul referred to in 1 Corinthians 14:2: "For anyone who speaks in a tongue does not speak to men but to God. Indeed, no one understands him; he utters mysteries with his spirit." The gifts discussed in the 1 Corinthians 12 passage are for messages from God to the church. In other words, when believers pray in tongues, it is the Holy Spirit praying through them to

God and according to His perfect will. When a message in tongues is given to the congregation, it is from God to the assembled people and must be interpreted so that people know what God said.

HOW TO LEAD A BELIEVER INTO THE BAPTISM OF THE HOLY SPIRIT

- Determine if the person is born again. This experience is only for believers.

- Determine the person's motive. If it is simply to speak in tongues, make sure the person has a scriptural understanding before you proceed.

- Explain that this gift is a free gift just as salvation is. You receive the gift the moment you ask in faith believing. (Note: Incomplete or wrong teaching, unforgiveness, or occult practices can hinder a person. If there seems to be a hindrance, give the person a scriptural understanding and lead in a prayer of repentance about these matters before proceeding.)

- Explain exactly what you are going to do. Say, "We will examine Scripture, pray to receive the Holy Spirit, and release a spiritual language."

- Instruct the person to pray, or lead the person in a prayer that asks the Lord Jesus Christ for the gift of the Holy Spirit and the ability to pray in languages they have not learned.

- Reassure the person that he or she will receive the moment they ask. Do not rush the person. Give "grace and space."

- Instruct the person to take a deep breath and allow the Holy Spirit to give the words. The best description is that it may sound like a baby learning to talk with nonsensical syllables. Jesus asks us to become like little children and speak words of praise to the heavenly Father. We simply speak the words the Holy Spirit prompts. Many people think they are "just making it up." We like to continue praying with people and encouraging them until they are speaking fluently and clearly understand that they cannot be making it up.

- Put your hand lightly on the person's shoulder and pray softly in your own prayer language. Do not push; give the person a few moments to respond to the Holy Spirit. Gently encourage the person not to be afraid or care what it sounds like. Simply keep encouraging him or her and validating the experience.

- Finally, encourage the person to pray in his or her new language as often as possible and to not get "religious" about it. Riding in a car, taking walks, or almost any other activity can lend itself to prayer.

Summary of speaking in tongues from 1 Corinthians 14:

It is a real language.

You are speaking to God.

You are speaking spiritual secrets.

You are being personally built up and edified.

Your spirit is praying.

You are giving thanks.

BECOMING MARKETPLACE MINISTERS

Because of the controversy that exists in regard to Holy Spirit baptism, we have attempted to give a brief, but fairly comprehensive, teaching about the experience. We hope it will be helpful in answering questions as you step out and begin to share this wonderful gift with those in your marketplace.

How this works in the marketplace

One day I (Sonja) was sitting in my office when a secretary from another building stopped by to chat. Knowing I was a Christian, she asked me what I thought about that speaking in tongues stuff. I responded by telling her that I happened to have had that experience. She was stunned, exclaimed her disbelief that I would do such a thing, and hurriedly exited.

I did not see her for a few days, but, when my company's reorganization was announced the next week, I found that she was going to be working with me. I am sure Lois thought I would be all over her, trying to convince her to speak in tongues. However, I had learned some "marketplace savvy." My practice was to let people come to me with a question; then I would share a little and change the subject. I always tried to leave them wanting more.

That was the way I handled the situation when Lois approached me. I gave my brief testimony of how I was baptized with the Holy Spirit and what had happened since. I then changed the subject. This went on for a couple of weeks. One morning she burst into my office and said, "I must be baptized with the Holy Spirit today! I can't wait any longer!" True to my convictions, I told her that we would have to wait until lunch time instead of doing it on company time.

Hamburgers and the Holy Spirit

Lois eagerly waited for the noon hour. I called a friend who worked in another building close by and asked her to pick up hamburgers and join us for lunch. I had previously led her into this wonderful experience, and she was thrilled to be able to help pray with someone else to be baptized with the Holy Spirit.

After we finished lunch in the conference room, we simply laid our hands on Lois and led her in a simple prayer. She immediately received a beautiful and fluent spiritual language. She went on to become one of the most dynamic marketplace ministers I know. She and her husband own a large real estate agency, and she is a powerful witness in her community.

This is one of many such marketplace experiences I had while in corporate America. Now most of my encounters are on airplanes, in hair salons, and with my neighbors.

Ministering one-on-one

Leading individual believers into the Holy Spirit baptism is easy. You can answer their questions and calm their fears while assuring them this gift is theirs for the asking. As the above illustration demonstrates, when seekers are properly prepared, we just lay our hands on them and pray a simple prayer and they receive!

Ministering to small groups

Both of us have had multitudes of opportunities to lead small groups of believers into this wonderful, life-changing experience. We always have the people who are responding to our invitation come forward so we can make eye contact with each person. If there are more than twenty, it is helpful to move to another room if possible.

I (Sonja) was recently ministering at a women's retreat. When I gave the altar call for Holy Spirit baptism, women flooded the front of the room. There was no stage, so I was trying to determine how to make eye contact with each of the women. Spontaneously, one woman grabbed a chair; I climbed on it, and led more than 20 women into the baptism with the release of their languages.

When people respond to our invitation, we explain exactly what we are going to do:

- We will pray for you.
- We will lead you in a prayer in which you will ask Jesus to baptize you with His Holy Spirit.
- We will lay hands on you while we are praying in our spiritual language.
- The Holy Spirit will come upon you, and you can begin speaking in your spiritual language.

The vast majority of those seeking, receive and release a spiritual language on the spot. We tell them they may leave when they have received what they came for. We keep praying for those who remain. If people have previously asked for the gift and did not have a satisfactory experience (such as not releasing their language), they usually have some type of mental blockage. Often they are expecting the Holy Spirit to do the speaking. We explain that the Holy Spirit gives the words, but we must do the speaking. Usually they are released into a beautiful spiritual language. We will address this more fully at the end of this chapter.

If you are teaching on Holy Spirit baptism and plan to give people an opportunity to respond, ask the Holy Spirit to show you ahead of time the type of response you can expect. He has shown us on numerous occasions that hundreds would respond. That allowed us to discuss logistics beforehand with the pastor so we could be assured every person would have a good experience. Teaching on the subject and having people respond on the basis of the Word instead of an emotional appeal makes it easy for them to receive.

Ministering to large groups

Leading large groups of 50 or more into Holy Spirit baptism requires significant planning. We recommend meeting with those in charge of the service well before the actual start time. Everyone needs to know ahead of time how the altar call will be done and how many are expected to respond. The pastor or leader in charge of the service, the main speakers, the worship team, the worship leader, and the altar workers need to be in agreement. Always plan to accommodate a maximum number, whether that situation materializes or not. People need to know what is expected of them once the altar call begins. Several things can be done to eliminate chaos and ensure that people who are responding to the Holy Spirit will have satisfactory experiences:

- Train altar workers to lead Christians into Holy Spirit baptism in a graceful way that ensures the release of a new spiritual language (speaking in tongues).

- Teach workers to gather a little group of three to five people and lead them through the process of receiving the Holy Spirit baptism. Give each worker a "Prayer Team" name badge. If 100 people respond, 20 to 25 altar workers would be advisable.

- When the altar call is given, have people move to the front of the auditorium. Next, tell them to proceed to a designated room or part of the auditorium that is well away from the sound of the concluding worship music. If that is not possible, do not begin the concluding music until after the group has received instructions and has prayed to receive the Holy Spirit baptism.

- Once the large group has responded and gathered together, designate one person (normally the speaker) to explain exactly what is going to happen and what they are going to do.

- Invite those seeking ministry to join with an altar worker in groups of three to five.

- Once people are in small groups, the speaker should have them pray out loud and invite the Holy Spirit to come upon them and baptize them in the Holy Spirit.

- The altar workers should pray and work with all members in their group until they have had a satisfactory release of their spiritual languages.

Training is the key

The biggest hindrance to ministering the Holy Spirit baptism in large groups is the lack of qualified altar workers. We recommend conducting a training workshop prior to the meeting to ensure a quality experience for each individual. We continually have people coming to us expressing negative experiences when they were part of a large crowd being instructed to speak in tongues all at once. A sizable number of people need personal, one-on-one ministry to release their new languages in an authentic and personal way.

Federal Way, Washington

We were privileged to talk to a large sanctuary full of eager Christians at Northwest Church in Federal Way, Washington. It was a special meeting dedicated to the Person of the Holy Spirit and the reasons we need His power for more effective witness.

Sonja received a word from the Holy Spirit that there would be an unusually large response. Two hundred Christians responded to the altar call, coming forward for empowerment. Sonja separated 120 of those who had asked for Holy Spirit baptism but had not released satisfactory spiritual languages. She took them into a separate meeting room, and John remained with the 80 who had never asked for the gift of the Holy Spirit. We took adequate time to explain fully what was to happen when they prayed for the free gift. We prayed and laid hands on each of them, and all but one released beautiful spiritual languages, personally confirming that they had been Holy Spirit-baptized.

Even with a sizable number of leaders helping us, it took an extra two hours for us to confirm that each one released an authentic spiritual language. It was a very exciting time. The pastor thanked us more than once and said, "The way you guys do it is unique, and it surely saves a lot of time and effort for the one ministering."

Bangkok, Thailand

I (John) was invited to speak at the three-day "Power Evangelism" conference near downtown Bangkok, Thailand. I spoke on why we need the power of the Holy Spirit to live a victorious Christian life. The daytime attendance was 3,000 and over 5,000 at night. The reason we stress having a lot of trained altar workers was clearly revealed at this conference. Speaking through an interpreter, I preached with everything I could muster. I was speaking in one of the largest auditoriums I have ever seen. The Holy Spirit was gracious and motivated 300 to respond to the altar call for the baptism of the Holy Spirit.

Now what?

I quickly realized I needed help. How could I ensure that all 300 would receive the power and speak in unknown tongues? I did not know Thai, and they did not speak English. My interpreter just shrugged his shoulders, indicating he did not know either. The Holy Spirit came to my rescue. He told me to call for the Thai believers who had already spoken in tongues to listen to their fellow believers speak in unknown tongues. I immediately invited about 50 Spirit-baptized Thai believers to merge into the crowd down front. I told them to listen carefully to each person as they spoke and worshiped in tongues. When they confirmed a new spiritual language being released in each person, they were to signal me. It was such a joy to see the workers going from one seeker to another carefully listening for an unknown language.

It only took about 15 minutes to confirm that all but a few had released genuine spiritual languages. The conference leaders came to me later and stated that they had never seen that done before. I had to say that I had not either! We were all praising the Lord for such an awesome move of God. In addition to the 300 who were baptized in the Holy Spirit, 500 people gave their lives to Jesus Christ by the end of the conference.

Let's do it right

We have many more stories about leading scores of hungry Christians into the baptism of power. Because we have been doing this for a long time, we forget that a whole generation of Christians has not heard about Holy Spirit baptism. In America today there are pastors who call themselves "Spirit-filled," yet they do not feel confident in leading the members of their congregation into the Holy Spirit baptism.

From our perspective as international evangelists primarily ministering to Pentecostal pastors and leaders, we feel something is missing. Where did pastors get their training? What kind of training have they received since leaving seminary? We feel that Holy Spirit baptism should be high on the list of personal priorities for all disciples attending a Spirit-filled church. It is the only way for new believers to have any chance of survival in witnessing to the hostile, twisted, and demonic world outside the church walls. So let's do it right! Let's become truly Spirit-filled in such a way that we can lead our fellow believers into the same power-filled experience we have received.

PRAYING FOR A SATISFACTORY EXPERIENCE

We are always sensitive to Christians who have previously prayed for the gift of the Holy Spirit, but did not have a satisfactory experience. The number of people in that category is usually double the number of people seeking the gift for the first time. After ministering to countless numbers of people for more than 35 years, we have come to the following conclusions:

- The teaching on this subject has been more experiential than scriptural.

- The believers did not realize that the gift of the Holy Spirit baptism is theirs for the asking and that they received the moment they asked in faith.

- The loud, emotion-based ministry in meetings can cause newcomers to become overwhelmed.

- People who did not release spiritual languages may feel that something is wrong with them and that God was withholding His gift from them.

When a person has an unsatisfactory experience, a mental barrier goes up. The barrier is reinforced with each negative experience. This always revolves around releasing a spiritual language.

God is not withholding His gift from them

I (Sonja) usually begin ministering to these people by saying that God is not withholding His gift of the Holy Spirit and a spiritual language from them. Further, I tell them He gave them the gift when they first asked in faith. I ask them if they have seen a change in the power of God in their lives. More often than not, they say they have seen a change, more power manifesting through them, but they know there is more. By then, many of them have tears in their eyes. They have felt like something was wrong with them, and I dispel that notion.

Hindrances are dealt with

Next, we explore what the hindrances might be—previous teaching against speaking in tongues, unforgiveness, or occult practices. A few may have these issues, and we simply have them pray a prayer of repentance, renouncing the sinful behavior. When they do so, the barrier is broken from their lives. Most often, however, the reason they have not released their prayer language is that they simply do not know how to yield to the Holy Spirit. They just cannot let go and begin speaking.

Sydney, Australia

We were ministering in a large church in Sydney, Australia. John was praying for the sick on one side of the church, and I (Sonja) was praying for believers to be baptized in the Holy Spirit on the other side. More than 30 people had received and released their spiritual languages. As we finished, I noticed an older man who had been standing off to the side carefully watching me minister. He told me he had been seeking the Holy Spirit baptism for over 25 years! He said he had requested every visiting high-powered evangelist to pray for him, but so far he just could not speak in tongues.

Are you afraid you will look and sound foolish?

I prayed and asked for wisdom. A word of knowledge came to me, and I shared it with the gentleman by asking this question: "Are you afraid you will look and sound foolish and be embarrassed?" With a shocked look on his face, he said that he had been tormented by that fear all those years. I reminded him that Jesus said we must become like little children if we want to see the kingdom of God. I then asked him if he would be willing to let go of his ego and his fear of looking foolish. Would he simply trust Jesus to give him a good gift?

He released a beautiful spiritual language

With tears in his eyes, he nodded his head and prayed a humble, simple prayer asking the Lord to forgive him for his lack of childlike trust. I laid hands on him, and he began to speak fluently in a beautiful spiritual language. He was thrilled and said, "Well, little lady, you did what the high-powered evangelists could not. Praise God!"

Home group ministry

This next incident happened in the small group that meets in our home each week. It is always interesting to see how the Holy Spirit arranges the mix of folks for a certain purpose. I (Sonja) am always extra curious when only a couple of people show up. Inevitably, He has a special need He is going to address.

One evening only Greg and Karen Fry attended. Since it was just the four of us, we asked the Frys if they had anything special to pray about. Greg immediately said that he wanted a greater release in his spiritual prayer language. He had received a few words, and had been prayed for multiple times, but with no satisfactory results. He was quite discouraged about the whole situation.

Shortly, the Holy Spirit was gushing forth from him

We began to worship the Lord, and, after a few minutes, we all became extremely joyful and even started laughing. In that environment, the Holy Spirit came upon Greg, who began to speak and laugh at the same time. Shortly, the Holy Spirit was gushing forth from him like "streams of living water." The dam of resistance had broken, and our dear friend has never been the same. A year later, Greg and Karen joined us in the ministry. He flows freely in teaching, and they both operate in prophetic prayer and healing gifts.

When working with people who are seeking to release their spiritual prayer languages, be respectful of their feelings, and ask the Lord to give you the key to unlocking the blockage.

I broke its power off them

Another time, I (Sonja) was teaching a group of people about the Holy Spirit baptism. Most of them had prayed for the gift before, but had not released their spiritual languages. I prayed for them as a group, taking authority in Jesus' name over the previous wrong teaching they had received. I broke its power off them and loosed them into the fullness of this wonderful experience. After I prayed, I led them in a prayer, and they all released their spiritual languages.

He had been raised as a Jehovah's Witness

During the break, a man came to me with a wonderful testimony. He had sought the Holy Spirit baptism for a number of years, but could never release his language. When I prayed and broke the power of the wrong teaching off of his life, he said it was as if "something actually broke off of me"—he felt it leave. He then explained he had been raised as a Jehovah's Witness, and he was sure that was what left him and allowed him to fully receive God's gift.

We can all do this

We hope you will be convinced of how easy this ministry really is. It can be done one-on-one or with a large number of Christians. All that is needed are the power and presence of the Holy Spirit as we minister. The same power and presence are needed as we learn how to heal the sick. This is the next ministry skill we will learn in chapter 3.

LET'S PRACTICE

James 1:22 says to do what we have heard (read).

Consider doing what is recommended in this chapter by referring to the "Let's Practice" in Appendix B, page 255.

Do the ministry skill assignment titled, "Leading Christians Into the Holy Spirit Baptism."

Ministry Skill Three

LEARNING HOW TO HEAL THE SICK

Jesus told us that He wanted us to do the things that He did—including healing the sick. In this chapter, we will carefully review what the Bible has to say about healing and learn how we, too, can be used to heal the sick.

(JOHN) BECAME A Christian in March 1973 and became a member of the Seattle chapter of the Full Gospel Business Men's Fellowship International (FGBMFI) two months later. I watched in amazement as members of this organization prayed for those who needed healing. In astonishment I saw people get healed. The men would pray with such conviction that I assumed they were sent directly from God. Not everyone was healed, but those who were healed got my attention. I thought the men who prayed for people to be healed had special powers from God. I had no idea where or how they received these special powers. I made it a priority to be up front where the action was. Christianity was new to me, and I wanted to experience everything that was going on. This began my journey of learning how to heal the sick.

Jesus healed the sick

One-third of Jesus' earthly ministry was healing the sick. In Matthew 9 and 10, Jesus taught, preached to, and healed the sick. If we are to do what Jesus did, healing the sick will be a part of our ministry. After demonstrating to His disciples how to do it, Jesus immediately gave them the power and authority to heal the sick. Healing the sick is a vital part of the Lord's evangelistic strategy to win the world to Himself. Healing grabs the attention of pre-Christians, softening their hearts to hear the way of salvation. It is a sign to them that the message the person is preaching while healing the sick is from God. It demonstrates that the Lord is working with them as an authentic ambassador of Jesus Christ.

Then Jesus went about all the cities and villages, teaching in their synagogues, preaching the gospel of the kingdom, and healing every sickness and every disease among the people.

—MATTHEW 9:35, NKJV

And when He had called His twelve disciples to Him, He gave them power over unclean spirits, to cast them out, and to heal all kinds of sickness and all kinds of disease.

—MATTHEW 10:1, NKJV

> As disciples of Jesus Christ, we have been authorized and empowered by Him to heal all kinds of sickness and all kinds of disease.

John's history

I will share some early snapshots of how I came to believe in divine healing and how I began praying for the sick. Your experiences may or may not parallel mine. The Lord's desire is that we all arrive at the same destination—a firm belief that Jesus Christ still heals the sick.

Growing Faith

My journey started within months of my becoming a Christian early in 1973. As the years progressed, I noticed a natural progression of faith as I saw God heal the sick. My coming to a full understanding about divine healing occurred in two stages: *surprise encounters* and *discovering the authentic*. Chapter 5 will thoroughly discuss the final stages where we minister healing by reliance on the Holy Spirit and His revelation gifts. In both stages, a compassionate, supernatural God progressively manifests Himself as a God who is willing to heal us. This is clearly illustrated in the following passages:

> Now a leper came to Him, imploring Him, kneeling down to Him and saying to Him, "If You are willing, You can make me clean." Then Jesus, moved with compassion, stretched out His hand and touched him, and said to him, "*I am willing*; be cleansed." As soon as He had spoken, immediately the leprosy left him, and he was cleansed.
>
> —MARK 1:40–42, NKJV, EMPHASIS ADDED

And behold, a leper came and worshiped Him, saying, "Lord, if You are willing, You can make me clean." Then Jesus put out His hand and touched him, saying, "I am willing; be cleansed." Immediately his leprosy was cleansed.

—MATTHEW 8:2–3, NKJV

And it happened when He was in a certain city, that behold, a man who was full of leprosy saw Jesus; and he fell on his face and implored Him, saying, "Lord, if You are willing, You can make me clean." Then He put out His hand and touched him, saying, "I am willing; be cleansed." Immediately the leprosy left him.

—LUKE 5:12–13, NKJV

- The preceding scriptures reveal God's will concerning healing. His will is plainly revealed in these three passages. They all say the same thing: He is willing to heal us!

- God is willing to heal leprosy, and He is willing to heal all manner of sickness and disease. Jesus has revealed His eternal compassion and mercy to heal the sick.

- Most believe that God is able to do anything He wants. These passages proclaim that God is able and also willing to heal those who come to Him in faith.

- Therefore, we can preach with confidence that diving healing is available through the mighty name of Jesus Christ.

- Sick people (like the leper) who are serious and determined to get healed, demonstrate the kind of faith that will set the stage for healing.

- The timing of when the healing will actually manifest is always left in the hands of the Lord. Even though He is willing to heal now, the full, physical manifestation may be instant or may take hours, days, or weeks.

- Nowhere in Scripture can we find a passage that permits us to demand an instant healing. That is foolish presumption. Because Jesus is willing, healing starts the moment we start praying for the sick.
- Our confession remains: "God is willing to heal you now. Your healing starts today. We will continue to thank Him until the physical manifestation comes to pass."
- Only God knows the sicknesses that will end in death (John 11:4). This is why we need revelation knowledge from the Lord about how to pray in these kinds of situations. We contend for healing until the Lord reveals otherwise.

SURPRISE ENCOUNTERS

My first attempt

I (John) will never forget the very first time I prayed for a person to be healed. He was an old man with a damaged knee. He and I attended a luncheon meeting of the FGBMFI in north Seattle. The speaker for the meeting was a fiery, faith-filled businessman who announced that God wanted to heal everyone who would come for prayer. I was seated on the first row and was excited that I could watch what was going to happen. By the time the elderly man limped to the front for prayer, all the chapter officers were busy praying for the sick. Assuming that I was one of the ministers, the man turned to me and rolled up his pant leg and showed me his bandaged knee. He asked me to pray for him, and, not wanting to disappoint him, I told him I would go get somebody so we could pray.

The man gripped my sleeve firmly and said that he wanted me to pray for him. I turned once more to those who knew what to do. They all waved me away, firmly indicating that I was interrupting their healing ministry. So I sat the man down in my chair. I looked at the mangled knee and said, "Oh God, help me. Do something here, please." Then I heard one of the men behind me boldly say, "In the name of Jesus!" I promptly added, "Oh, that's right, God, please do it in the name of Jesus. Amen."

I did not know what to believe

I was afraid to open my eyes, and I did not know what to do next. With my hand still on the man's injured knee, I kept my eyes closed and silently hoped I could exit gracefully. I felt the man stand up. And then I heard him shout, "I'm healed! I'm healed!" When I opened my eyes, I was stunned to see him jumping up and down exclaiming that God had just healed him. With no limp, he confidently marched back to his seat and testified to his friends that God had just healed his knee.

I left the meeting in a state of awe. I had no idea how that man got healed. All I knew was that Jesus Christ had set up a situation where people could get healed, and the man simply needed someone to help him release his faith. I was a reluctant participant in what Jesus had set in motion 2,000 years earlier. It was the elderly man's faith that healed him, not mine. The woman in the following scriptures illustrates the principle of this kind of unwavering faith in Jesus Christ as the source of divine healing.

> A woman was there who had been subject to bleeding for twelve years, but no one could heal her. She came up behind him and touched the edge of his cloak, and immediately her bleeding stopped. "Who touched me?" Jesus asked. When they all denied it, Peter said, "Master, the people are crowding and pressing against you." But Jesus said, "Someone touched me; I know that power has gone out from me." Then the woman, seeing that she could not go unnoticed, came trembling and fell at his feet. In the presence of all the people, she told why she had touched him and how she had been instantly healed. Then he said to her, "Daughter, your faith has healed you. Go in peace."
>
> —LUKE 8:43–48
> (ALSO MATTHEW 9:20–22 AND MARK 5:25–34)

- There will be times when those we pray for will be exercising a high degree of faith toward God for healing. Any kind of physical contact with another believer will cause them to release their faith and receive an immediate healing.

- In these cases our faith is superfluous. We simply make physical contact, agree with what they believe will happen, and then watch God do the rest.
- Note: Jesus did not initiate the healing. Power transferred from Jesus to the woman when she touched Him, not vice versa.
- Everyone was crowding around Jesus, yet He only acknowledged that one person touched Him. Her faith was based totally on the divine presence of a healing Lord who is willing to heal anyone whose hope is found in Jesus Christ.

My quest begins

That was the beginning of my quest to find out how God operates through His people. Over the years I participated in rallies, conventions, and meetings with the FGBMFI, watching ordinary businessmen exercise their faith in Jesus Christ. During that time my faith for the miraculous steadily increased. Each week I heard the leadership say, "Anyone filled with the mighty power of the Holy Spirit can do what Jesus did!" Slowly my understanding about kingdom principles changed. One day I finally convinced myself that if they could do it, so could I. I tentatively began praying for the sick just as the other men were doing.

Do what Jesus says you can do

Eventually I came to understand that Jesus Christ Himself was the source of divine healing power. The FGBMFI men believed the healing promises in the Bible proclaimed both in the Old and New Testaments, and I began to believe them, too. I heard people quote Scripture, and then I saw them doing what it said. Sometimes healing would manifest, and sometimes it would not. But I saw enough results that I began to see that doing what the Word says will yield results.

I began to do it

At first I began to assist people who prayed for others. I laid hands on people and said "amen" to whatever the lead person prayed. I got used to hearing certain words and phrases, and I became more and more confident that something was going to happen. Faith comes by hearing, and faith for healing was beginning to manifest in my mind. Eventually I began to think I could try it for myself. My thinking was similar to the disciples in Luke 17. I needed the Lord to increase my faith:

> And the apostles said to the Lord, "Increase our faith." So the Lord said, "If you have faith as a mustard seed, you can say to this mulberry tree, 'Be pulled up by the roots and be planted in the sea,' and it would obey you."
>
> —LUKE 17:5–6, NKJV

> Faith is increased by constant use. Taking Jesus at His Word by continuing to pray for the sick over and over again will eventually cause faith to increase. We will experience success if we continue to pray for the sick.

Overflowing meetings

In the spring of 1973, I attended meetings at a hotel in Seattle's University District. These meetings were spectacular! We were packed in like sardines, and our expectation of what God would do knew no bounds. The praise and worship were electrifying. It was there that I learned to sing in my spiritual language. The presence of the Lord was strongly manifesting, and the crowds continued to increase. We had to move to the largest hotel ballroom in downtown Seattle. It was there that I began praying with conviction for the sick. I did not see too much happen at first, but I continued to pray for the sick like the other men I had been watching the past months. If you were part of the group, you were expected to pray for the sick at every meeting.

The Word changed my thinking

By mid-1974, I had read through the Old Testament once and the New Testament a couple of times. I began to concentrate on the promises of Jesus and what He said we should be doing. I underlined the scriptures that were being preached by various speakers at FGBMFI and other faith-filled preachers. They all were saying the same thing: "You can do what Jesus says you can do." I began to understand how faith comes as stated in Romans 10:17. My faith was increasing as I witnessed the spoken Word of God produce healing as people incorporated the Word into their prayers for the sick.

> So then faith comes by hearing, and hearing by the word of God.
> —ROMANS 10:17, NKJV

- Faith for doing the miraculous increases as we meditate on what Jesus said we can do.
- Faith will also increase when we act on what He says we can do and begin praying for people to receive what He promises.
- Faith will grow when we continue to associate with those who operate in the supernatural and boldly pray for the sick.

The man called Miracle

One of the businessmen I associated with was aptly named Ken Miracle. Ken was about 10 years older than I and had come to Christ quite a few years earlier. He encouraged me to practice the Word. I followed his lead and did as he did, and it began to work. He kept saying, "The Word works. Just act like it's so." He, and others like him, continued to reinforce what I was reading and highlighting in Scripture.

I teamed up with Ken and began ministering with him. We would pray for anyone who needed healing. I began to see evidence of what he was talking about. Pains left people as we prayed. Headaches were gone; broken bones were healed; sore backs became normal; sinuses cleared up. Some of the healings took a while; other healings were instant. To me they were all miraculous. Ken even went to the local hospital looking for people to pray for. The nurses found out what he was doing and firmly insisted he leave. He did, but not before the doctors recorded a series of "unexplainable" miracles. Ken and his devotion to biblical truth changed my thinking. I finally did what Jesus said I could do. I boldly began to pray for the sick.

Jesus prayed for the blind man twice

We tend to give up too soon when learning how to heal the sick. Mark 8:22–26 depicts Jesus praying twice before the blind man saw clearly. Jesus worked with the man until his sight was totally restored. This is an excellent lesson for those desiring to pray for the sick. If it took two prayers for Jesus to see results, we can expect to offer two or more prayers before we see results. Sometimes we may pray multiple prayers over a period of time before the healing finally manifests.

> Then He came to Bethsaida; and they brought a blind man to Him, and begged Him to touch him. So He took the blind man by the hand and led him out of the town. And when He had spit on his eyes and put His hands on him, He asked him if he saw anything. And he looked up and said, "I see men like trees, walking." Then He put His hands on his eyes *again* and made him look up. And he was restored and saw everyone clearly. Then He sent him away to his house, saying, "Neither go into the town, nor tell anyone in the town."
>
> —MARK 8:22–26, NKJV

Jesus showed us some important ministry techniques to ensure success in healing the sick:

- Lead the person away from doubt and unbelief.
- Listen to and follow the Holy Spirit's instructions. If the Holy Spirit say, "Spit and lay on of hands," do it.
- Ask the person what is happening as you continue praying. Jesus asked the blind man if he saw anything. We should do the same.
- Jesus prayed a second time! If it does not work on the first prayer, pray again. Offer to keep praying until the Holy Spirit says you are through.

> ● Caution those you pray for to avoid an atmosphere of unbelief. Instruct the people to continue thanking God for their healings until the medical community has given confirmation of them.

Sharing my testimony

In 1975 I was invited to speak at my first FGBMFI dinner meeting in Mount Vernon, Washington. I earnestly prayed that God would use me. After telling how I became a Christian and how I was baptized in the Holy Spirit, I had the privilege of praying with two men that gave their lives to Christ. I also prayed for some men who needed healing. One was healed from pain. The others left without acknowledging any change. That was the beginning of my speaking and ministering at FGBMFI meetings all over the Northwest U.S. and Canada. I was privileged to be one of their speakers for over 25 years. Sonja and I were very grateful when the Seattle chapter inducted us into the "Hall of Faith" in the fall of 1998.

Another surprise

FGBMFI meetings became a spiritual shot in the arm for many men in Seattle. I remember one in 1976 where I arrived spiritually drained. I had not read the Word in a week; I had not prayed. I had done nothing to bolster my faith. I showed up to get blessed, not to be a blessing. Toward the end of the meeting I saw a man I had never met. The Holy Spirit told me that the man had a pain in his back. He told me to go to the man and he would be healed. God's voice sometimes comes spontaneously, sometimes when we are least expecting it. This happened to Peter:

> While Peter was still thinking about the vision, the Spirit said to him, "Simon, three men are looking for you. So get up and go downstairs. Do not hesitate to go with them, for I have sent them."
> —ACTS 10:19–20

> Whenever we hear words in our minds that are out of the ordinary and come as a "jolt," it is most likely the Holy Spirit urging us to do something. Obey!

I went to the man and told him what I had heard from the Lord. He verified that he had back pain, so I laid my hands on his back and said, "Pain, leave in the name of Jesus Christ." The pain left immediately. The man who was healed became a regular at Full Gospel functions from then on. You may think God cannot use you because of a negative circumstance, but that is when He is likely to take command of the situation and surprise you. God works best when we acknowledge total dependence on Him.

Hanging around those who are doing it

During the early years, I was invited to accompany some key Full Gospel individuals on speaking engagements that accelerated my learning curve for operating in the supernatural power of God. The first was Don Ostrom, the president of the Seattle chapter, who was a mentor to many men through the years. On one particular trip to a Bremerton, Washington chapter meeting, Don encouraged me to be sensitive to the Holy Spirit and do whatever God led me to do. It was that night I first prophesied in a public meeting. Don gave me some positive advice and gave me some pointers for the next time I exercised that gift. Good feedback from those who precede us in the ministry help us learn to do things right. The early disciples received such feedback from Jesus:

> Then the disciples came to Jesus privately and said, "Why could we not drive it [the demon] out?" And He said to them, "Because of the littleness of your faith; for truly I say to you, if you have faith the size of a mustard seed, you will say to this mountain, 'Move from here to there,' and it will move; and nothing will be impossible to you." ["But this kind does not go out except by prayer and fasting."]
> —MATTHEW 17:19–21, NASB

> When learning how to heal the sick, watch
> how your mentor does it. Jesus' disciples were
> quick to ask Jesus why their attempts to drive
> out a demon did not work. Jesus used the sit-
> uation to teach them how to do ministry. He
> told them that prayer and fasting should be
> employed.

Valuable mentor

Another early mentor was Steve Lightle, a completed Jew who sold out to Jesus about five years before I did. Steve eventually became the European coordinator for FGBMFI and lived in Brussels, Belgium, for a number of years. He did not like to travel alone and invited others to accompany him. I went with him to a Kent, Washington, men's meeting. It was a turning point in my life. Steve had a prophecy for me that confirmed my calling and future in the ministry. It has come to pass just as he prophesied.

Grab a toe and pray

Steve called a person whose heart had stopped beating back to life. It happened outside a Full Gospel convention in a downtown Seattle hotel lobby. A woman passed out and fell to the lobby floor. First aid workers responded quickly and hooked the woman up to a heart monitor. The woman had no heartbeat. Steve maneuvered close to the woman's feet and laid hands on the only place he could—her big toe. Steve boldly grabbed her toe and commanded life back into her body. To the astonishment of those who observed the incident, the heart monitor immediately started beeping. Most would classify the event as a miracle, close to raising the dead. Steve considered it as such, even though they had not declared her clinically dead. Either way, it demonstrates the power of speaking life-giving words that release the healing power of God, similar to what Peter experienced in Acts 9:

> Peter sent them all out of the room; then he got down on his knees
> and prayed. Turning toward the dead woman, he said, "Tabitha,
> get up." She opened her eyes, and seeing Peter she sat up. He took
> her by the hand and helped her to her feet.
>   —ACTS 9:40–41

- Jesus mentored Peter. Peter had seen Jesus raise the dead. When it came time for Peter to do it, he knew what to do. Like Jesus, Peter first prayed, and we assume he received instructions from the Father of what to do (John 5:19). Then, he addressed the dead person by name and commanded her to get up.
- Peter had seen Jesus take Jairus' daughter by the hand. So, he did it just like Jesus, his mentor. Peter gave her his hand and lifted her up.
- As Peter obeyed what the Holy Spirit wanted to do, all doubt and disbelief were removed from him. He could do what Jesus had taught him, and a miracle transpired.
- Because Peter was obedient, the Lord was glorified. Acts 9:42 states, "This became known all over Joppa, and many people believed in the Lord."

Steve helped shape my early ministry skills. He was good at improvising ministry techniques that few would dare try. He believed that God that would honor anyone who operated according to the whole counsel of the Bible. One other important thing I learned from Steve was to always give God all the glory and credit for the victories that are achieved in ministry.

Receiving what they believed for

FGBMFI chapter officers prayed that God would do the miraculous at every meeting. They invited speakers that had personal testimonies that included exciting moves of God. Ordinary businessmen who had encountered a miracle-working God testified to how God had changed their lives. They would always say, "God is no respecter of persons. If He did it for me; He will do it for you." This resulted in some very exciting meetings. It would cause astonishment to the skeptics, similar to the next Scripture passage.

When they [the high priests] saw the courage of Peter and John and realized that they were unschooled, ordinary men, they were astonished and they took note that these men had been with Jesus. But since they could see the man who had been healed standing there with them, there was nothing they could say.

—Acts 4:13–14

When we give testimony of an authentic healing, it closes the mouths of the skeptics and produces an atmosphere of faith toward God. Always be open for opportunities to share what God has done, especially when He heals you or someone you know.

The FGBMFI meetings produced an atmosphere of faith and expectancy. The leaders always invited the Holy Spirit to do whatever He wanted to do. People were always invited to receive Christ, and many did. Then altar calls were made for those who wanted to receive the Holy Spirit baptism and be prayed over for healing. That is when most of the miracles took place. People got what they believed for. We never cared about the time because there was so much going on. These meetings were similar to Paul's, described in the following passage:

Paul, ready to depart the next day, spoke to them and continued his message until midnight. There were many lamps in the upper room where they were gathered together. And in a window sat a certain young man named Eutychus, who was sinking into a deep sleep. He was overcome by sleep; and as Paul continued speaking, he fell down from the third story and was taken up dead. But Paul went down, fell on him, and embracing him said, "Do not trouble yourselves, for his life is in him." Now when he had come up, had broken bread and eaten, and talked a long while, even till daybreak, he departed. And they brought the young man in alive, and they were not a little comforted.

—Acts 20:7–12, NKJV

> Jesus still wants to heal the sick even in the middle of the night. God never sleeps. We can be sure that Eutychus was glad the meeting did not dismiss until after Paul had raised him from the dead.

Believing in spite of the circumstances

In 1978 one of my clients heard me speak and asked me to go pray for his mother who was in a Seattle hospital. Still basking in the faith of the meeting, I told him that I would love to pray for his mother, and that I believed she would be healed. I went to her bedside and found her in a coma. But I had learned that God's healing was not bound by outward circumstances. I was to release my faith and believe that God would perform a miracle. I anointed my client's mother with oil and prayed the prayer of faith.

When I returned the next day, her room was empty. I began to rejoice, thinking that she must have been healed and released from the hospital. My joy quickly turned to bewilderment, however, when the nurse informed me that the patient had died during the night. I sat in the car and asked God what had happened. I heard Him tell me that I did not know everything. I was to continue to obey Him and keep doing what He instructed me to do. I learned a big lesson: I was to be obedient and leave the final results up to a merciful God.

Eternity awaits everyone

When Christians die, they immediately enter into the glorious destination promised by the Lord Jesus Christ, eternity with Him! For Christians, dying is the consummation of the promise of eternal life, where there is no more death, mourning, crying, or pain. Our responsibility is to pray for those who are asking for prayer, including those who may be dying. Our goal should be to lead them into relationship with Jesus Christ before they die so that they can enter into the glorious promise of eternal life.

Start with something easy

In learning how to heal the sick, we sometimes have to start with something that does not seem to require much faith. Headaches, high fevers, neck pains, or sore backs may be easier to tackle than praying for someone dying of terminal cancer. All healing is easy for God; however, Christians who have never prayed for the sick may need to start with something similar to the next passage.

> Now [Jesus] arose from the synagogue and entered Simon's house. But Simon's wife's mother was sick with a high fever, and they made request of Him concerning her. So He stood over her and rebuked the fever, and it left her. And immediately she arose and served them.
>
> —Luke 4:38–39, nkjv
> (also see Matthew 8:14–15 and Mark 1:29–31)

This is a great example of how many Christians begin healing the sick. Do it just like Jesus did:

- Respond to a request for healing by going to where the sick person is.
- Take charge of the situation by going directly to the sick person.
- Rebuke the fever, sickness, or pain by speaking to the problem area in the name of Jesus Christ.
- Act on the prayer you just prayed by encouraging the person to do something that could not be done previously because of the sickness or pain.
- Keep expecting the fever, sickness, or pain to leave the person at any moment. Eventually, the healing will manifest.

The crooked elbow

Also during 1978, I had a surprise encounter that I will never forget. About 2:00 one wintry afternoon, I got a call from the president of the Kelowna, B.C., Canada, FGBMFI chapter. He requested that I find a way to get from Seattle to Kelowna by 7:00 to speak at their evening meeting. The scheduled speaker had canceled the day before because of a scheduling conflict. Larry Day, the president of the Bellevue chapter, checked out a Cessna 210 from his flight club at Boeing Field and got me to the meeting just as the praise and worship were ending. It was a sold-out house because of the reputation of the scheduled speaker. God had something He wanted to do and He wanted us in on it.

Larry gave a riveting testimony about Jesus' healing the sick. Then I spoke about similar healings. About a dozen people received Christ. Then people formed three lines when it came time to pray for the sick. One by one, we began to pray for the sick and hurting. The one healing miracle I will never forget was a young woman who had fallen as a child and had broken her arm at the elbow. She could not straighten her arm. It was permanently crooked. She asked me to pray for her arm. Like Paul in Acts 14, I looked directly at her and saw something in the Spirit.

> In Lystra there sat a man crippled in his feet, who was lame from birth and had never walked. He listened to Paul as he was speaking. Paul looked directly at him, saw that he had faith to be healed and called out, "Stand up on your feet!" At that, the man jumped up and began to walk.
>
> —ACTS 14:8–10

- When we are preaching, teaching, or testifying about the Lord's desire to heal people, we must be sensitive to listeners.
- Because of the Word's ability to penetrate people's hearts, faith will rise up in those in need of healing.
- The Holy Spirit is strongly at work when the Word is preached. Pause and allow Him to speak regarding any who need healing.
- As you look at the people around you, the Holy Spirit may cause you to "see" the ones who have faith to be healed.

- We "see" through the eyes of the Holy Spirit when He says to us, "That one, over there—call out to him to stand up on his feet!"
- When the Holy Spirit initiates the ministry, people are always healed.

I saw that she had faith to be healed

I asked the woman, "Do you believe God will straighten your arm when we pray?" She quickly said yes. I agreed with her and commanded her arm to be straightened in the name of Jesus. We heard a gentle snapping sound as the arm came into normal position. The woman's arm was completely straight, and appeared as normal as her other arm. The woman and her mother shed tears of joy, and I must admit that tears came to my eyes. Until that time, I had never witnessed such a profound healing miracle. The woman's faith made her whole. It was similar to what Jesus did in Mark 3:

> And He entered the synagogue again, and a man was there who had a withered hand. So they watched Him closely, whether He would heal him on the Sabbath, so that they might accuse Him. And He said to the man who had the withered hand, "Step forward." Then He said to them, "Is it lawful on the Sabbath to do good or to do evil, to save life or to kill?" But they kept silent. And when He had looked around at them with anger, being grieved by the hardness of their hearts, He said to the man, "Stretch out your hand." And he stretched it out, and his hand was restored as whole as the other. Then the Pharisees went out and immediately plotted with the Herodians against Him, how they might destroy Him.
>
> —MARK 3:1–6, NKJV

There may be occasions when the Holy Spirit urges us to pray for the sick in front of religious leaders who do not believe in healing. We must obey God. God would have us to heal the sick instead of arguing whether or not divine healing is appropriate in the church.

DISCOVERING THE AUTHENTIC

As I (John) grew in my faith and understanding, God continued to confirm His Word with signs and wonders. In the late 1970s and early 1980s I began to discover the importance of operating by revelation knowledge. This seems to be the missing ingredient that eludes most ministers seeking to operate in God's supernatural arena. Jesus promised to speak to all believers who seek a deep, personal relationship with Him. This became evident when I realized that healing miracles were more frequent when I obeyed God's voice and did what He revealed.

I began to examine the methods others employed as they prayed for the sick. Some seemed to operate by revelation; others did not. I noticed peculiarities in style and mannerisms that were sometimes suspect. It was as if some people relied more on what had worked in the past than on what God wanted to do at the moment. I needed to take Paul's advice to the Thessalonians:

> Do not quench the Spirit; do not despise prophetic utterances. But examine everything carefully; hold fast to that which is good.
> —1 THESSALONIANS 5:19–21, NASB

> Now John answered and said, "Master, we saw someone casting out demons in Your name, and we forbade him because he does not follow with us." But Jesus said to him, "Do not forbid him, for he who is not against us is on our side."
> —LUKE 9:49–50, NKJV

- Jesus grants more grace to us than we do to each other. Just because a minister displays an unusual style in healing the sick, we should not necessarily discount his or her ministry.
- Jesus reminded us to examine the fruit of people's ministries. Are people genuinely healed? Do they give God the credit? Are people being saved? We shall know them by their fruit.
- Remain on the side of Jesus by following His examples from the written Word.

I discovered that those acting on what God was revealing at the moment were seeing authentic and lasting healing miracles. Those acting in their own faith or on past experience were having results, but not nearly to the same degree as those operating by revelation.

Doing the "circuits"

By 1980, I was invited to speak at more and more of the FGBMFI chapters in the Western USA and Canada. Because of a career change, I was available to speak to multiple chapters over three to five days in one trip. We called those meetings a "circuit." In any case, one of the more memorable "circuits" I was privileged to do was in Northeastern Washington State.

I kept a journal of what happened

I was invited to speak at three different chapters: one located in Sandpoint, Idaho; one in Colville, Washington; and another in Newport, Washington. Each chapter held its meetings in the same week (Tuesday, Thursday, and Saturday evenings). On that trip I kept a journal of what happened. If you do not keep a journal, you quickly forget the marvelous things God does. Meeting agendas were always the same: a buffet dinner; worship; a few short testimonies; a main speaker who gave his testimony; an altar call for salvation, Holy Spirit baptism, and healing.

Tuesday evening in Sandpoint, Idaho, was a relaxed time of ministry. Two men got saved, one couple was baptized in the Holy Spirit, and five people were healed from various ailments. When I read the following scripture, I could almost envision the story:

> He went down with them and stood on a level place. A large crowd of his disciples was there and a great number of people from all over Judea, from Jerusalem, and from the coast of Tyre and Sidon, who had come to hear him and to be healed of their diseases. Those troubled by evil spirits were cured, and the people all tried to touch him, because power was coming from him and healing them all.
>
> —LUKE 6:17–19

- When we are asked to go and speak about the wonderful things God is doing, we must ask the Lord for His anointing to manifest in the meeting place. Without the strong presence of the Lord, nothing much will happen.
- Multitudes came to Jesus, expecting great things to happen because of the news that He was healing the sick. Healing miracles are the best advertisement.
- The power spoken of here is the tangible presence of the Lord in full manifestation. When this begins to happen, move quickly and minister to as many people as possible, keeping in the flow of revelation from the Holy Spirit.
- Be aware of people with religious spirits announcing that you are special. Avoid allowing people to "puff you up" by praising you for what is happening.
- Respond by having people lift their hands and voices in praise and thanksgiving, glorifying the Lord Jesus Christ for what He is doing.

Thursday night at Colville was the meeting I will never forget. I had prayed hard that God would use me for His purposes, and I was not disappointed. As I gave my testimony, the Lord began to interrupt my thoughts with pictures, words, and a strong pull toward certain individuals. When I stopped speaking, the Holy Spirit brought to my remembrance each person He wanted to minister to. I boldly obeyed even though I was not sure what would happen.

Holy Spirit radar

As I scanned the group of about 80 people, the Holy Spirit directed my attention to a middle-aged man, and He said to me, "He is not saved. Go to him and ask him if he wants to become a Christian." I obeyed. The man and his wife said that they wanted to be saved. I grasped their hands, and we prayed the sinner's prayer right at their table. Afterward, with tears and smiles, they giggled through the rest of the meeting. A teenage boy also gave his heart to the Lord.

Woman with a cane healed

A hush of expectancy came over the crowd, and the fear of the Lord fell upon everyone in the room. The gift of faith came upon me, and the Holy Spirit showed me a picture of a woman with a cane and a little white dog on a leash. The Lord told me that He would heal the woman when she came forward for prayer. I stated that to the crowd, and an elderly lady with a cane stood. Her husband helped her make her way to the front. She could hardly stand by herself and told me she had angina of the throat and a weak heart. She could barely function anymore, but she believed God wanted to heal her. As I placed my hand on her shoulder, a surge of power went through her. She immediately raised her hands, dropped her cane, and began walking back and forth, loudly praising and magnifying God for instantly healing her.

Healed collarbone

A man came forward with his arm in a sling. He had fallen and broken his collarbone and was unable to raise his arm. I asked, "When will God heal you?" He said, "Right now!" I laid my hands on the broken side and said, "I agree. In Jesus' name, receive your healing!" He immediately lifted his arm, removed the sling, and walked away completely healed.

Severed nerve repaired

A young man stood in front of me and said an illness had left him completely deaf in his right ear. The doctor said the nerve seemed to be severed and nothing could be done to restore hearing in the ear. The Holy Spirit created a picture in my mind: I saw myself spitting on my finger, placing it in his right ear, and commanding hearing to return. I did exactly that, and the young man's hearing was instantly restored. He could hear perfectly with both ears.

The little girl on a swing

A young woman and her husband asked for prayer for their relationship, saying that they were having great difficulties being intimate.

I had no idea how to pray for them, so I asked if I could use my prayer language. They were in agreement, and I began to pray in tongues as I had my hands on their shoulders. The Lord showed me a picture of a happy little girl on a swing. Then I saw a dark adult male figure take her off the swing and carry her away behind some bushes. I heard the words, "Her stepfather molested her. Command the unclean spirit to depart." I relayed those words to the woman, who began to cry uncontrollably. When I commanded the unclean spirit to depart, she immediately began to smile, rejoice, and praise God that the "ugly" feeling was no longer in her. I later saw them leaving the meeting happily embracing each other with big smiles on their faces.

Saturday night at the Newport, Washington, FGBMFI meeting, three people gave their lives to Christ. A man came with severe pain in both shoulders. In one prayer he was healed and then filled with the Holy Spirit. He walked away praising God in a new prayer language. Two women and a young man were also healed. Everyone went home from those meetings praising God for demonstrating His presence in signs and wonders.

God strongly manifested Himself in those meetings by saving, healing, and filling people with the Holy Spirit. The intensity of God's presence was directly related to two things: the amount of intercession that occurred, and our obedience to what we saw in the Spirit. I moved from being surprised, to expecting God to move. Similar to the account in John 5, people gathered their sick friends and family members and went wherever healing was happening. Ultimately, they discovered that Jesus Christ is the source for all healing.

> Now there is in Jerusalem by the sheep gate a pool, which is called in Hebrew Bethesda, having five porticoes. In these lay a multitude of those who were sick, blind, lame, and withered, [waiting for the moving of the waters; for an angel of the Lord went down at certain seasons into the pool and stirred up the water; whoever then first, after the stirring up of the water, stepped in was made well from whatever disease with which he was afflicted.] A man was there who had been ill for thirty-eight years. When Jesus saw him lying there, and knew that he had already been a long time in that condition, He said to him, "Do you wish to get well?" The sick man answered Him, "Sir, I have no man to put

me into the pool when the water is stirred up, but while I am coming, another steps down before me." Jesus said to him, "Get up, pick up your pallet and walk." Immediately the man became well, and picked up his pallet and began to walk.

—John 5:2–9, NASB

- Before praying for a person with a chronic illness, make sure the person has faith to be healed.
- Remain sensitive to what the Holy Spirit wants to do. Obey whatever He says.
- Ask the person what Jesus asked the sick man: "Do you wish to get well?"
- Listen for any kind of response that has faith in it.
- Finally, ask when the person wants God to heal. When you hear "Now," immediately agree with the person that God is starting the healing process and will continue to restore health according to His timetable.
- God will sometimes heal immediately. Always leave the results up to God.

Do only what God says

As I discovered the authentic, I learned a critical lesson every evangelist should know: Never get ahead of the Holy Spirit during public ministry. I was invited to speak at an Aberdeen, Washington, monthly chapter meeting, and I invited another evangelist to accompany me. We felt somewhat smug and a bit proud having our friend Larry fly us to Aberdeen in a Cessna from the Boeing Flight Club. Perhaps that was the mistake that resulted in what happened next. God was about to make an obvious distinction between ministering in presumption and operating by His leading.

Just before I was to speak, my evangelist friend called my attention to a man in a wheelchair. He said, "I feel like we are to minister healing to that man and get him out of that wheelchair." I thought it would really be great for that to happen. So, I made opportunity for him to be wheeled to the front so we could minister to him. We both commanded the man to get up and walk. He could not get up, so we tried to pull him up and make his legs work. He finally fell; fortunately, he fell back into his wheelchair. We tried to save the meeting by singing a few more choruses. It did not help. The meeting was over. We left embarrassed, refusing the normal honorarium.

We learn by making mistakes

Listen to God's instructions, not man's instructions! Do only what the Holy Spirit tells you to do. If you have no direct revelation of what to do, always ask the people you want to pray for what they believe God is willing to do. Then agree in prayer at their level of faith. If the person wants God to remove a headache, that is as far as you go. When God wants us to command someone to rise up and walk, He will tell us how and when. The Holy Spirit does not honor religious zeal that is birthed in the flesh. Jesus illustrated that principle when He asked the blind men what they wanted Him to do for them:

> Now as they went out of Jericho, a great multitude followed Him. And behold, two blind men sitting by the road, when they heard that Jesus was passing by, cried out, saying, "Have mercy on us, O Lord, Son of David!" Then the multitude warned them that they should be quiet; but they cried out all the more, saying, "Have mercy on us, O Lord, Son of David!" So Jesus stood still and called them, and said, "What do you want Me to do for you?" They said to Him, "Lord, that our eyes may be opened." So Jesus had compassion and touched their eyes. [Luke 18:42 says, "Then Jesus said to him, "Receive your sight; your faith has made you well."] And immediately their eyes received sight, and they followed Him.
> —MATTHEW 20:29–34, NKJV

- The Holy Spirit initiated healing of the blind by revelation.
- Notice: Jesus asked the blind men, "What do you want Me to do for you?" Jesus already knew what the Father wanted to do, but He was testing their faith for healing. We should do the same.

- We should ask what people believe God will do for them. We should not attempt to go beyond what a person believes God will do.
- Jesus touched the blind men's eyes. When appropriate, we too, should lay our hands on the part of the body needing healing, using discretion, of course.
- In Luke 18:42, Jesus said, "Receive your sight; your faith has made you well." We should do the same.
- Jesus was moved with compassion. When people come earnestly seeking healing, we will also be moved with compassion.
- The men immediately regained their sight. The timing is always up to the Lord. We should not be surprised if the healing takes a while to manifest.

My first mission trip

In 1979 a businessman offered to pay for my plane ticket to Seoul, Korea, so that I could be part of a four-man team representing the American FGBMFI at the annual Asian Christian Layman's Conference. My room-mate, Gil Bean, was an old prayer warrior from Seattle. Two evangelists from California rounded out the team. Slomo Isaac, an Israeli from Jerusalem was one of the main speakers. During Slomo's sermon, the Lord called me to the "nations." I was transfixed and only able to hear him say, "You will be going into all the world!" I quickly wrote these words on a napkin that I keep in my prophetic word journal to this day.

All of us on the team had speaking engagements; Gil and I had two. The first was a Sunday morning service in a Presbyterian church. The second service was at a Pentecostal church. What a contrast! They both preach Jesus Christ as Savior, but the Pentecostal church expected God to move supernaturally in every service. I did not know that, even though I was advertised as the main speaker for that morning.

The unexpected happened

I had prepared a three-point sermon on the grace and love of God. I did my best through the Korean interpreter, but it seemed they were expecting something more. The members sat on the floor while the pastors sat in big chairs on the stage. As I finished, people were very polite and seemed to like what I said. Then something unexpected happened. The senior pastor gave some kind of invitation for people to come forward, and the whole church began to crowd toward the stage.

Gil waved me over to center stage and told me that the service had been advertised as a healing service. We were expected to heal the sick! We had no idea how we would pray for people who spoke a different language. Gil and I decided that we would lay hands on people and pray in tongues for their healing.

We could not pray fast enough

I went to the right, Gil to the left, and we began laying on hands and praying. The people were like a bunch of hungry baby birds when mamma bird shows up with the food. We could not pray for them fast enough. Many fell under the power of God, causing an obstacle course for the next wave needing healing. It was the most unusual healing meeting I had ever attended—and I was supposed to be in charge!

I tried using my little felt oil pad, but it ran out in about five minutes. Those who wanted healing did not care. There was such an atmosphere of faith that no matter how we prayed, they knew God was going to heal them. All we had to do was touch them or allow them to touch us. We were experiencing what Jesus did in Mark 3:

> Because of the crowd he told his disciples to have a small boat ready for him, to keep the people from crowding him. For he had healed many, so that those with diseases were pushing forward to touch him.
>
> —MARK 3:9–10

- Always give all the honor and praise to the Lord for healing the sick.
- Avoid anyone who wants to "puff you up" by praising you for what happened.
- The Bible says, "Man is tested by the praise he receives" (Proverbs 27:21).

Intercession was the key

Gil and I were still praying for the sick when the leaders took us by the arm and ushered us out the side door for our drive to lunch. We learned that the whole church had been fasting and praying for an outpouring of God's healing power during the meeting. No wonder we experienced what we did! It was because of intercessory prayer. This was something Koreans have been doing for decades. Unlike Americans, they knew how to break down barriers of unbelief, and usher in the presence and favor of God. We just happened to be participants in their reward. The price had already been paid—on their knees.

CHRIST'S AMBASSADORS INTERNATIONAL

In 1979 the Lord gave me the vision for what Sonja and I are now doing. While I was in an intense time of prayer, the Lord showed me a brilliant sunset over the Olympic Mountains west of Seattle, Washington. In the sun's rays, I saw the words, "Christ's Ambassadors."

> Therefore, we are ambassadors for Christ, as though God were making an appeal through us; we beg you on behalf of Christ, be reconciled to God.
> —2 CORINTHIANS 5:20, NASB

> We are ambassadors for Christ with delegated authority and power to do what Jesus did. He sealed our ambassadorship with His blood.

A maker of Timothys

As I WAS transfixed in the vision, the Lord said, "You will be training ambassadors for Me, and they will be going into all the world. Prepare yourself for the task." That vision was confirmed over and over again as I attended various prayer meetings and FGBMFI conferences. The same prophetic word became commonplace in our life. "You will be a maker of Timothys. You will affect nations. You are called to prepare the saints for the work of the ministry. You will do this together as a team." We continue to rejoice and thank the Lord for all these confirming words over the many years. Today, we know for sure that we are in the middle of God's will. We purpose to stay there.

Sonja and I hold bachelor's degrees in business administration, but, at the time of the initial vision, neither of us had a formal theological education. We read every book we could find about the supernatural power of God. We felt an urgency to be better grounded in the Word. I enrolled in Bible school by correspondence, earning a diploma in a little over a year. The next few years I attended every Christian ministry seminar, church seminar, conference, crusade, and FGBMFI function within driving distance of Seattle. Healing the sick was usually a part of these conferences.

Later, both Sonja and I attended seminary at Regent College graduate school in Vancouver, B.C., Canada. We also became very active ministering in our local church. Sonja taught the new believers' class, and I became a staff pastor and taught various classes, all pertaining to equipping believers for ministry. We both ministered weekly in the prayer ministry at our church.

We began ministering in other churches in the Seattle area and, eventually, much of the Northwest. We participated in major evangelistic events that came to town. Often we directed the prayer and ministry teams for visiting ministries. Healing was the major ministry focus for most of those meetings. We continued to witness miracle after miracle, and we were no longer surprised when God healed the sick. We were discovering the authentic move of God and expected Him to continue healing. People who came for healing had a high expectation, similar to the centurion in the following passage:

> Now when He concluded all His sayings in the hearing of the people, He entered Capernaum. And a certain centurion's servant, who was dear to him, was sick and ready to die. So when he heard about Jesus, he sent elders of the Jews to Him, pleading with Him to come and heal his servant. And when they came to Jesus, they begged Him earnestly, saying that the one for whom He should do this was deserving, "for he loves our nation, and has built us a synagogue." Then Jesus went with them. And when He was already not far from the house, the centurion sent friends to Him, saying to Him, "Lord, do not trouble Yourself, for I am not worthy that You should enter under my roof. Therefore I did not even think myself worthy to come to You. But say the word, and my servant will be healed. For I also am a man placed under authority, having soldiers under me. And I say to one, 'Go,' and

he goes; and to another, 'Come,' and he comes; and to my servant, 'Do this,' and he does it." When Jesus heard these things,
He marveled at him, and turned around and said to the crowd
that followed Him, "I say to you, I have not found such *great
faith*, not even in Israel!" And those who were sent, returning to
the house, found the servant well who had been sick.

—Luke 7:1–10, nkjv

- When we meet people with great faith in Jesus Christ as their Healer, it becomes much easier to agree with them for healing. Their eyes are on Christ and not us.
- If we do only what we see the Father doing (just like Jesus), then we will see the manifestation of what He wants done.
- If the Father says, "Go, come, do that, do this" and you obey, then your commands are backed up by the power and authority of God Himself! You are operating in the gift of faith that comes with obeying what the Father is saying via the Holy Spirit.

Experience convinced us

By the mid–1980s, our belief in a healing God was firm. We had
witnessed so many authentic healings that we could no longer deny
the fundamental truth that God is willing to heal anyone coming to
Him in faith. By that time, we could discern the genuine from the
contrived. We respected people's unwavering faith in a God that heals.
But, to be authentic, we encouraged those convinced of a healing that
was "in process," to get confirmation from the medical community.
Upon returning with a good report, everyone could rejoice in a bona
fide miracle. This practice is illustrated in Luke 17:

> Then as He entered a certain village, there met Him ten men who
> were lepers, who stood afar off. And they lifted up their voices and
> said, "Jesus, Master, have mercy on us!" So when He saw them, He
> said to them, "Go, show yourselves to the priests." And so it was
> that as they went, they were cleansed. And one of them, when he
> saw that he was healed, returned, and with a loud voice glorified

God, and fell down on his face at His feet, giving Him thanks. And he was a Samaritan. So Jesus answered and said, "Were there not ten cleansed? But where are the nine? Were there not any found who returned to give glory to God except this foreigner?" And He said to him, "Arise, go your way. Your faith has made you well."

—LUKE 17:12–19, NKJV

- People with incurable diseases are no different to God than people with headaches. All healing is easy for God.
- Faith in Jesus as Healer is the key. The lepers demonstrated faith by crying out to Jesus for healing. They earnestly sought Jesus to heal them.
- As they obeyed what Jesus commanded, to "go," they were cleansed as they went. Strict obedience to what the Holy spirit reveals is necessary.
- One leper returned, giving thanks and glorifying God. Because of this, he was 100 percent healed (not just cleansed).
- Jesus said to the one who returned, "Your faith has made you well." Continually giving thanks to God completes a healing that is in process.

God gets the credit

Moving from surprise encounters to authentic manifestations of God's healing power was a process that took more than 10 years. We observed all kinds of healings. Some were questionable, and some were obvious. Some were routine, and some were spectacular. Regardless of who was ministering or how they prayed, we learned one vital truth: we are very careful to point to an awesome God and give Him all the credit and glory. We received no acclaim for how we or anyone else achieved the various healings. Prolonged intercessions with fasting may have played a part; however, the ultimate reason for the healing lies in a compassionate God who is willing to heal those who rely on His Word, His mercy, and His grace.

We went fishing

Some years ago, a pilot friend from church mentioned we could rent a plane and fly to a remote British Columbia lake to do some trophy fishing. I (John) love to fly fish and persuaded my friend Dr. Larry Shelton, a theologian, to share expenses and come along. We loaded our gear into a Cessna 170RG and began our journey from Snohomish, Washington, to a remote fishing lodge on Bear Lake, Northern B.C., Canada. Once airborne, Larry reminded the pilot to stay at about 5,000 feet because he suffered from congestive heart failure. Any higher altitude would cause breathing problems, putting undue pressure on his heart. It was a relief to finally locate the lake after flying for over an hour without seeing any roads or signs of civilization. We buzzed the lodge twice, assuming they knew who we were and would pick us up at the airstrip.

We landed on the rough, gravel strip alongside an abandoned railroad track about two miles from the lodge. We waited and waited, but no one came to pick us up. Finally, we decided to carry all of our gear down the old tracks in the general direction of the lodge. We had trudged for about half a mile when Larry suddenly dropped all of his gear, saying that he could go no further. We knew it was his heart, and we agreed to return with help.

The maintenance man from the lodge found us. We went back and got Larry and proceeded to the lodge. The pilot apologized to everyone for failing to contact the lodge properly, and all of us were thankful to finally be at the lodge, especially Larry.

Call for a helicopter

Two days later Larry had a heart attack. It happened early in the morning as we were getting ready for a major fishing expedition to a remote river. Larry had missed breakfast, and I went to his bedroom and saw him sprawled on his bunk looking very weak and pale. We were hundreds of miles from anywhere! If we tried to get Larry back to the plane, it would kill him. Using the lodge radio, the host called the nearest hospital, 150 miles away. Upon learning the symptoms, the doctor told us that Larry was having a heart attack and needed to be taken to the hospital immediately. We finally got a response from a logging company helicopter, the only aircraft in the area that could be at the lodge within an hour. He was on his way.

Larry was not looking good. Suddenly, I heard the Holy Spirit say, "John, you know what to do. Pray for him!" I laid my hands on Larry and began commanding the spirit of death to leave; I commanded his heart to function normally, and prayed that healing and health would return to him. I even prayed that God would give him a new heart. This was my friend. I was not going to stand around and let him die. His wife, Vangie, would want to know that we did all we could to save him. She would not think much of any of us if we had not at least prayed for him before he died. I said a loud "amen" and then we waited. The chopper came in about 45 minutes. I do not remember if it was the Holy Spirit's prompting or my idea, but I began taking pictures of the whole event. I snapped some of Larry on the bunk, some more of the men carrying him up a hill on a chair and loading him in the chopper. I even took one of him looking very shaky as he lifted off. My reasoning had something to do with being able to tell the complete story to Vangie, should the worst happen.

Take the shortcut

The closest hospital was 150 miles away. The pilot asked Larry if he wanted to go straight over the mountains with altitudes exceeding 10,000 feet or go around them, which would take an extra 45 minutes. Larry said, "Go up and over. I don't know how much time I have left." They arrived safely and rolled Larry into the emergency room over three hours after his heart attack. The doctor on duty just happened to be a heart specialist. Working very quickly, the medical staff stabilized Larry in about two hours. Later, the doctor told Larry that the damage to his heart had been severe. The doctor was amazed that he had survived the trip to the hospital, stating that most people would have died en route to the hospital. Larry said, "I had a Christian friend who prayed for me. That's how I made it!" God did give him a new heart three years later, when he received a heart transplant!

Healing those who are deaf and mute

It may seem hard at first to minister to those who are deaf, mute, or both. We discovered that the source of some of these difficulties is spiritual rather than physical. The key is allowing the Holy Spirit to reveal which it is. When there is a spirit involved, we have learned to pray in similar fashion to how Jesus did in the following passage:

Then they brought to Him one who was deaf and had an impediment in his speech, and they begged Him to put His hand on him.
And He took him aside from the multitude, and put His fingers
in his ears, and He spat and touched his tongue. Then, looking up
to heaven, He sighed, and said to him, "Ephphatha," that is, "Be
opened." Immediately his ears were opened, and the impediment
of his tongue was loosed, and he spoke plainly. Then He commanded them that they should tell no one; but the more He commanded them, the more widely they proclaimed it. And they were
astonished beyond measure, saying, "He has done all things well.
He makes both the deaf to hear and the mute to speak."

—Mark 7:32–37, nkjv

- When the Holy Spirit is leading us, He may
  indicate doing something that may seem
  strange.
- This may involve doing something as unusual
  as putting your fingers in someone's ears,
  spitting, and touching the tongue.
- Always speak to the problem area and command it to be healed.
- You will have success when you obey the
  Holy Spirit.

Deaf-mute boy healed

I (John) had the privilege of spending six weeks with Dr. A. L. Gill
in Malaysia in 1988. I helped him conduct five healing crusades during
this trip. The first major miracle happened in the city of Kuantan, and
it was similar to what happened in Mark 7:32–37 above. Dr. Gill and
I trained healing teams over a period of three days prior to each crusade. During the final one or two nights, citywide invitations were
sent out inviting the public to come and be healed.

One of the healing teams, composed of two Chinese ladies, was
selected to pray for an eight-year-old boy who was a deaf-mute. The
boy's mother brought him forward so the ladies could pray for him.
The Spirit evidently led them, because they put their fingers into his
ears and touched his tongue with their fingers. They commanded the
boy's ears to open and his tongue to be loosed. In a matter of minutes

he could both hear and speak. His first words mumbled included thanks to "Jesus," in Chinese. His mother was amazed and gave her life to Jesus Christ that night. Ministering healing two by two is a biblical principle found in Mark 6.

> And He called the twelve to Himself, and began to send them out two by two, and gave them power over unclean spirits. He commanded them to take nothing for the journey except a staff—no bag, no bread, no copper in their money belts…So they went out and preached that people should repent. And they cast out many demons, and anointed with oil many who were sick, and healed them.
>
> —MARK 6:7–8, 12–13, NKJV

- Where two or more are in agreement, there is more power for ministry. While one is praying, the other is hearing from the Holy Spirit.
- We already have authority over all evil spirits. We do not go in our own power and authority. We go in the name of Jesus as our authority.
- Travel light. God will supply your needs as you go.
- Notice the order of events: Preach, repent, cast out demons, anoint with oil, and then heal the sick.
- Always carry a vial of anointing oil. It gives a point of contact so people can release their faith for healing.

Miracles multiplied

The trip to Malaysia moved me into the absolute realm of the authentic, supernatural healing power of God. There were only two of us, but a lot happened. It may be hard for readers to grasp the totality of what I am about to relate. I was an eyewitness with twelve rolls of film and one-on-one personal interviews with those healed over a period of six weeks in a phenomenal move of God. Each of the five meetings averaged over 400 in attendance. I documented over 130 miraculous healings, 190 true conversions to Jesus Christ, and

740 people receiving the baptism of the Holy Spirit. I personally witnessed four totally demon-possessed people set free and returned to their right minds. I documented all of this with photos and a journal as the people testified to being completely healed and set free by the power of Jesus Christ.

Forget the numbers

Jesus said we would do greater things than He did. We experienced this personally in Malaysia. The two of us, working separately at times, were experiencing simultaneous miracles. Church leadership and trained healing teams would then go into action praying for the sick. By this time, multiple miracles were manifesting all over the auditorium. We were experiencing the "greater works" and did not realize it. I tried to keep track of everything, going from one healing team to another, overseeing prayer for the sick, and taking pictures. I was overwhelmed with joy and wonderment for what was happening. I was experiencing authentic manifestations of a God who loves to heal the sick. Suddenly, in the middle of the miracles, it came to me. Forget the numbers! Just enjoy doing what Jesus did!

I lost count

Somewhere during the fifth week I lost count. I tried to reconstruct the numbers later as I reviewed my audiotapes, pictures, and journal. At that point I heard myself say, "Tonight was incredible. We experienced 20 people getting saved, many more got baptized in the Holy Spirit, and a whole bunch of people received all kinds of healing miracles. Praise the Lord!"

Today, I will occasionally revert to my old ways and try to keep track of who got what. The Holy Spirit will gently remind me it is His business. He says, "John, forget the numbers and just keep doing what Jesus did. I'm keeping track. We'll review everything after the final trumpet has sounded."

THE BOOK OF ACTS IS NOT FINISHED

The following stories are representative of what continues to happen in and around our ministry. We never stop being totally surprised and thrilled when God decides to intervene and heal somebody. We often desire that more pastors and Christian leaders would experience what we do, especially in America. In our exuberance, we sometimes will give an unsolicited testimony about an incredible miracle that just happened a few days earlier. They look at us with blank stares, slightly smiling, wanting to believe, but giving the impression that we may have "stretched" the story a bit. They sometimes make us feel slightly guilty for testifying to the great things the Lord is doing. The book of Acts is not finished! Healing and miracles are more numerous today than they were in the book of Acts! We hope the following stories will build your faith.

Biker gets healed

Recently, we conducted a workshop on hearing God's voice and healing the sick. A biker attended the workshop and responded to an invitation to receive prayer for healing. He said his body hurt all over from being hit and partially run over by a truck while riding his Harley. He also said he could not breathe properly from crushed ribs, and he had a history of smoking too much. When asked what he wanted God to heal first, he said, "All of it, today!" When we hear a response like that, we immediately begin to pray. John laid hands on the man's chest and commanded healing to manifest in the name of Jesus Christ. Then John told the man to take a deep breath. He did, and, to his amazement, he could breathe deeper than ever before, and there was no pain in his body. He immediately began to tell everyone about God's healing him, and he began witnessing to all who would listen. We called the pastor of the church a month later and asked how the biker was doing. The pastor confirmed that the man was still healed and was continuing to witness.

Business executive begins screaming

One day I (Sonja) was sitting in my office when one of the executives limped through the door. I took one look at him and knew he was in a great deal of pain. He said, "Sonja, I've got spasms in my back, and I'm leaving to go to the doctor." I expressed my concern and asked if he needed someone to drive him to his emergency appointment. He thanked me, but said he was sure he could make it and turned to leave. As he did, he had another spasm, and he began screaming from the unbearable pain.

All of the vice presidents' offices were down one hallway, and we all had ceiling-to-floor glass windows by the doors. As my colleague began screaming, all eyes from the work area outside my office focused on him.

That's impressive

I jumped up and ran around my desk because he looked like he might pass out. As I reached him, I said I did not know what to do except pray. I laid my hands on his back and commanded the muscles to relax and the pain to subside, in Jesus' name. I then said, "You were asking me about speaking in tongues the other day, and I'm going to pray that way also." I interceded for just a few moments in my spiritual language, and then he began to straighten up—the pain was gone! He slowly turned around, his eyes as big as saucers, and exclaimed, "That's impressive!" I told him I serve an impressive God! As I glanced out of my office, I saw many curious stares and smiles at my brand of "first aid."

This coworker and his wife and little daughter began to attend a little community church. The pastor apparently did not preach a clear salvation message, but, over the months that followed, I was privileged to confirm this man's salvation as he continued to ask questions. What a joy!

One morning he rushed into my office and asked if I had a minute. He related how the night before his daughter had such a high fever that they were bundling her up to rush to the emergency room. All of a sudden he remembered how I had prayed for him. He had not received any teaching on divine healing—his only experience was in my office that day. He said he gathered his little one into his arms and told her he thought Jesus wanted to heal her. She had been learning about Jesus in Sunday school and in childlike faith agreed with her daddy. He said he shouted, "Fever, get out of her!" Then he remembered I had said, "In Jesus' name!" so he added that to his heartfelt prayer. His eyes were glistening with tears of joy as he related how the fever broke, she was healed, and things were normal that morning.

True Christianity that expresses the power of God in our everyday lives gets people's attention. It should be the norm to see healings wherever they are needed; and they should be done in such a way that people are drawn to salvation and "gifts of healing" in their own lives.

Woman healed of uterine cancer

One Sunday a woman came to us for prayer after the morning service. She had been diagnosed with uterine cancer and was going the next day for a pre-operative appointment. She was terrified by the whole ordeal. We prayed a simple prayer and cursed the cancer in Jesus' name and commanded healing to her uterus. She seemed relieved and left in much better spirits.

A couple of months later she rushed up to us with the wonderful news that she had been healed. There was no sign of cancer and no surgery! We rejoiced with her.

Why isn't everyone healed?

As we drove to lunch that Sunday, we were happy for our friend's good news, but we also discussed once again the mystery of healing. As we shared in chapter 1, we do not have all the answers. We just know that we are to pray and leave the results up to God.

Recently, a dear friend of ours died from cancer. We had contended for healing with her and her husband for over four years. Yet, she went to be with Jesus. The following morning, I asked the Lord about her death. I recorded the following thoughts in my journal: "Sonja, you and My friend, Nina, fought a good fight, and she has been received into glory where every question has been answered; every doubt cast off. Everything, yes everything, now makes perfect sense to her. For those of you who are still in this dimension, you can only rest in My faithfulness and know that one day it will also make perfect sense to you."

Grace healings and the sovereignty of God

God remains sovereign. It is His choice if He decides to miraculously heal someone without any involvement of man. We call that a "grace healing." Perhaps the person who was sick looked to God, prayed a simple prayer, and "wham" they were healed! We wish God would do that more often. Then this book would not have been necessary. The truth is that the Lord has provided a means by which His body, working with the Holy Spirit, can facilitate healing in those coming to Him in faith. He is not just able to heal us; He is willing.

We contend in prayer with the best understanding and leading we have and leave the rest in the hands of a gracious and loving Lord.

When people are not healed

God in His infinite wisdom has the answer for those who are not healed. This remains a mystery to any honest minister who preaches that Jesus Christ is our Healer. Our experience is that not everyone is healed. Many are, but not all. We must defer to the One who in the very beginning said to the nation of Israel and to us:

> There the Lord made a decree and a law for them, and there he tested them. He said, "If you listen carefully to the voice of the Lord your God and do what is right in his eyes, if you pay attention to his commands and keep all his decrees, I will not bring on you any of the diseases I brought on the Egyptians, for I am the Lord, who heals you."
>
> —Exodus 15:25–26

When we carefully examine the God of the old covenant, there were sometimes conditions surrounding the God who heals. Jesus Christ inaugurated the New Covenant with better promises, one of which is healing. He is the same sovereign God of both covenants. We must rely on His mercy and not on our desire, our effort, or our faith formulas. In regard to that topic, Paul quoted from the Old Testament in the following passage:

> What then shall we say? Is God unjust? Not at all! For he says to Moses, "I will have mercy on whom I have mercy, and I will have compassion on whom I have compassion." It does not, therefore, depend on man's desire or effort, but on God's mercy.
>
> —Romans 9:14–16

Not to include this biblical principle in our discussion regarding divine healing would be to ignore the sovereignty of a loving God who ultimately decides who receives healing and who does not. We do not pray for the sick because He guarantees healing; we pray because He has declared that He is willing! The final outcome rests with Him.

Blind woman healed

We were with the Lahu tribal people in northern Thailand and were teaching about the God who heals. After the preaching, an elderly blind woman was led to the front for prayer. One of our team members was Steven Darrow, who owned a large software company in the Northwest. He and his wife, Dorinda, had been through our training, and they were full of faith. Steven and a missionary from Australia began to pray for the woman. In a short while, she began looking around in wonderment as her vision returned. This remarkable miracle caused quite an uproar in the village. Two days later, a witch doctor showed up at the meeting. He had heard of the astounding things that were happening. (His story is related in chapter 6.) The thrilling thing for us was seeing a corporate executive healing the sick! We are all called to do what Jesus did.

Lame-from-birth woman walks

Dorinda Darrow was quite timid about ministering healing when she first arrived in Thailand. However, the gift of faith came upon her, and she became fearless! A woman was brought for prayer who had been lame from birth. Her legs hung limply, even turned backwards, when she was held upright. Dorinda and another team member, Kathy Knox, practically ran to the woman, took her from those who were holding her up, and began to minister. The gift of faith on Dorinda expressed itself with commands in Jesus' name for healing and strength to manifest in the woman's legs. A creative miracle was needed, and they believed for one!

To the village people's utter amazement, the woman began to receive strength, her legs turned forward, and she began to take halting steps unassisted. Soon Dorinda was out a few feet in front beckoning the woman to walk to her, much like people do with a baby who is learning to walk. The woman took her baby steps to Dorinda. It was a tremendous healing for the woman and an unforgettable experience for all of us.

Native Americans learn to heal the sick

Recently, we were invited to assist Dr. A. L. Gill in conducting a healing crusade on the Rose Bud Indian Reservation at Mission, South Dakota. We spent several evenings teaching the Christians how to heal the sick. They practiced on each other during the teaching sessions, and many people were healed. That stirred their faith for others, and they were ready to minister when the first night of the crusade began.

After the preaching, people came forward for healing and John had all of our two-person healing teams ready. It was exciting to see people who had never before prayed for the sick, until our training, do so with great results.

Rancher's rotator cuff healed

An older man, a rancher, came for healing. The doctor had diagnosed a torn rotator cuff in his shoulder. He was in so much pain he was not able to do his work. After prayer, he had full motion of his shoulder, and he was extremely happy.

The next evening I (Sonja) was greeting the people as they arrived. I recognized the rancher, and I asked him how his shoulder was doing. He said he had worked all day and it felt great! I then asked him if he would be willing to tell the people what had happened.

I have never done such a thing

I saw stark terror in his eyes at the thought of getting up on the stage and using a microphone to testify about his miracle healing. "Oh, no, ma'am. I have never done such a thing. I just couldn't!" I explained how it would likely help the faith of others and perhaps they, too, would be healed. He was such a humble man and obviously loved the Lord, so I finally persuaded him.

Before the preaching the next evening, we had several people testify to healings that they had received. When the rancher's time came, he said, "I know you folks are like me when you see healing stuff on TV, and you wonder if it's the real thing or not. Well, last night my shoulder was healed—I had a torn rotator cuff. You believe me! I'm telling you I was healed, and I'm not putting you on!" The audience broke into approving applause. They all knew the humble man who was testifying to God's healing power at the hands of his neighbors who were on the healing teams.

Child healed of eczema

We are coaches over home groups for our church, and we occasionally visit the other groups we oversee. We recently learned of a tremendous healing that happened through prayer at one such meeting.

A single mother of three had a beautiful two-year-old daughter who was covered with bleeding, oozing sores due to eczema. She was not responding to any of the medication, and the doctors were confounded. Meanwhile, her condition was worsening. We gently prayed a simple prayer and commanded healing to manifest in the child's body. From that hour healing began, and, over the next several days, she was completely healed and has had no recurrence. Jesus is our Healer!

Yes, you can heal the sick

We hope by reading these accounts, your faith will be stirred to heal the sick just like the people we have been telling you about. You may just need a little practice with some people who know how much the Lord wants to use you. Learning how to heal the sick requires a progressive revelation of what Jesus promised to every one of His followers. Those who have submitted themselves to the baptism of the Holy Spirit simply need to begin to release gifts of healing whenever it is appropriate.

It is "gifts," not "gift"

When a believer receives the gift of the Holy Spirit, gifts (plural) of healing are immediately available to be released to those who are sick. Other gifts are also available to be given away to those who need them. With a little training, believers can begin to operate in any gifts the Holy Spirit deems necessary for each occasion. When a believer decides to step out in faith and begin praying for the sick, the Holy Spirit is there to help complete the ministry. The Holy Spirit disperses gifts of healing when and where He sovereignly wills. This is promised in 1 Corinthians 12:

> Now to each one the manifestation of the Spirit is given for the common good…to another *gifts of healing* by that one Spirit…All these are the work of one and the same Spirit, and he gives them to each one, just as he determines.
> —1 CORINTHIANS 12:7, 9, 11, EMPHASIS ADDED

- When the Holy Spirit indicates He is willing to start healing people, gifts of healing are already being dispersed.
- Healing gifts are not a single great gift for special individuals.
- Gifts of healing are available to whoever will believe, step out in faith, and pray for the sick.

There are no "special" ministers with privileged "inside" information—though some well-publicized evangelists would want you to believe that. The Scriptures are open for any believer to read and believe what is promised. Jesus promises that every Christian can pray for the sick and believe God for healing. As we close this chapter and move on to hearing God's voice, we pray that you will move from doubt and timidity to doing what Jesus said you could do. He promised it. He will help you do it.

LET'S PRACTICE

James 1:22 says to do what we have heard (read).

Consider doing what is recommended in this chapter by referring to the "Let's Practice" in Appendix B, page 257.

Do the ministry skill assignment titled, "Learning How to Heal the Sick."

HEARING FROM GOD

Jesus Christ said His followers will hear His voice. In this chapter, we will examine the biblical references and accounts of people who heard and obeyed God's voice. We will learn how to hear from God and to do what He says.

HEARING GOD'S VOICE is a spellbinding experience. He knows how to grab our attention. He surprises us. He speaks in ways so unexpectedly, so spontaneously, that we attribute the voice to Him. Though it seems irrational and runs contrary to modern thinking, and though it is extremely difficult to prove, deep down we know we are hearing from the Holy Spirit. When we were born of the Spirit we were given "ears to hear." We can now hear what the Spirit is saying to the church. Christians are continuing to hear from God in a multitude of ways. Whether direct or indirect, God's voice is being heard. He speaks through His Word, sermons, other Christians, prophecy, books, tracts, CDs, and many other ways. By design, we have dedicated this chapter to hearing from God in a personal way. We will concentrate on personally hearing the voice of the Holy Spirit. Jesus said:

> My sheep hear My voice, and I know them, and they follow Me.
> —JOHN 10:27, NASB

> Everyone who is of the truth hears My voice.
> —JOHN 18:37, NASB

> I have other sheep, [He was speaking about the Gentiles] which are not of this fold; I must bring them also, and they will hear My voice; and they will become one flock with one shepherd.
> —JOHN 10:16, NASB

> God is speaking to us. Hearing His voice is a
> privilege, and we must discover how to hear
> God's voice and then obey what He tells us
> to do.

We must hear His voice and do what He says

The most important factor in doing what Jesus did is hearing His voice and doing what He says. If ministers are looking for the key to fruitful ministry, this is it. The most effective way to meet the needs of those around us is to have God tell us what the *real* need is and then have Him reveal the solution. That is how Jesus did it. As we stated in the introduction, John 5:19–20 is foundational to this book. We believe the secret to Jesus' perfect ministry of healing and setting people free was that He did everything by revelation.

> Truly, truly, I say to you, the Son can do nothing of Himself,
> unless it is something He sees the Father doing; for whatever
> the Father does, these things the Son also does in like manner.
> For the Father loves the Son, and shows Him all things that He
> Himself is doing; and the Father will show Him greater works
> than these, so that you will marvel.
> —John 5:19–20, NASB

God always knows the source of everyone's problems and how they got into the situation. Whether the problems are physical, emotional, or spiritual, God knows everything about everyone and holds the solution to each need. When we approach Him with a sincere heart, crying out for an answer, God not only listens but also may reveal the solution.

> I cry to you, O Lord; I say, "You are my refuge, my portion in the
> land of the living." Listen to my cry, for I am in desperate need.
> —Psalm 142:5–6

> Whether it is pleasant or unpleasant, we will listen to the voice
> of the Lord our God.
> —Jeremiah 42:6, NASB

We need to hear from God regardless of what He might say. We will receive His words any way He wants to deliver them. As young

Samuel did, we say to the Lord, "Speak, for your servant is listening" (1 Samuel 3:10). For those who have paid the price and have disciplined themselves to hear from God, answers will come. However, for the majority of believers, it is difficult to hear God's voice personally. This chapter is intended to help those desiring to hear directly from God.

JOHN LEARNS TO HEAR FROM GOD

They seemed a little "spooky"

The first time I (John) heard a Christian say, "God speaks to me," I thought they were nuts. After all, I held a Bachelor of Science degree in business administration. If you could prove it scientifically, fine, but it was to convince me of something I could not understand. The thought of hearing directly from an unseen God was incomprehensible. I was a brand-new believer and wanted everything God had for me, but all that was new. I was naturally skeptical of those who said they could have a two-way conversation with God; they seemed a little "spooky" to me. I wanted God to speak to me in an authentic encounter—something I knew was real and not some bogus experience.

So I prayed, "God, speak to me like You do to these other Christians. I'm one of Your sheep. I want to hear Your voice. So, speak." There was no answer. No matter how hard I listened, there was only silence. After a few months, I presumed that people who heard directly from God were God's anointed. They must be super spiritual to have that privilege. I found out later that every Christian could hear from God. We just had to learn how. We needed to incorporate some personal disciplines into our lives that would allow us to hear. I was to discover how to hear by obeying scriptures that would lead me into a deep, personal relationship with Him. It would take years to master, but I had the rest of my life to work on it. I sought out Christian leaders who had successfully made the journey. Perhaps they could guide me to where I could hear. I will relate the next story from the perspective of how I perceived things as a brand new Christian.

It was a startling experience

The very first FGBMFI meeting I attended was a luncheon near downtown Seattle. It was a startling experience. First-timers were asked to stand and introduce themselves. That was easy. What came next was unexpected. After giving my name and what I did as a businessman, I was asked how long I had known the Lord. I said, "About a week." I was surprised when the whole room erupted into applause. I smiled, sat down, and wondered what I had gotten myself into. Then everyone began to sing songs I did not know, and everyone raised their hands and sang with their eyes closed. Then they seemed to murmur and hum some words in unison; then the guy right next to me started speaking foreign words that made no sense. Everyone kept their hands in the air, listening. Then there was silence.

Thus saith the Lord

All of a sudden, on the far side of the room a rather large Jewish man said, "Thus saith the Lord." The rest of the message spoke directly to my heart. Up to that time I wanted to get out of there. However, I could understand these words and they made me feel good. I wanted to stay and hear more. It was like he really was speaking on behalf of God. I did not understand the protocol for that kind of meeting, but I knew the man had somehow heard from God and was relating what he heard. Afterward, I was introduced to him. His name was Larry Bullock. He seemed nice, outgoing, and not weird at all—that is, until he and the other men firmly gave me brotherly "bear hugs." That was hard for me to do because I had been taught to stay away from men like that.

I left the luncheon and returned to work in a state of excitement. I did not understand what had happened. All I knew was that Larry heard God's voice and spontaneously related the words to us. I was blessed, even though I was having difficulty interpreting what was happening. I wanted to return to their meetings and find out what else they knew about God, and especially how I could hear God's voice. I later found out that I had encountered the spiritual gifts of speaking a message in tongues and the companion gift of interpretation of tongues as described by Paul in 1 Corinthians 12. That experience began my journey toward a supernatural God who speaks to His people.

> But to each one is given the manifestation of the Spirit for the common good. For to one is given...various kinds of tongues, and to another the interpretation of tongues. But one and the

same Spirit works all these things, distributing to each one individually just as He wills.

—1 Corinthians 12:7–11, nasb

The Holy Spirit distributes supernatural gifts each time Christians gather. We should remain open and available to receive or give words that are prompted by the Holy Spirit.

The school of trial and error

I started to grow in my understanding of the Bible. I read and meditated on it and then watched, listened, and tried to apply it to my life. I experimented with the things Jesus said we could do. Something wonderful was happening. I was gradually being led into a deeper understanding of how God speaks to His people. First, I watched as others heard from God. Second, I compared what I was witnessing to passages in the Bible. They seemed to be the same. Then I tried to listen to God for myself. As I tried to do what I saw the other men doing, it did not work very well. At first, the words that I thought were from God turned out to be my own thoughts. The majority of the "revelations" ended in disappointment and frustration. I was learning through trial and error.

One of my early Bible teachers said we should journal what we think God may be saying. So I sat down, prayed, and asked God to fill my mind with His thoughts. By faith, I began to record paragraph after paragraph of what was transpiring in my mind. I invited a longtime friend of the FGBMFI, Pastor Harley Goodwin, to my home to examine my work. He had baptized me in water the year before, so I respected his spiritual input. He reviewed the many pages of hot "revelations."

I threw it all away

After reading my stuff, he smiled and said, "Brother John, some of this sounds good. But, it's about half God and half you. If I were you, I'd throw it all in the trash. That means your soul nature is competing with your spirit. If you don't know what the Bible says, you record what you think it says and what you want to hear. The result is a mixture of what *you* want God to say with parts of what His Word already says.

This is dangerous. Instead, allow His Word to renew your mind to what He's already established as truth and obey what the Word already says."

I threw all of it away and started reading the Bible in earnest. I began to differentiate between religious zeal and operating with the gentle coaxing of the Holy Spirit. I learned valuable lessons by stumbling through the process. Delivering what we think are inspired words from the Lord in the presence of discerning and mature leaders is a safe way to learn. Allowing mature believers to critique your words is a sound way to learn what is and is not from the Lord. The same Holy Spirit is upon everyone. By allowing the Lord to give a positive witness to the majority of those present, agreement is reached, confirming the authenticity of the content. This may have to be done over and over again. It takes time to truly hear from God. We need others to confirm the words we are hearing from God. It is critical to have mature Christians around us who will correct, critique, and guide us in the process. This also affords us the opportunity to judge ourselves: Am I teachable and submitted to authority?

HOW DO YOU PROPHESY?

During the early years of attending all kinds of FGBMFI meetings, I noticed that quite a few men would spontaneously deliver inspired words from God. Sometimes the words would be for the whole group, and at other times they were for individuals. I asked the president of the chapter how I could learn to do that. His response was puzzling at first. He said, "Brother, you can't give it out unless you have it in you." I asked what he meant by that. He wisely said, "You cannot speak on behalf of the Lord until He has something to draw from. You must spend a lot of time renewing your mind in the Word of God." He went on to say, "The best way to deliver an encouraging word is to know the Bible backwards and forwards. That comes with years of meditating and memorizing the Word of God." That sounded like a lot of hard work and I thought that there must be an easier way. But the Bible says that meditation is the key.

> I will meditate on Your precepts And regard Your ways. I shall delight in Your statutes; *I shall not forget Your word.*
> —PSALM 119:15–16, NASB, EMPHASIS ADDED

> Meditation and memorization of the Word of God are important processes. The Lord uses His Word implanted in our hearts to bring forth phrases that resonate God's plan for our lives.

Dick Mills

A prophet named Dick Mills, a frequent speaker at FGBMFI meetings, came to town. I had never seen a prophet before, and I was utterly amazed by his ministry. He would stare at various individuals, point to them, and say, "What is your name? The Lord has a word for you." He would then repeat the person's name and spontaneously quote a series of scriptures from both the Old and New Testaments. Another person would follow him around recording the scriptures on a notepad and pass them to the person. We would look these up later and marvel at the confirming nature of the words to our personal lives.

Walking Bible

Dick Mills knew the Word of God so well that he was literally a walking Bible. He had committed hundreds and hundreds of scriptures to memory, and he relied upon the Holy Spirit to bring them to mind as he fixed his gaze on certain individuals. Dick knew the importance of fixing his gaze on people before delivering what God had given him to speak. We will revisit this ministry truth later, but it is mentioned in Acts 3:

> But Peter, along with John, *fixed his gaze on him and said,* "Look at us!" And he began to give them his attention, expecting to receive something from them. But Peter said, "I do not possess silver and gold, but what I do have I give to you: In the name of Jesus Christ the Nazarene—walk!"
>
> —ACTS 3:4–6, NASB, EMPHASIS ADDED

> The Lord desires to meet our needs, and He may use mature believers to confirm His intentions.

Young man, stand up

Dick looked my way, pointed to me and said, "Young man, stand up. Give me your hand. The Lord has a word for you." I stood up, told him my name and took his hand. He then gave me the following verses:

> Have I not commanded you? Be strong and courageous! Do not tremble or be dismayed, for the Lord your God is with you wherever you go.
> —JOSHUA 1:9, NASB

> Behold, I am with you and will keep you wherever you go, and will bring you back to this land; for I will not leave you until I have done what I have promised you.
> —GENESIS 28:15, NASB

> Now then go, and I, even I, will be with your mouth, and teach you what you are to say.
> —EXODUS 4:12, NASB

> Jesus will use people to confirm what the Lord may be speaking to people's hearts. Scripture is the best starting point to give guidance to others.

Dick finished with a short exhortation about how God was going to use me in a future ministry. I wrote the verses in my first Bible and recopied them over and over through the years.

A confirming word

Within six months, another prophet came through town. His name was Dick Joyce, and he had a similar ministry. Like Dick Mills, he pointed at me and asked me to stand. Then he spontaneously gave me a set of scriptures that exhorted me in much the same way as Dick Mills had previously done. He said, "I see a man called to serve the Lord." Then he gave me the following passages:

> Hear, you deaf! And look, you blind, that you may see. Who is blind but My servant, Or so deaf as My messenger whom I send?

Who is so blind as he that is at peace with Me, Or so blind as the
servant of the Lord?
—Isaiah 42:18–19, nasb

Brethren, I do not regard myself as having laid hold of it yet; but
one thing I do: forgetting what lies behind and reaching forward
to what lies ahead.
—Philippians 3:13, nasb

"For I the Lord will speak, and whatever word I speak will be performed. It will no longer be delayed, for in your days, O rebel-
lious house, I will speak the word and perform it," declares the
Lord God…Therefore say to them, "Thus says the Lord God,
'None of My words will be delayed any longer. Whatever word I
speak will be performed,'" declares the Lord God.
—Ezekiel 12:25, 28, nasb

I will give you utterance and wisdom which none of your opponents will be able to resist or refute.
—Luke 21:15, nasb

God will open up to us a door for the word, so that we may
speak forth the mystery of Christ, for which I have also been
imprisoned.
—Colossians 4:3, nasb

> One way the Lord confirms His intentions
> for us is by delivering the same or sup-
> porting scriptures through two or more ma-
> ture Christians. The Lord does this to assure
> us that He is personally speaking to us.

At the time, I did not understand the significance of these two prophetic encounters. God's plan for my life was just beginning to unfold.

BE FULL OF THE WORD

By this time I knew both Dick Mills and Dick Joyce were hearing
from God. There was too much compelling evidence. The presence of
the Holy Spirit accompanied their activities. There seemed to be an
unusual atmosphere of faith and sense of expectation as these men
delivered what God gave them. Then it dawned on me that these men

were full of the Word of God. They had spent years memorizing thousands of scriptures. No wonder they were anointed. God's Word had renewed their mind. It was like they really were speaking on behalf of God because they thought like God's Word. This revelation hit me like a flash. *This may be my answer,* I thought. I wondered what would happen if I memorized Scripture. It certainly could not hurt. I did not know the Bible all that well anyway.

Combining business with pleasure

I was an account representative for a large business envelope manufacturing company in Portland, Oregon. My sales territory included all the counties from north Seattle to the Canadian border. I had attended many business seminars to sharpen my sales and marketing skills. A principle that was recalled to me was how to acquire a new personal sales skill. The presenter said if you would practice it for 21 days, it would become a part of your daily life, thus improving your presentation. I decided to apply the same principle to memorizing Scripture. I selected my favorite scriptures from both the Old and New Testaments. I then spoke each scripture seven times into a tape recorder. I would do this until I filled a 90-minute tape. Then I would start a new tape. I was treasuring the Word of God in my heart.

> Do not let me wander from Your commandments. Your word I
> have treasured in my heart.
> —PSALM 119:10–11, NASB

> The Word of God is permeated with the Holy Spirit. The Word will never pass away. It is eternal. It is alive. When we memorize His Word, we are replacing human understanding with eternal truth that will change our thinking to the way God thinks.

I listened to myself

During my drive time to and from work and between appointments, I listened to nothing but the Bible. By the end of 21 days, I was amazed at how easy it was to speak the complete series of scriptures out loud as I was hearing it. After only hearing the first few words, I could perfectly finish speaking the scripture. What was remarkable to me was after only six months, I had memorized 130 key passages from the Bible. I must have been led by the Holy Spirit to do this. The passages I chose to memorize were eternal promises pertaining to salvation, eternal life, the power of the Holy Spirit, healing, deliverance, and what Jesus said we could do. I still can recall most of them today, word for word.

Then something wonderful began to happen. What I had prayed for came to pass. As people asked for prayer or voiced concerns about their situation, I would suddenly be reminded of a promise from Scripture that would meet their need. The Holy Spirit would often remind me of a set of scriptures that would be the answer to people's problems. It happened so naturally that I felt confident that the Lord was speaking through me. He was using the deposit of His Word in my spirit to bless others. It was extremely gratifying. The Lord was using me in a way I never thought possible. Finally, I was hearing God's voice in a safe and reliable way. It was like I was being used as an echo of the written Word of God when and where it was needed.

I HEARD THE VOICE OF THE HOLY SPIRIT

I will never forget the first time I delivered an "inspired" word from the Holy Spirit at a public gathering. It happened in a FGBMFI luncheon at the Galilean Restaurant in north Seattle. During worship, one of the leaders gave a public message in tongues. The master of ceremonies told us to wait until there was an appropriate interpretation of the message. We needed to be in order and understand what the Lord said. We waited and waited. In the meantime, I was enjoying the Lord's presence on the other side of the room. It seemed the Lord was causing an explosion of words and accompanying pictures to manifest in my mind. It was great. I was having my very own Holy Ghost party.

> If anyone speaks in a tongue, let there be two or at the most three, each in turn, and let one interpret.
>
> —1 CORINTHIANS 14:27, NKJV

> It is best to allow the Holy Spirit to use more than one person when the gifts of tongues and interpretation are manifesting together in a public gathering.

What do I do?

The man standing next to me received a word of knowledge, and I had the interpretation to the message in tongues. He firmly nudged me with his elbow and told me to interpret the message. I opened my eyes and said, "What do I do?" He said, "Just speak what you are hearing and seeing in the Spirit." The party was over. With hesitant words I related to the group what I had just seen and heard. The room erupted in spontaneous applause to the Lord of lords. For the first time in a public setting, I heard the voice of the Lord and was privileged to deliver what He wanted said. The Holy Spirit had created an atmosphere that brought edification to those gathered.

> How is it then, brethren? Whenever you come together, each of you has a psalm, has a teaching, has a tongue, has a revelation, has an interpretation. Let all things be done for edification.
> —1 CORINTHIANS 14:26, NKJV

> God the Holy Spirit is present when believers gather. Everyone should come expectant and ready to contribute something that will edify and build up those who are gathered.

Gaining sensitivity to the Holy Spirit

The more I memorized the Word, the more God used me to give an encouraging word to others. As the months and years rolled on, I noticed an ever-increasing sensitivity to the ministry of the Holy Spirit. This happened as I prayed with certain individuals. It was as if I knew things about their lives and how best to pray for their situations. It was sparked into action when I either looked directly at them or laid my hand on their shoulders. It took a long time of trial and error to master cooperating with the Holy Spirit in this way, but

I kept doing it. Sometimes I heard correctly, sometimes not. When I hesitated and failed to obey the subtle leading, I immediately knew I was grieving the Holy Spirit. He gently lets us know when we hesitate and begin doubting His leading. If we continue doubting too long, the anointing ebbs away, and we are left feeling miserable.

The safe approach

I have learned how to apologize when I miss what God wants to do. Christians are quick to forgive you when you are trying to obey God's voice. I recommend the "safe approach" to people who are not sure they are hearing correctly. You may say something like this: "Sir, I may be wrong. But, I would like to tell you what I 'think' I am hearing from the Lord. Is that OK?" When we approach ministry like that, people will most always respond positively. After delivering the word I ask, "Did that make any sense to you? Did the word fit your situation?" I allow them to respond honestly. I am ready to ask forgiveness if I missed God. We have discovered that 95 percent of the time it is God leading us. We are apologizing less and less as we learn to do it right.

The occasions of disobedience were also becoming less. I was gaining confidence to minister as I felt I was being led. Eventually, I decided to go ahead and assume I was being led by God's voice. Whether it was a weak leading from the inner voice, or the firm, commanding voice of the Holy Spirit, I resolved to go ahead and act on what I thought was manifesting in my mind. At the same time, I always remained open for critique from those to whom I ministered. I wanted to obey Paul's admonition in Ephesians 6.

> Pray at all times in the Spirit.
>
> —EPHESIANS 6:18, NASB

Jesus said believers would speak in tongues. Paul said that when we speak in tongues, we are actually praying in the Spirit. Praying in tongues allows the Holy Spirit to activate our mind to hear a response from God.

Praying in tongues

Ephesians 6:18 is a primary avenue to hear from God. It is not an option. Praying in tongues is a must, and it should be pursued aggressively. The more we pray in the Spirit, the more we will hear from God. When coupled with memorization of Scripture, praying in tongues keeps the channel open to hear God's voice on a daily basis. This is part of abiding in Christ. To abide means to get so close to the Lord that we will pray unselfishly.

> If you abide in Me, and My words abide in you, ask whatever you wish, and it will be done for you.
> —JOHN 15:7, NASB

Jesus desires for us to pray using His words as we ask for things. Praying in the Spirit allows us to pray with His words. When we do this, we are praying His words and asking according to His will, and He will do whatever we ask.

PRAY AT ALL TIMES IN THE SPIRIT

I learned a vital truth from a number of leaders in the Charismatic movement during the 1970s and 1980s. They all agreed on one thing: "The way we hear from the Holy Spirit is to pray at all times in the Spirit. If you are not praying in tongues at every opportunity, then you are really missing God's best." They would challenge us to pray in tongues for as long as possible. I remember what happened when I exceeded about a half-hour praying this way. Something happened within me. It was as if I became supercharged deep within. I experienced a feeling of spiritual euphoria. It was as if I was connected with the Holy Spirit in a way otherwise not possible.

> He who speaks in a tongue does not speak to men but to God, for no one understands him; however, in the spirit he speaks mysteries…He who speaks in a tongue edifies himself.
> —1 CORINTHIANS 14:2, 4, NKJV

> Paul strongly encouraged believers to pray in
> tongues at every opportunity. The more we do
> this, the more the mysteries of God begin to
> flow from our spirit nature, thus edifying and
> recharging us for ministry.

Stop and listen

Believers who are willing to spend quality time praying in tongues will inherit a little known promise found in 1 Corinthians 14. When I pray for extended times in the Spirit and then stop abruptly and listen, I can hear words of praise and adoration to the Lord in my mind, intelligible words that concur with what I have just been praying in tongues. I assume this is most often the interpretation of the mysterious words I have been praying.

> Therefore let one who speaks in a tongue pray that he may interpret. For if I pray in a tongue, my spirit prays, but my mind is unfruitful.
> —1 CORINTHIANS 14:13–14, NASB

- Paul revealed a profound truth about praying in tongues. He said that people who speak in tongues should pray to interpret what they say.
- Praying in tongues is a supernatural transaction generated from our spirit nature, not our mind.
- Paul encouraged us to allow the Holy Spirit to interpret what we have been praying so our mind can understand what was said.
- When we are alone we should practice this way of praying.

Personal worship

The context of 1 Corinthians 14 is almost exclusively related to the public gathering of the church body. But how do we learn how to express these gifts when they manifest at church? May we suggest practicing at home? If we cannot learn how to edify ourselves, how can we ever learn how to edify the church? Let us attempt to apply the principles of speaking in tongues and interpretation of tongues in the safety of our own home, alone.

An exciting way to pray

The preceding scripture says we can expect to receive the interpretation of what we have been praying in unknown languages. It says, "Pray that he may interpret." I discovered this while alone with God, praying for prolonged times in the Spirit. I would pray, "Lord, what am I saying?" Words would then manifest in my mind, and I would speak those back to the Lord. The words were most often praise, exaltation, and magnification of the Lord. They seemed to be words that needed to be said to the Lord. This became a regular exercise that strengthened my faith and belief that I was on track. I eventually concluded that I was hearing what the Holy Spirit was saying. He then encouraged me to express these words to the Father. It was as if the Holy Spirit were giving me the kind of words that would bless and magnify the Father more than what I could come up with.

Caution

I also found that, when I continued to exercise faith and speak words that were manifesting in my mind, occasionally the message would pertain to things the Lord wanted me to do. The communication was personalized and intended for me to apply to my situation. There is a danger in accepting words that come this way as being from God. In our zeal to hear from God, we must always test the words we are hearing, especially if they apply to us personally. I learned quickly to write down what I thought the Holy Spirit was saying. As I wrote I would always pray, "Lord, if this is from You, please confirm it any way You want." I would never act on the message until I received multiple confirmations. A good indication that we are hearing from the Holy Spirit is when we hear the same message or see the same images in our thoughts and dreams over and over again. This is especially true when we pray for extended times in tongues.

When confirmation comes

As soon as God confirmed what He had said, I learned to act immediately on what He wanted me to do. With few exceptions, the leading turned out to be from the Lord. When He multiplies His confirmations, you can be more assured it is from Him.

> Your word is a lamp to my feet and a light to my path. I have sworn and I will confirm it.
>
> —PSALM 119:105–106, NASB

> After you have suffered for a little while, the God of all grace, who called you to His eternal glory in Christ, will Himself perfect, confirm, strengthen and establish you.
>
> —1 PETER 5:10, NASB

When Jesus wants you to do something, the Holy Spirit will provide multiple confirmations. Most confirmations will be spontaneous surprises.

HOW THIS WORKS OUT IN OUR DAILY LIVES

Hearing God's voice can be a great advantage to staying on course in our daily lives. It would be wonderful if we could hear His voice hour-by-hour just as Jesus did. That is just not how it works for most Christians. Even the holiest, most spiritual and most mature pastors we know do not hear from God to that extent. We do not, but we want to. All of us should be working toward this goal. If every Christian leader were totally honest, we would have to admit we are a long way from hearing the Father's voice like Jesus did. Knowing it is possible is the driving force that keeps us seeking an even closer, more personal relationship with the heavenly Father. The following are some real-life examples of how we have heard from God and attempted to obey.

We must be deliberate

Learning to hear God's voice requires deliberate action on our part. I (Sonja) am a Word person, and by being in the Word daily for almost 40 years, I have had the Holy Spirit teach me many wonderful spiritual principles. I have learned from the Word what pleases God and how I can show Him I love Him. Learning to hear God's voice through His Word is very exciting, and it can shape the very direction our lives will take. The following scriptures have guided me through the years.

For the word of God is living and active. Sharper than any double-edged sword, it penetrates even to dividing soul and spirit, joints and marrow; it judges the thoughts and attitudes of the heart.

—HEBREWS 4:12

To obey is better than sacrifice.

—1 SAMUEL 15:22

If you love me, you will obey what I command.

—JOHN 14:15

The Word of God is living and active. God makes it clear in His Word that we show Him we love Him by our obedience. We must know His Word so that we can live a pleasing life before Him.

Renewing the mind

Over the years He has dealt with my (Sonja's) sinful, carnal behaviors through His Word. It is as if a spiritual spotlight shines on certain passages and causes them to illuminate and give me personal insight, conviction, and understanding. This is the supernatural nature of the Bible as revealed by the Holy Spirit.

On many occasions it has been a fierce struggle between my soul nature (mind, emotions, and will) and my spirit. One of the greatest areas of spiritual warfare is self-justification. What stinking thinking that is! I always wanted to be right, always wanted my point of view to prevail. The following incident reveals how I have struggled in this area.

Corporate executive needs to hear from God

I was employed as a corporate officer of an electronics firm, and I enjoyed my job very much. As the company grew, the board of directors agreed with the top executives that it was time to hire a new chief executive officer to take the company to the next level. In this reorganization, four new executives were hired. In my position I had to interface with each of these people on a daily basis.

Since I had always had excellent working relationships with their predecessors, I naively assumed it would be "business as usual." What a rude awakening I experienced! From day one, the new "inner circle" began to shut me out. Since I was dependent upon them for timely information to do my job, I was in a most untenable situation. As the weeks progressed, the situation went from bad to worse. Nothing I did or said seemed to change things. It was obvious that new executives did not like me and wanted me out of there.

I was fervently praying about the deteriorating circumstances in which I found myself, and I had no answers and no reasons why. I had watched the job I loved deteriorate into one that was miserable, to the point that I dreaded going to work. It all came to a head one Friday afternoon when the data I needed for a board of directors' meeting was not forthcoming, consequently making my report late. I was rudely told the information would not be available until after the meeting. That was the last straw.

Fire was shooting out of my eyes

I became so angry I think fire was shooting out of my eyes! Shaking with anger, I somehow managed to mumble something like, "I cannot believe you can be so unprofessional!" I then went into my office and slammed the door with all my might. Every wall in the executive suite shook at the force of my fury. I grabbed my briefcase and purse, threw the door open, marched out, and slammed the door again. By then, I had everyone's attention. Thank God, no one said a word as I stomped out to my car and left for the weekend.

Very few times in my life have I been so completely out of control. It was sickening. We had planned a weekend trip to a quaint Bavarian town in eastern Washington. I vented my anger and frustration, my self-justification, my uncontrolled soul nature to poor John. It became clear that I had three choices:

1. I could resign and leave the company I had helped build along with the lucrative stock options, bonus programs, etc.

2. I could stay and fight the executives on their own terms. After all, I reported directly to the chairman and person-ally knew all of the directors of the board. I could cause

my "enemies" considerable grief and feed the demon of self-justification.

3. I could stay, and through God's grace, be myself—not responding in like manner.

After I was finally able to calm myself to where I could listen, I went to the Bible and was led to the following passage:

> Love is patient, love is kind. It does not envy, it does not boast, it is not proud. It is not rude, it is not self-seeking, it is not easily angered, it keeps no record of wrongs. Love does not delight in evil but rejoices with the truth. It always protects, always trusts, always hopes, always perseveres.
> —1 Corinthians 13:4–7

This paragraph is one of the most powerful passages in the entire Bible. Jesus, our perfect example, exhibited this type of love.

He spoke through His Word once again

I had been rude, self-seeking, easily angered, and I was keeping a record of every little offense! I was extremely sensitive to how I was being treated. The kind of love the apostle Paul wrote about can only come from God. I asked Him for it, and He immediately softened my heart. He spoke through His Word once again. I felt led to purchase a small, but meaningful gift for the woman who had treated me so rudely on Friday.

I was myself as I walked into the office on Monday morning and put the beautifully wrapped gift on the woman's desk as I said a cheery "Good morning!" Honestly, her mouth dropped open as I walked into my office. She obviously was ready for a knock-down-drag-out encounter, and my actions totally disarmed her.

I quit the ugly self-justification

Things began to change that very day. I quit the ugly self-justification and determined that, if the Lord allowed me to continue to be treated badly, then He must need to work some things into or out of my character, and I would declare, "Your grace is sufficient."

Two months later one of the executives stuck his head in my office and asked if he could meet with me in a few minutes. As I said, "Of course," I honestly thought to myself, "What now?" This particular man had been especially abrasive in our communications.

He thought I was a phony

I went to his office, sat down and braced myself. He began by thanking me for coming, and said he needed to tell me something before he went into the matter he wanted to discuss. I nodded my head, and he proceeded to tell me that he had not liked me from the moment he laid eyes on me. He thought I was a phony—no one could be that cheerful and considerate day in and day out. However, he had come to the conclusion that I was who I appeared to be and that he had been mistaken. He then leaned forward, smiled, and said the most unbelievable thing: "Actually, Sonja, I really like you!"

I was dumbfounded and sat there in utter amazement as he moved on to the matter he wanted to discuss. It involved a very serious situation with one of his employees, and he wanted my advice on how to handle it. Together we were able to come up with an excellent solution that was a win-win for the employee and the company.

My remaining time at that company was enjoyable. We all ended up being friends and supportive co-workers. Yes, we can hear the voice of the Lord through His Word and His Holy Spirit for our everyday life experiences! The following story relates a more dramatic way the Lord can speak.

"JOHN, I CALL YOU TO PREACH THE GOSPEL!"

Then I heard the voice of the Lord saying, "Whom shall I send? And who will go for us?" And I said, "Here am I. Send me!"
—ISAIAH 6:8

One of the highest callings that anyone can receive is being called to preach the gospel. We should have only one response: "Yes, Lord! Here am I. Send me!"

Jack-in-the-Box

It was noon on November 3, 1975. I (John) had just been handed my lunch at the drive-up window of a Jack-in-the-Box near downtown Seattle. I decided to save time by eating lunch in my car because I had a busy day of making sales calls. Parking close to the ordering window, I unwrapped the biggest, juiciest hamburger on the menu. As I put it up to my mouth, God's voice suddenly filled the car. He said, "John Decker, I call you to preach the gospel!" Shocked, I lost my grip on the burger. The tomatoes, lettuce, and onions fell to the napkin on my lap. Then He said it again: "John Decker, I call you to preach the gospel!" Stunned, eyes wide, and holding my breath, I stared at the big plastic Jack-in-the-Box statue with the two-way speaker on his chest. The voice was not coming from the speaker. The speaker was the King of kings and the Lord of lords! I slowly placed what remained of the burger back into its box.

Ask for confirmation

A pastor once told me to ask for multiple confirmations if you think the Lord is speaking to you about a major life change. This one certainly qualified, so I asked the Lord to confirm three times what I thought I had I had heard Him say. I thought that, if I made it hard for God, I could really know for sure if it was Him. I barely finished my question when I heard, "Drive up to the park on the top of the hill and I will confirm it!" The voice was so clear, so forceful, and so spontaneous that I started the car and drove to the park. Turning off the engine, I said, "OK, what now?" Again, as before, His words loudly exploded inside my head. He said, "Turn to Hebrews chapter 3." I fumbled around the boxes of envelope samples in the backseat and finally found my Bible. Turning to chapter 3, my eyes immediately fell on:

> The Holy Spirit says, "Today, if you hear His voice, do not harden your hearts as when they provoked Me, as in the day of trial in the wilderness."
>
> —Hebrews 3:7–8, nasb

I knew the Holy Spirit was personalizing this passage to me. I said, "OK, that's one confirmation." Then He said, "Turn the page!" I turned the page. There it was again, not only once but two more times!

Today if you hear His voice, do not harden your hearts, as when they provoked Me.

—HEBREWS 3:15, NASB

Today if you hear His voice, do not harden your hearts.

—HEBREWS 4:7, NASB

When the Holy Spirit speaks, He may repeat the same message over and over until we accept that it is from God.

I said, "OK, that's twice." Then I was startled when I heard a loud knocking on the passenger side window. I jerked to the right and saw the face of my prayer partner smiling at me. He motioned for me to unlock the door. I could not believe what was happening. Sitting down he said, "God told me to drive up here, find you, and tell you that He is calling you to do something very important."

I said, "OK God, that's three"

When I told my prayer partner what was happening and that he was the third confirmation God had orchestrated to get me to believe that I had heard from Him, we began to pray and cry together. With hands raised, sitting in the front seat of my car we began praising God and rejoicing that the Lord had boldly called me to preach the gospel in such a convincing way that I knew it was Him. This bold encounter with God was just the beginning of a series of events that put me into the equipping ministry. The following scriptures showed me that Peter had a bold encounter with the Lord where he was told something three times.

And a voice came to him, "Rise, Peter; kill and eat." But Peter said, "Not so, Lord! For I have never eaten anything common or unclean." And a voice spoke to him again the second time, "What God has cleansed you must not call common." This was done three times. And the object was taken up into heaven again. Now while Peter wondered within himself what this vision which he had seen meant, behold, the men who had been sent from Cornelius had made inquiry for Simon's house, and stood before the gate. And they called and asked whether Simon, whose surname was Peter, was lodging there. While Peter thought about the vision, the Spirit said to him, "Behold, three men are seeking you. Arise therefore, go down and go with them, doubting nothing; for I have sent them."

—ACTS 10:13–20, NKJV

- This is one of the best scriptures in the New Testament regarding how the Holy Spirit can speak to believers today.
- We can expect the Holy Spirit to arrange circumstances that will coincide with His commands. He does this to convince us that it is the Lord speaking.

More confirmations

It was but a few months later, after I spoke at the Tacoma chapter of the FGBMFI, where a man I had never seen before appeared in front of me. He took my hand, and, looking deep into my eyes he said, "The Lord says to you to be bold as never before. You shall not delay any longer. You shall preach the gospel in the mighty power of the Holy Spirit. The power of almighty God shall be in you and in your words!" I closed my eyes for a moment and began thanking the Lord. When I opened my eyes, I could not see the man. I quickly went looking for him but to no avail. The other men did not know who he was or where he came from. This began a series of similar confirmations over the next two years that firmly convinced me to surrender my life to preach the gospel. I finally did it in the spring of 1977. I began to understand the mysterious way the Holy Spirit works. I saw in Acts 13 where the Holy Spirit spoke concerning Barnabas and Saul.

Now in the church that was at Antioch there were certain prophets and teachers: Barnabas, Simeon who was called Niger, Lucius of Cyrene, Manaen who had been brought up with Herod the tetrarch, and Saul. As they ministered to the Lord and fasted, the Holy Spirit said, "Now separate to Me Barnabas and Saul for the work to which I have called them." Then, having fasted and prayed, and laid hands on them, they sent them away.

—ACTS 13:1–3, NKJV

> When we get serious about hearing from God, He will reward us. Fasting, praying, and ministering to the Lord are scriptural ways to create an atmosphere where we can hear the Holy Spirit.

HOW I LEARNED TO HEAR GOD'S VOICE THROUGH JOURNALING

I (Sonja) often ask pastors and leaders at our workshops if they are regularly hearing the voice of the Lord. Almost without exception, all hands are affirmatively raised. I then ask them if they remember from one day to the next what He has told them. That gets some inquisitive looks. Next, I ask them if they would agree that, yes, the Lord is speaking to us, but because we are not disciplining ourselves to record what He is saying, we cannot remember what He told us yesterday. His thoughts become intermingled with our own, and there is no clear message.

Besides reading the Word, the most significant way I have learned to hear and know His voice is through recording what I hear Him saying to me. I have been journaling for almost 40 years. Every morning I read my Bible and then I write down my worship (simply exclaiming God's worthiness), my thoughts, and often my prayers. Next, I discipline myself to listen for His voice, and I diligently record what I am hearing and the impressions I am receiving.

Lord, is this really You?

I remember early on when He told me something that was going to happen. I could hardly believe it. In fact, I put a big asterisk in the margin with a note that said, "Lord, is this really You? It seems so preposterous!" Imagine my amazement when that very thing came to pass a short time later! I remember thinking, "It was You! It was You, Lord! Even though I doubted at the time, it was Your voice!"

Over the years, this has happened time and time again. This is my vital, one-on-one connection time with the magnificent, triune Godhead—heavenly Father, Lord Jesus Christ, and the precious Holy Spirit.

God's voice can be heard around the world

On one of our mission trips to the refugee camps in Northern Thailand, John was wearing a money belt that contained all of our cash for the team's expenses. On our trip back to the no-star hotel this particular afternoon, it was extremely hot, and John removed the money belt. He put it over the back of the seat directly in front of him. When we returned to the hotel and I stretched out on the bed, God's voice immediately called my attention to John's missing money belt! John had left it in the van. He raced down to the van, and, by God's grace, it was where he had left it.

He was addicted to pornography

One Sunday morning we arrived early at a church in California where we were to speak. The pastors introduced us to the worship team, and we discussed how we wanted to close the service. One young man on the team was like a son to the pastors, and John and I both immediately liked him. He was cute, personable, and very talented.

There was a tremendous response to our altar call—people accepted Jesus as their Savior, many were healed, and another group was baptized in the Holy Spirit. In the midst of all that wonderful ministry, my eyes fell on the young man I described earlier. On a human level, John and I had instantly liked him, so I was shocked when I discerned that he was addicted to pornography and living a life of deception. I mulled this over for a few minutes, and then I went to John and shared what I had heard. He had not picked up on that, so I thought I was not hearing correctly.

A few more minutes passed, and I knew I had to say something. The young man walked over to the woman pastor who was standing next to me and was talking much like a son with his mother. I took a deep breath, breathed a prayer, and then asked him if I could ask him a question. "Sure," he said, never imagining what I was about to expose. "Are you hooked on pornography?" I asked. He looked like someone had just hit him with a two-by-four. The color drained from his face, and he burst into tears. "Yes! It's true. I'm just sick about it."

He was sleeping with two young women

I immediately went and got John, told him what I had heard was true, and asked him to minister to the young man. John got the associate pastor to assist him so that he could provide accountability after we left. It was an ugly story. The young man had played around with porn and had become addicted; he was currently sleeping with two young women in the congregation. It was unbelievable! What a web of deception he had allowed Satan to weave. John dealt with the unclean and lying spirits and set accountability in place. We then shared with the senior pastors who were also blindsided and broken-hearted by the revelation.

When we checked back on the situation, we were saddened to learn that the young man had left the church. Apparently, he was still struggling and was unable to resist the temptations. We know that men often need a strong program and/or support group to break the bondage of pornography. We are finding this deplorable conduct in more and more churches. How we need the revelation gifts of dis-cerning of spirits and words of knowledge and wisdom so we can unmask the enemy and get people the help they need. Oh, that a holy reverence for God's house would fall upon us!

Supernatural strategies

Recently the Lord challenged both of us to enter a fresh and very serious phase of spiritual warfare and intercession. He indicated that, if we would dedicate a significant amount of time each day praying in and with the Holy Spirit, He would reveal glimpses of future events. We would not become prophets, but we would be enlightened so that we could direct our energies to stay as close to God's will as possible. The Lord also indicated that, if we paid the price to stay in close, intimate relationship with Him, He would reveal the strategies of the enemy before they were implemented. We would be able to sidestep potential tragedy and stay on track with God. He said we would need to join the ranks of the truly committed intercessors for this to become a reality.

Paying the price

True intercessors pay an enormous price to stay in touch with the Lord. It is neither cheap nor intermittent. It is a serious undertaking, often for life. It is a thankless task to spend hours of quality time crying out before God on behalf of others, some who are enemies of the cross. The alternative is not attractive. We would have a comfort-able life of status quo, business as usual, and an occasional blessing because of the grace of God. We are reminded of the Scriptures that say obedience is better than sacrifice. So we have chosen intercession as the best course of action. We are spending more and more time entreating the Lord, exercising our spiritual languages, and listening for His response. The rewards are worth the price.

We have only just begun

We are beginning to hear incredible things that will affect our future and the future of those affiliated with our ministry. Our journals are filling, and our spirits are rejoicing for what the Lord continues to reveal. We are both in our mid-sixties as of the writing of this book, and we become more energized as each year passes. We have learned one truth that keeps us going: hearing God's voice is the key to productive ministry. He knows the end from the beginning. He knows where each of us will be five or ten years from now. If we will surrender everything we are and ever will be into His hands, it is easy for Him to catapult us into exactly what He wants us to do. It is easy for Him to place us precisely in His will when we constantly remind Him that is where we want to be.

LET'S PRACTICE

James 1:22 says to do what we have heard (read).

Consider doing what is recommended in this chapter by referring to the "Let's Practice" in Appendix B, page 259.

Do the Ministry Skill Assignment titled, "Hearing from God."

HEALING THE SICK BY REVELATION

Jesus healed the sick by doing what He saw the Father revealing through the Holy Spirit. We will learn how to do the same in this chapter. When we follow the Holy Spirit's leading and obey what He is revealing in regard to praying for the sick, healing will manifest and miracles will result.

JESUS ONLY DID what He saw the Father doing. It is reasonable for us to believe that Jesus operated perfectly by revelation knowledge emanating from the Father. It would stand to reason that, even though He was moved by compassion, the only people He healed were those the Father selected. Sometimes it was the whole crowd. Other times, "many" were healed. Sometimes only one received healing. From this, we can begin to understand the reason everyone He prayed for was healed. It was because in the Father's infinite wisdom and foreknowledge He will have mercy and compassion on whomever He chooses. The only ones Jesus prayed for were those revealed by the Father through the Holy Spirit.

> Then Jesus answered and said to them, "Most assuredly, I say to you, the Son can do nothing of Himself, but what He sees the Father do; for whatever He does, the Son also does in like manner. For the Father loves the Son, and shows Him all things that He Himself does; and He will show Him greater works than these, that you may marvel."
>
> —JOHN 5:19–20, NKJV

> Learning to heal the sick by relying on the leading of the Holy Spirit is a difficult skill to master. It is the way Jesus conducted His healing ministry. And it is available to every Spirit-filled believer around the world. More and more believers are discovering the Holy Spirit's willingness to guide them to those who will be healed.

When God starts revealing, He starts healing

We have coined the above statement to explain a more sure way to minister healing to others. When we receive a word or picture from God regarding the situation about those around us, God is initiating ministry. If we act on these impressions, the people most often receive the things God revealed. This is especially true regarding healing. We firmly believe this is the key to supernatural ministry. We should always pray for those requesting healing. However, without a leading from the Holy Spirit, we are not surprised when our prayers yield no visible result. We should always remain expectant because of God's willingness to heal. But, when we are operating with an authentic word or revelation from the Holy Spirit, the healing most always manifests.

Stop and listen

Healing of chronic disease, serious pain, or life-threatening ailments needs to be carefully confirmed by a thorough medical examination. We want our testimony to be based on fact, not emotion. Whenever and however God wants to heal us is just fine. But, every minister should learn this truth: When God starts revealing things about people, stop and listen. Then act on what is being revealed and minister accordingly. Everyone gets blessed and God gets all the glory.

> Do not worry about what to say or how to say it. At that time you will be given what to say, for it will not be you speaking, but the Spirit of your Father speaking through you.
> —MATTHEW 10:19–20

> We should be so connected with the Holy
> Spirit that He will tell us what to speak. We
> are to rely on the Spirit of the Father speaking
> through us to those in need. This is the way
> Jesus wants us to respond: Only do what you
> hear from the Father.

Obey the Word and the Spirit

The Word of God authorizes us to heal the sick. The Holy Spirit tells us when and in whom healing will manifest. The Word tells us we can; the Holy Spirit tells us when.

God initiates the ministry

When God starts revealing specific words, thoughts, pictures, or symbolic images that are relevant to the people to whom we are ministering, we should carefully observe what is being revealed. It only takes seconds to stop, watch, and listen. When we proceed with the revelation and act on what we are discerning, the healing is only seconds away. The only thing God requires is strict obedience to what is being revealed. When we obey and act on what we are being shown, the healing most often manifests. That is because we are not initiating the ministry; God is. Both the person and the minister know it was all God. Everyone is quick to give God all the praise for initiating and completing the healing. We see below in 1 Corinthians 12 that it is the Holy Spirit who manifests these supernatural gifts through God's people for the common good.

> But to each one is given the manifestation of the Spirit for the
> common good. For to one is given the word of wisdom through
> the Spirit, and to another the word of knowledge according to the
> same Spirit; to another faith by the same Spirit, and to another
> gifts of healing by the one Spirit, and to another the effecting of
> miracles, and to another prophecy, and to another the distin-
> guishing of spirits, to another various kinds of tongues.
> —1 Corinthians 12:7–10, nasb

- Jesus wants His ministers to operate by revelation, just as He did.
- When the Holy Spirit comes upon believers, He imparts various gifts. Three of these gifts allow us to minister to others by "seeing or hearing" what needs to be done from God's perspective.
- These are called revelation gifts because the Holy Spirit is revealing hidden wisdom, knowledge, and spiritual activity.
- When we act on these revelations, we are ministering according to God's perfect will.

The lady wearing the blue blouse

While teaching a ministry training workshop in Abidjan, Ivory Coast, Africa, I (John) received a word of knowledge. The Holy Spirit wanted to accentuate what I was teaching about ministering by revelation by giving a real-life example to all of the pastors and leaders. The Holy Spirit gently interrupted my teaching by saying, "John, I want to heal someone." I stopped what I was doing, closed my eyes, and waited for further words from the Lord. I told my interpreter to tell the pastors, "The Lord wants to heal someone. Let's wait on Him." With my eyes still closed, in my mind I began to see a woman wearing a blue blouse. I had to assume she was in the gathering of pastors. Then I saw the woman rubbing her back as if in pain. That was it. No more words or pictures. I have learned that, when this happens, I do not try to analyze the word of knowledge. In faith, I quickly act on what I am receiving. I said, "There is a lady here with severe back pain and God wants to heal you. You are wearing a blue blouse. When you come forward, God will instantly heal you!"

She came up smiling

I have also learned to be very bold when a revelation is manifesting because the Lord is initiating the miracle, not me. The wait between when you call out what you think the Lord is saying and when the people finally respond seems like an eternity. In this case, she only took thirty seconds to get up and come forward. Greatly relieved and once again full of faith, I laid one hand on her shoulder and said, "I command the back pain to go in the name of Jesus Christ! Amen." Then I told the interpreter to tell the woman to bend all the way over because the pain was gone. Not knowing French, I encouraged her by smiling and quickly bending over myself a few times to give her the idea. She bent over and came up smiling. She said the pain was all gone. She demonstrated it by swaying back and forth and up and down. She came to us during the break and thanked us over and over again. She had been in almost unbearable pain for a long time.

DEFINING THE WORD OF WISDOM

The word of wisdom is a divine revelation from God revealing to man His plan and best course of action for a given situation. This wisdom is communicated spontaneously from God to man, through the Spirit, revealing how to proceed in His will. It provides wholeness, restoration, peace, and/or strength to overcome in times of perplexity, trial, persecution, or danger.

It will reveal the future

The word of wisdom and the word of knowledge are very similar. The word of wisdom will reveal God's will concerning what should or will happen. It will reveal what the future should be, either in a few minutes, days, or months. We are to simply obey what we are either seeing or hearing from the Holy Spirit. God's infinite wisdom is revealed in the form of what He desires to be accomplished. When we hear or see correctly about what is yet to come, we simply act out what we are hearing or seeing. That is what Jesus did. We are working with the Spirit of truth (Holy Spirit) who will tell us what is yet to come.

> But when he, the Spirit of truth, comes, he will guide you into all truth. He will not speak on his own; he will speak only what he hears, and he will tell you what is yet to come. He will bring glory to me by taking from what is mine and making it known to you.
> —JOHN 16:13–14

- As you pray for others, the Holy Spirit will reveal what you should do or say in the form of pictures or words in your mind.
- When we obey and proceed according to what is being made known to us through the Holy Spirit, we will experience a miracle.
- It takes a lot of trial and error and hours of practice to master cooperating with the Holy Spirit in this way.

What is heard or seen

We will see pictures in our mind of what should happen. We will hear instructions regarding what to do about the people standing in front of us. We are given God's will in advance. We are being given what God desires to happen. We may not understand it at the moment, but our mission is to obey in faith and fully trust that God knows what He's doing. The word of wisdom very often will manifest with the word of knowledge. The two go together. God will reveal the root problem and then give us the solution, all in one word. This is exciting when it happens. The minister seems to be suspended for a moment, in total dependence on God's will as it is being revealed. God is calling all the signals. We simply act out His signals and bring His will into fulfillment in the natural realm.

The lady with the white headband

While teaching in Malawi, Central Africa, I (John) received a word of wisdom. During the Sunday pre-service prayer, the Holy Spirit began to reveal that I was to preach on healing. I had prepared a good sermon, but the Lord had a better one in store. While I was praying, in my mind I saw a lady with her hair piled on top of her head and held together with a white headband. I kept seeing her over and over. All I heard from the Lord was that He was going to heal her. The Lord seldom gives me any more details than I need to know. I went into the service looking for the lady with the white headband. She was not there. I began preaching on divine healing and was about halfway through when I began to think that I had misunderstood the word from the Lord. Then the door opened and another group of people came in. There she was! I preached ten more minutes and then I heard, "John, call her forward."

Through the interpreter I said, "There is a lady here with a white headband, and God wants to heal you." I saw her and another woman begin to argue with one another. The lady with the white headband kept shaking her head no. I thought, "Oh no, Lord, is she really the one?" Then the Holy Spirit gave me the rest of the word of wisdom. I have learned to proceed with what is given to me even though it may only be a part of the unfolding picture. He said, "Yes, that's the one. She has pain in her ovaries and is afraid. I will heal her."

New ovaries

Wow! At that point I knew what to do. With boldness I looked at the woman, pointed to her and repeated what I had just heard from the Lord. She looked amazed, hesitated for a moment, and then came forward. I had Sonja lay hands on her lower abdomen as I prayed. Because the Lord always heals what He reveals, I boldly prayed, "In the name of Jesus Christ, I command brand new ovaries in this woman. Satan, you cannot have her. I command you to loose her, now! Pain, leave now in the name of Jesus Christ! Amen." I told the interpreter to tell her she was healed and to go get a doctor's report to confirm it. She said the pain was no longer there and she would go get the doctor's diagnosis. She returned at the end of the week and announced to everyone that the doctor said she no longer had the ovary problem and gave her a clean bill of health.

Jesus is our perfect example

Jesus perfectly operated in words of wisdom as an example for us. He did these things as a man, filled with the mighty power of the Holy Spirit. He was demonstrating how to operate in the supernatural by relying totally on the Holy Spirit. He said we would do the same things He did. All four Gospels have beautiful examples of Jesus' operating by revelation from the Father. Below are two examples of "seeing" into the future by words of wisdom:

> Now a man named Lazarus was sick. He was from Bethany, the
> village of Mary and her sister Martha. This Mary, whose brother
> Lazarus now lay sick, was the same one who poured perfume

on the Lord and wiped his feet with her hair. So the sisters sent word to Jesus, "Lord, the one you love is sick." When he heard this, Jesus said, "This sickness will not end in death. No, it is for God's glory so that God's Son may be glorified through it."

—JOHN 11:1–4

Peter replied, "Even if all fall away on account of you, I never will." "I tell you the truth," Jesus answered, "this very night, before the rooster crows, you will disown me three times."

—MATTHEW 26:33–34

- In both of these examples Jesus showed us how to cooperate with what the Father is revealing through the Holy Spirit.
- He repeated what He was hearing and seeing from the Father.
- We should do the same when the Holy Spirit begins revealing words of wisdom and knowledge.

The lady from South Whidbey Island

When I (John) first began operating by revelation it was a scary experience. I remember a particular dinner meeting where I was the speaker for the FGBMFI in 1977. The Holy Spirit urged me to call out a woman for healing while I was speaking. This was new to me. I thought I heard the Holy Spirit say, "She needs healing. Speak to her." I kept on telling my story, not wanting to make a fool of myself, but every time I looked her way the same inner urging would prompt me to speak to her. I had seen this done by mature speakers and evangelists at these kinds of meetings and on television. It seemed God was testing me to see if I would obey.

I may be wrong, but...

In faith, I stepped way out of my comfort zone and said to her, "I may be wrong, but, sister, I believe you need to be healed. Right?" To me, the next five seconds of silence seemed like an eternity as everyone awaited her response. With a surprised look, she said, "Yes, I do." I was incredibly relieved, and my faith reengaged. I stepped off the platform, laid hands on her, and said, "Be healed in the name of

Jesus Christ!" It only took a moment of stretching and bending for the woman to declare that all of the pain was gone.

God knows everything about everybody

God changed the course of that meeting. People spontaneously came forward to be prayed for. Other healings must have taken place, but the only one I remember was the lady from South Whidbey Island. The event showed me something new. The Holy Spirit always knows everything about everybody. He chose that meeting to activate a word of wisdom and knowledge through a vessel that was almost too scared to do anything about it. I learned a big lesson. When God starts revealing who needs healing, they get healed! When we relinquish our agenda for His and obey His voice, miracles begin to happen.

Philip received a word of wisdom

The Holy Spirit spoke directly to Philip and told him God's plan in advance. He was to take a hike on the road to Gaza. When he got to a certain point, the Holy Spirit delivered a second word of wisdom, telling him to go to the eunuch's chariot. His obedience was rewarded supernaturally:

> Now an angel of the Lord said to Philip, "Go south to the road—
> the desert road—that goes down from Jerusalem to Gaza." So he
> started out, and on his way he met an Ethiopian eunuch, an impor-
> tant official in charge of all the treasury of Candace, queen of the
> Ethiopians. This man had gone to Jerusalem to worship, and on his
> way home was sitting in his chariot reading the book of Isaiah the
> prophet. The Spirit told Philip, "Go to that chariot and stay near it."
> —ACTS 8:26–29

- We can expect the Holy Spirit to speak to us exactly as He did to Phillip.
- The voice of the Holy Spirit will be strong and directive when you are ministering to others. Expect Him to speak.

- Ask for direction and revelation by praying in tongues before and during ministry to others.
- Pray, "Lord, what do You want to do next? Lord what do You have for this person? Lord, how do I pray for this person?"
- Just do what Jesus did.

Paul received a word of wisdom

In times of intense ministry or even in distress, the word of wisdom is a welcome revelation from the Spirit of God. Paul received advance information that no one was going to die because of the storm raging against the ship he was on:

> After the men had gone a long time without food, Paul stood up before them and said: "Men, you should have taken my advice not to sail from Crete; then you would have spared your-selves this damage and loss. But now I urge you to keep up your courage, because not one of you will be lost; only the ship will be destroyed. Last night an angel of the God whose I am and whom I serve stood beside me and said, 'Do not be afraid, Paul. You must stand trial before Caesar; and God has graciously given you the lives of all who sail with you.' So keep up your courage, men, for I have faith in God that it will happen just as he told me."
>
> —ACTS 27:21–25

- We may not get a visit from an angel, but the Holy Spirit is always with us to give insight and information concerning the outcome of our current situation.
- He knows the end from the beginning and will reveal what we need to know to minister healing and comfort to those God places be-fore us.

The revelations do not have to be dramatic

Our receiving a word of wisdom may not be as dramatic as with Jesus, Philip, or Paul. But we can receive foreknowledge that will show us the way into God's perfect will. We simply expect the manifestation to come in the timing and at the discretion of the Holy Spirit. This gift is very helpful when we are ministering to people and have no clue what to do. By keeping our mind focused on what heaven wants, there will be times when heaven will respond.

BEST GIRLFRIEND RECEIVES BEST GIFT!

My (Sonja) best girlfriend is Janie Gibson. She has been my best girlfriend since junior high school in 1952. (That is over 50 years!) Although we have not lived in the same town since college days, we have remained the dearest of friends. Can you imagine exchanging 50 birthday and Christmas gifts! I have lovely things all over our home that daily remind me of her. We recently agreed we would only give "consumables" (stationery, etc.) from now on.

It was as though I knew the time was right

In 1970, Janie and her husband, Glynn, were visiting in our hometown, and I was concerned that they did not yet personally know the Lord. They had attended church while growing up but never understood the need for a personal Savior. I sensed they were open as I shared about my recent experience with the Holy Spirit baptism. It was as though I knew the time was right.

Then came the Holy Spirit baptism

I invited Janie and Glynn to our home Bible study. Janie wanted to go, but Glynn was hesitant. After a little gentle persuasion, he agreed to accompany Janie. I cannot remember exactly what we talked about or studied, but, at the close of the meeting, we asked them if they would like to invite Jesus into their hearts and receive Him as their personal Savior. They wholeheartedly responded, and it was a joyous time for all of us. I later had the privilege of leading them and another couple into the Holy Spirit baptism. It was wonderful to share this additional common ground in our friendship.

We have since walked through some extremely difficult life experiences together. One involved their infant grandson, Brittain, who developed Kawasaki disease and was in critical condition at Children's Hospital in Seattle for four months. I remember going into his room with his parents, Brian and Kim Gibson, and speaking healing over his swollen, lifeless little body. I kept declaring, "Brittain, one day I will watch you play basketball."

A spirit of death

In the middle of the night, I received a call from Brittain's daddy, Brian. The doctors had said Brittain would not live through the night, and Brian was sensing the spirit of death in the room. Frantically, he said, "Sonja, what do I do? I'm not willing to let him go!" I silently prayed and then instructed him to put everyone out of the baby's room except Janie, his grandmother. I then explained his spiritual authority as head of his household and instructed him to exercise that authority by submitting himself to God in prayer. He was then to boldly address the spirit of death in the name of Jesus Christ and command it to depart. He hung up the telephone and did exactly as I had told him. Even though Brian had limited understanding about spiritual warfare, he acted in total and bold faith, and the spirit of death departed! Little Brittain had a worldwide prayer covering that resulted in his total recovery. And, yes, he plays basketball!

DEFINING THE WORD OF KNOWLEDGE

The word of knowledge is a divine revelation originating with God about situations either past or present of which God makes us aware. This knowledge is communicated spontaneously from God to man, through the Holy Spirit, to bring clarification, wholeness, and restoration to the lives of those present.

Words come spontaneously

The word of knowledge comes in the form of words directly from God and is given to us by the Holy Spirit. These words spontaneously manifest in our minds. Sometimes the words are weak; at other times they are strong; it just depends on the urgency and nature of the situation. The word of knowledge is communicated directly from the Holy Spirit. Because it is spontaneous and will relate to a current situation of ministry, we can assume it is from God. We act on what the words reveal.

God reveals the past and the present

God sees all and knows all. A word of knowledge reveals the missing facts that are needed to successfully conclude a situation of ministry. We can use an analogy by picturing a very large symphony with God as the conductor. We are the gifted players with our many instruments. Each of us has a part to play, but we await His cues and timing to release our gifts and talents. When the time is right, He gives us a sign in the form of words that fit perfectly into the melody of ministry. The following scripture illustrates how Peter operated by words of knowledge given by the Holy Spirit:

> Now when Simon saw that the Spirit was bestowed through the laying on of the apostles' hands, he offered them money, saying, "Give this authority to me as well, so that everyone on whom I lay my hands may receive the Holy Spirit." But Peter said to him, "May your silver perish with you, because you thought you could obtain the gift of God with money! You have no part or portion in this matter, for your heart is not right before God. Therefore repent of this wickedness of yours, and pray the Lord that, if possible, the intention of your heart may be forgiven you. *For I see that you are in the gall of bitterness and in the bondage of iniquity.*" But Simon answered and said, "Pray to the Lord for me yourselves, so that nothing of what you have said may come upon me."
> —Acts 8:18–24, NASB

- At times we will "see" images or hear the Holy Spirit say, "That person is in the gall of bitterness and in the bondage of iniquity."
- Respond to the revelation by telling the person what the Lord just revealed and what the Lord said to do.

Apply it to the situation

The information pertains to certain facts that must be known so that we can clearly understand what needs to be done. For instance, we may be praying for someone to be healed and but not seeing anything happening. Suddenly we hear the words, "He has not forgiven his brother." We immediately and boldly apply the information, but we also use wisdom and sensitivity. We could say, "I am sensing that you have not forgiven your brother. Am I correct?" The person's response will confirm whether we heard correctly or not. Our prayer ministry will take a definite turn for the better from that point forward.

The Yelm experience

My (John's) most phenomenal time of operating by revelation was in Yelm, Washington, in the mid-1980s at a dinner meeting of the FGBMFI. While eating fried chicken, I suddenly heard the Lord's voice. He said, "Go outside, behind the building. I want to tell you what will happen tonight." The chicken was good, but hearing from God was much better. I got up from dinner and went outside, where it was pitch black. I prayed in tongues for a while and then said, "What did You want to tell me, Lord?" As I stared into the night, I heard the Lord say, "I want to do many things tonight. If you will obey Me without hesitation, I will cause My glory to be revealed. You must rely totally on Me and obey My voice in everything that happens."

God's agenda can be specific

I went back in and sat down. As I ate a little more chicken, I looked around the room at each person. When I fixed my gaze on certain ones, the voice of the Lord manifested words in my mind for that person. The words were specific: "That one needs Me. She will give her life to Me tonight. I'm going to heal that man's back when you lay hands on him. That couple is having serious marriage problems. They will be set free through a prophetic word I will give that man over there. That lady has an eating disorder and will be set free through prophetic prayer."

God does it all

It was as if I had earphones on. I heard the Lord very clearly. I had said "yes" to the Lord, but this was more than I expected. The gift of faith dropped on me just as the president of the chapter introduced Sonja and me. I walked to the podium and started giving my testimony. Right in the middle of my speaking, the Lord interrupted me and told me to start calling out the people that He had showed me. With total confidence I began, to point to those people. I told them what the Lord had earlier said about them. Without exception, all received what the Holy Spirit said they would. Couples received salvation, many people were healed, a lady was completely set free of the eating disorder, and many people were baptized in the Holy Spirit. God initiated everything and used me in the process.

Notice the fruit of the word

We can always evaluate our prayer ministry by the fruit that results. We are surprised how many times the Holy Spirit has delivered a word of knowledge. Our humanness will resist proceeding with information that seems to come out of nowhere. But as we become more experienced, we can look back and see that God was leading us more often than we thought. Sometimes we may have to wait weeks or months for reports to filter back to us on the times we acted on an unsure word of knowledge. This is more reason for us to simply obey what we think we are hearing and believe God to come to our rescue. It is better for us to step out and believe God for the impossible than to play it safe so we can avoid being embarrassed.

Jesus saw their faith

The following account of healing shows how Jesus "saw" a man's faith by revelation and then healed him. Jesus also "perceived in His spirit" what the scribes were thinking.

> Immediately many gathered together, so that there was no longer room to receive them, not even near the door. And He preached the word to them. Then they came to Him, bringing a paralytic who was carried by four men. And when they could not come near Him because of the crowd, they uncovered the roof where He was. So when they had broken through, they let down the bed on which the paralytic was lying. When Jesus saw their faith, He said to the paralytic, "Son, your sins are forgiven you." And some of the scribes were sitting there and reasoning in their hearts, "Why does this Man speak blasphemies like this? Who can forgive sins but God alone?" But immediately, when Jesus perceived in His spirit that they reasoned thus within themselves, He said to them, "Why do you reason about these things in your hearts? Which is easier, to say to the paralytic, 'Your sins are forgiven you,' or to say, 'Arise, take up your bed and walk'?
>
> But that you may know that the Son of Man has power on earth to forgive sins"—He said to the paralytic, "I say to you,

arise, take up your bed, and go to your house." Immediately he arose, took up the bed, and went out in the presence of them all, so that all were amazed and glorified God, saying, "We never saw anything like this!"

—Mark 2:2–12, nkjv

- Jesus gave us an example of how to rely on the Holy Spirit. Jesus responded to the revelation of faith in the paralytic and his friends. We can "see" faith in someone through the gift of the word of knowledge.
- Jesus "saw" the men's faith and healed the paralytic by speaking words of authority: "Rise, take up your bed, and go home!"
- The Holy Spirit also revealed the negative perceptions of the religious leaders. Jesus showed us how to rely on the Holy Spirit to reveal what was going on and how to deal with it.
- The Pharisees' mind-set was that both forgiveness and healing were impossible. The Holy Spirit led Jesus to perform both to make His point: God can both forgive sin and heal the sick.

Do it like Jesus did

When you preach and teach like Jesus did, the power of God will manifest, and power will be available for healing and deliverance. When faithless, critical people are there, just ignore them the same way Jesus did in the Mark passage. The power of God will still be present to effect miracles. Act within the anointing, and flow with what the Holy Spirit indicates. When you see people's faith, pray in agreement with them. Jesus came into agreement with what the men were expecting to happen—healing! So minister to those demonstrating faith, and bypass those who are not operating in faith. God desires to accomplish His works through us to cause astonishment and awe in people so that they will open their eyes to receive Christ as Lord and Healer. The Holy Spirit points directly to Jesus Christ. We must be careful to glorify God at the signs and wonders He causes to happen.

Doing the supernatural stuff

The late John Wimber coined the phrase, "Doing the Stuff," in 1985 in his book, *Power Evangelism*. As a new Christian he asked a pastor after a service, "When do you do the stuff?" He was referring to healing and miracles that he had just found in the Bible. He never got a satisfactory answer.

Sonja and I recently taught a one-day seminar on doing the supernatural stuff at a Foursquare pastors' conference in central California. One of the pastors wanted to attend but could not, so he invited us to Carson City, Nevada, to present the same seminar at his church. The seminar was composed of four areas that seem to be overlooked in many churches: One, how to lead other believers into the Holy Spirit baptism; two, how to heal the sick; three, how to minister by revelation knowledge; four, how to set people free from demon bondage. In the morning sessions, 15 leaders received the Holy Spirit baptism, and many people were healed of all kinds of problems. The afternoon session became even more exciting as the Holy Spirit began to cause words of knowledge and wisdom to flow freely among the people.

We are not special

During the teaching on how to release revelation gifts, the Lord began giving both Sonja and me words of knowledge and wisdom about specific healings He wanted to do. Each time, Sonja and I would say, "Hey, we are not special. All of you leaders can do this. It just takes a lot of nerve to be willing to be wrong a few times as you learn how to move with the Holy Spirit." We would then put them into groups of 10 so they could practice releasing words of knowledge and wisdom for each other.

God began to do some awesome things. John announced that a lady needed a healing on her lower shin. The Holy Spirit was specific as to which leg and where the sore was located. A lady close to the front boldly stood up and said, "That's me! I've had a terrible staph infection on this shin." She then pointed to her right shin and began to pull up her pant leg. The black sore was completely gone! We took a picture of her for our newsletter, showing that the skin was normal and scar-free.

We try to get the audience involved whenever the Holy Spirit starts revealing things. One way we do this is to call out what the Holy Spirit is indicating He wants done. If it is some kind of healing, we have people with that particular problem stand at the front. Then we ask for those who have never prayed for the sick to face the ones needing healing. Because the Lord always heals what He reveals, it amazes both those who pray and those who receive. This is one of the best ways to demonstrate that God is in charge, not the one ministering.

Thirty years of pain

One such case involved an older gentleman dressed in western clothes. The Lord revealed that there were people with pain, starting in their backs and going down their legs. About five people, including the older gentleman, responded. I (John) then called forward five believers who had never experienced divine healing through their hands. Sonja matched each person needing prayer with a person who would pray. Sonja led them in the prayer of faith, and we watched as God healed them. The pain left instantly in all but the gentleman in western attire. I had everyone else sit down, and then I asked how long the pain had been in his back and legs. He said, "Thirty years!" He had been prayed for so many times that he had lost count, but he estimated that he had been prayed for 100 times. His response indicated that he did not have much faith.

Suddenly the Holy Spirit said to me, "Infirmity. It is a spirit of infirmity." Without hesitation I said, "The Lord has just revealed that we are dealing with a spirit of infirmity. I am going to loose you and you will be healed." We laid hands on his back, and I commanded the spirit of infirmity to leave in Jesus' name. I said, "Tell me when all the pain is gone." He said, "It's going!" I said, "Amen. And it will continue until it's all gone." Over the next half-hour, the man kept testing his back and legs and announcing the percentage of pain that was leaving. He finally said, "It's 99 percent gone. I think what's left is just stiffness from never being able to bend over." With that, we all gave the Lord a long and loud praise of thanksgiving for what He accomplished in Carson City.

What is revealed is healed

Christians in the West like to focus on all the sick and hurting people that never seem to receive their healing. The revelation gifts, especially the word of knowledge, change all this. When the revelation gifts are in operation, the healing statistics go from 50 to 100 percent. When a true word of knowledge is involved in ministry to the sick, the person always receives healing. It happens immediately or within a few hours or days. When God begins to reveal, He heals. We can trust the Holy Spirit to do what He says. When He comes upon us and reveals a word of knowledge concerning a person's bodily condition, healing is imminent. God is directly involved. We simply obey and get out of the way. Healing will manifest.

Jesus operated perfectly

Jesus is the author and finisher of our faith. He authored the word of knowledge and showed us the perfect way to operate in it. Jesus said we could do what He did. How? We do only what we see the Father doing. This will come in the form of words or images in the word of wisdom and knowledge just as Jesus received them:

> Jesus gave them this answer: "I tell you the truth, the Son can do nothing by himself; he can do only what he sees his Father doing, because whatever the Father does the Son also does. For the Father loves the Son and shows him all he does. Yes, to your amazement he will show him even greater things than these."
> —JOHN 5:19–20

We should pray, "Lord, I want to do only what I see the Father doing by the Holy Spirit. Help me to do that." Then we can pray, "Lord, show me even greater things than these. I want to do what Jesus did!"

The Lord knows the source of the sickness

When we pray for the sick, we often are unsure what is causing the sickness or pain. Sometimes the person does not know either. It could be a virus, a chemical imbalance, heredity, or even a spirit. The Lord always knows, so we should wait to hear from Him. When we do, the healing will always manifest. Below is the same story from the combined perspective of both Matthew and Mark. Notice that Jesus ignored the people's request to have Him lay His hands on the deaf-mute. Instead, He followed the instructions from the Father:

Again, departing from the region of Tyre and Sidon, He came through the midst of the region of Decapolis to the Sea of Galilee. Then they brought to Him one who was deaf and had an impediment in his speech, and they begged Him to put His hand on him.

And He took him aside from the multitude, and put His fingers in his ears, and He spat and touched his tongue. Then, looking up to heaven, He sighed, and said to him, "Ephphatha," that is, "Be opened." Immediately his ears were opened, and the impediment of his tongue was loosed, and he spoke plainly.

Then He commanded them that they should tell no one; but the more He commanded them, the more widely they proclaimed it. And they were astonished beyond measure, saying, "He has done all things well. He makes both the deaf to hear and the mute to speak."

—MARK 7:31–37, NKJV

...and went up on the mountain and sat down there. Then great multitudes came to Him, having with them the lame, blind, mute, maimed, and many others; and they laid them down at Jesus' feet, and He healed them. So the multitude marveled when they saw the mute speaking, the maimed made whole, the lame walking, and the blind seeing; and they glorified the God of Israel.

—MATTHEW 15:29–31, NKJV

- When the Holy Spirit is leading us, we only do what He indicates.
- Jesus followed what the Father indicated by putting His fingers in the person's ears, spitting, and touching his tongue. At the same time, He said to him, "Be opened!"
- Note: Jesus returned to Decapolis, a region where previously people did not want Him. The people were no longer afraid—they wanted His ministry of healing. This was because the demoniac had been delivered of spirits and had spread the gospel that Jesus was the Christ (Mark 5:18-20).

MINISTRY EXAMPLES

The Chiang Mai healing crusade

I (John) was the main speaker at a two-night healing crusade in Chiang Mai, Thailand in early 2002. Our associate ministers Greg and Karen Fry also shared and ministered at this crusade. The first evening God healed 25-30 people of pain, asthma, infections, poor eyesight, and high fevers. So many miracles were happening, and we quickly prayed for everyone who came forward. In three separate instances, the Holy Spirit spoke to me that spirits were causing people to experience severe headaches or chronic pain in their bodies. As soon as I looked these people in the eyes, the Holy Spirit would firmly say, "Spirits of infirmity are causing it." When I commanded the spirits to leave, the people were instantly healed of their sickness.

Deaf men instantly healed

The second evening, I waited on the Holy Spirit to identify and initiate the kind of healing that was to be done. Twenty-five people were healed in about an hour as the Holy Spirit called out various pains and illnesses. Again, spirits caused some of the people's problems. The Holy Spirit graciously healed those people after the spirits were identified and commanded to loose them. The highlight of the evening was two men who were 85 to 90 percent deaf in both ears. The first man came up, took out his hearing aids, and said he was ready to be healed. Greg and I began to pray for him with no success. We stopped and wondered what we needed to do. The Holy Spirit quietly said to me, "It's a spirit of deafness." I smiled at the man, and looking intently into his eyes, I said, "You foul spirit of deafness, be gone!" Total hearing was instantly restored to the man.

Spit on your fingers

The other deaf man was closely watching the first deaf man receive his hearing. His faith was high and he was ready. I had the interpreter yell into his ear, "How long have you been deaf?" He said, "Twenty years." I looked at Greg and Karen, and we agreed that this was easy for God.

The Holy Spirit then firmly spoke to me and said, "Spit on your fingers, put them into the man's ears, and say, 'Be opened!'" Without hesitation I obeyed. I spit on both of my index fingers, put my fingers in the man's ears, and loudly said, "Be opened, in the name of Jesus!" It took the man about a minute to realize he was hearing perfectly without his hearing aids. He, too, was instantly healed by the power of God. I realized that this was what Jesus did in Matthew 15:29–31 and Mark 7:31–37. Greg, Karen, and I went back to our hotel praising God for the incredible move of the Holy Spirit. We later discovered that many of the people who were healed are now part of the Foursquare Church and have made Jesus Christ their Savior. We had learned how to hear from the Father and obey what He wanted us to do so that He could bless many of His people.

The Holy Spirit speaks the words He hears

The word of knowledge is the Father's speaking to us through the Holy Spirit. We are hearing the words the Holy Spirit is hearing from the Father. We are hearing words and seeing things that the Father wants us to hear and see.

> But when he, the Spirit of truth, comes, he will guide you into all truth. He will not speak on his own; he will speak only what he hears, and he will tell you what is yet to come. He will bring glory to me by taking from what is mine and making it known to you.
>
> —JOHN 16:13–14

- Jesus told us how He interacted with the Father through the Holy Spirit. He revealed how to do what He did.
- He waited to hear words from the Father that were relayed to Him by the Holy Spirit.
- He heard words that revealed what was yet to transpire.
- He heard the Father's perfect will in advance!
- We can expect the same when we serve God with all of our heart, mind, and soul. We can do what Jesus did!

Miracles in south Seattle

A few years ago, Sonja and I were invited to teach on how to heal the sick at a large Foursquare church south of Seattle, Washington. We always pray, study, and seek the Lord before attempting to teach on the miraculous. We placed our agenda before the Lord and reminded Him and ourselves that He can do anything He wants in every meeting. We felt confident and ready as we drove up, parked, and proceeded to the pre-service prayer gathering with the leaders in charge. During the prayer time I noticed the chairperson of the event was really sick. She almost did not come because of unusual pain in her body and a severe headache. The others turned to her and suggested that we pray for her so that she could enjoy the meeting. We all agreed and began to pray. As I approached her, the Holy Spirit said, "Not now, John. I will heal her later." Wondering what He meant, I backed off and prayed in the Spirit. No one seemed to notice that I was the only one not laying my hands on her.

The Holy Spirit took charge

The meeting started with great worship. I noticed there was standing room only with a lot of the youth sitting on the floor. As usual, Sonja and I continued to sing and pray in tongues up until time to teach. There was a strong anointing as we taught. Then the Holy Spirit began to take charge. I heard Him say, "Call the chairperson to the stage." I obeyed. Then He said, "Ask who would like to be used in healing and invite the first one to raise their hand to come and pray for her." I obeyed. A young lady down front and to the right quickly raised her hand. I had her lay her hands on the chairperson and repeat a prayer after me. She did exactly what I told her. Then I told her to ask the woman for whom she had prayed what was happening. The new recruit said, "What's happening?" The chairperson said, "Oh my! Oh my! It's gone! The pain's gone and my headache is gone, too. I'm healed! God just healed me!" The crowd broke into spontaneous praise and applause. Faith rocketed throughout the auditorium. I asked the recruit, "Who did that?" Over the microphone she quickly said, "Jesus!" We found out later that she had been a Mormon who had just been saved the Sunday before. Many of the church folks knew that and were praising God and rejoicing that a new Christian had been used to heal the sick. It gave great hope to everyone that God is not a respecter of persons when it comes to praying and believing for miracles.

Forbid the pain to remain

I heard the Holy Spirit say, "Have them pray for each other and I will heal them." We had planned to individually pray for those needing healing, but the Holy Spirit changed the agenda. I instructed anyone who had noticeable pain to stand. About 75 people stood. I told those around them to lay hands on those who were in pain and pray this prayer: "In the name of Jesus, pain I command you to leave this body. I forbid this pain to remain. I call it done in the name of Jesus Christ! Amen." I then asked for everyone whose pain was gone to sit down. Over three-quarters of them sat down. The crowd again erupted in applause. I asked the people still standing to allow those around them to again pray like before. We did this two more times. After this, three remained standing. I instructed those three to allow the others to minister to them until they were healed. They, too, went home feeling better than when they came.

EXAMPLES OF WORDS OF KNOWLEDGE

Everybody gets to participate

These kinds of meetings are faith builders to many Christians who never get a chance to practice what the teachers are teaching. The Holy Spirit has led Sonja and me to get as many in the audience as possible to personally experience the healing power of God. By encouraging them to minister and pray for those needing healing in an atmosphere where the Holy Spirit is directing the meeting, multiple miracles are sure to manifest. Instead of the evangelist being the focus of power, the people look more to Jesus Christ as the source of power and miracles. When Sonja and I step aside and allow the Holy Spirit to freely work through us, it is obvious to everyone that Jesus wants to use anybody and everybody to get the job done. This way everyone gets blessed and God gets all the glory. That is the way it should be.

Peter relayed a word of knowledge

Peter received a word of knowledge from the Holy Spirit and he spoke to Ananias and Sapphira. It was confirmed immediately as coming from God when both died in front of him:

Now a man named Ananias, together with his wife Sapphira, also sold a piece of property. With his wife's full knowledge he kept back part of the money for himself, but brought the rest and put it at the apostles' feet. Then Peter said, "Ananias, how is it that Satan has so filled your heart that you have lied to the Holy Spirit and have kept for yourself some of the money you received for the land? Didn't it belong to you before it was sold? And after it was sold, wasn't the money at your disposal? What made you think of doing such a thing? You have not lied to men but to God."

—Acts 5:1–4

Whoever speaks a word against the Son of Man, it shall be forgiven him; but whoever speaks against the Holy Spirit, it shall not be forgiven him, either in this age or in the age to come.

—Matthew 12:32, nasb

- Jesus mentored Peter. Peter heard Jesus say that whoever speaks against the Holy Spirit will not be forgiven.
- Peter also had learned from Jesus to act on whatever the Holy Spirit revealed.
- The judgment of God was pronounced against a man and his wife who lied about giving everything to the work of the Lord when they, in fact, held back money for themselves.
- The presence of the Holy Spirit was so strong that death came to both Ananias and Sapphira.
- We must be careful at all times not to lie to the Holy Spirit.

Ananias relayed a word of knowledge

Paul was rescued from blindness by a Damascus disciple named Ananias. The Holy Spirit told Ananias facts he did not know about Paul. Then the Spirit told him what to do with the word of knowledge—to speak the word to Paul:

In Damascus there was a disciple named Ananias. The Lord called to him in a vision, "Ananias!" "Yes, Lord," he answered.

The Lord told him, "Go to the house of Judas on Straight Street and ask for a man from Tarsus named Saul, for he is praying. In a vision he has seen a man named Ananias come and place his hands on him to restore his sight."

—ACTS 9:10–12

> When the Holy Spirit calls us by name and gives strong instructions for us to do something, we must obey.

Paul healed the sick by a word of knowledge

Paul received a revelation about a crippled man having enough faith to stand up and be healed. Paul obeyed what he was hearing from the Holy Spirit, and a miracle healing manifested.

In Lystra there sat a man crippled in his feet, who was lame from birth and had never walked. He listened to Paul as he was speaking. Paul looked directly at him, saw that he had faith to be healed and called out, "Stand up on your feet!" At that, the man jumped up and began to walk.

—ACTS 14:8–10

> - The word of knowledge given to Paul resulted in the healing of a man lame from birth.
> - The only way we can "see" a person having the faith to be healed is through a word of knowledge.

Miracles in Korea

Sonja and I were invited to conduct a teacher intensive near Seoul, Korea. Sixty pastors and leaders attended the weeklong training. During one of the healing workshops, a woman in leadership came forward complaining of chronic sickness and depression that had plagued her for years. The moment she looked at me (John) a word of knowledge manifested in my mind. I heard the Holy Spirit say, "She has a spirit of infirmity. Command it to go and she will be healed."

I obeyed. I spoke to the spirit and said, "Spirit of infirmity, you are bound. I command you to loose this woman in the name of Jesus Christ!"

Before I could say anything else, she fell to the floor, writhing and rolling from side to side as she coughed repeatedly. I left her there and went on praying for others. Eventually, I returned to where the woman was lying still, seemingly free of whatever had her bound. The next day, she returned with a big grin on her face and announced that she was totally healed of her sickness and was totally free of the depression. She had slept the whole night through for the first time in years without using the usual drugs.

She called her sick sister

The woman leader was so elated for what Jesus had done that she called her Buddhist sister who was to have back surgery the next day. Her sister had been in excruciating pain for months and was desperate for relief. At the first break in the meeting, the woman leader led us to where her sister was lying on a pew, unable to sit up without terrible pain. As I set my gaze on her, the Holy Spirit said, "Tell her I love her so much that I will heal her back. All she needs to do is acknowledge that the Lord Jesus Christ is her Healer." This was relayed to her through our interpreter. She nodded her head "yes."

At that moment I commanded her back to be healed in Jesus' name. I then told her to stand up and that the pain would be gone. She slowly sat up, then stood up; she twisted back and forth, expecting pain. She then looked at us with a smile and boldly exclaimed, "There is no more pain. I've been healed by God!" A woman pastor promptly led the sister into a prayer, asking Jesus to become her Lord and Savior. I had obeyed a word of wisdom and knowledge, and a woman had been healed and saved by the grace and power of God.

Contend for the best

As ministers, we must pursue God until we are operating competently in words of wisdom and knowledge. They can be the difference between victory and defeat. These gifts are available to all serious believers, and we should contend in prayer, meditation in the Word, and even fasting until we begin to hear from God. Consecration brings revelation. When we get serious about being able to minister by the leading of the Spirit of God, powerful ministry begins. Operating in words of knowledge and wisdom will produce the kind of results Jesus experienced.

Remember that Jesus and His Word have already declared that we can heal the sick. We only have to wait for the Holy Spirit to indicate to whom and when. Learning to work in harmony with the Holy Spirit and His gifts is the most rewarding service to our fellow man we can ever experience. There is none better. It places us in the passenger seat as the Holy Spirit drives the car. We are along for an exciting ride that will take us on a journey of matchless ministry.

The next chapter is the final step in learning how to cooperate with the Holy Spirit in setting people free of demon bondages. Jesus did not prioritize physical healing over spiritual healing. He treated both with equal compassion and concern. We will learn to do the same.

LET'S PRACTICE

James 1:22 says to do what we have heard (read).

Consider doing what is recommended in this chapter by referring to the "Let's Practice" in Appendix B, page 261.

Do the Ministry Skill Assignment titled, "Healing the Sick by Revelation."

DEALING WITH DEMONS

Jesus intended for His followers to learn how to deal with demons and set people free of the bondages demons cause. This chapter is divided into two parts: Demons in Foreign Lands and Setting the Captives Free in America.

DEMONS IN FOREIGN LANDS

A s I (JOHN) entered the door of the meeting place, two ushers were carrying a demon-possessed woman to the back of the auditorium. They were holding the young woman tightly by both arms as she was screaming, spitting, and twisting her body uncontrollably. The worship service had started, and apparently the demons did not like people worshiping the Lord Jesus Christ.

It happened in Africa

We were in Abidjan, Ivory Coast, West Africa, and Sonja and I had been asked to preach in different churches. We had just finished five days of teaching over 100 French-speaking pastors on effective discipleship principles from our *Ambassador Series*. As I entered my assigned meeting place, I saw the ushers dealing with a demonized lady. I then remarked, "Well, Lord, this ought to be interesting." The Lord had already told me to preach on healing. I wondered what else He had in mind.

I presented the gospel to this newly planted church of more than 100 people, emphasizing that Jesus wanted to heal people of all sorts of diseases and pain. The Holy Spirit began revealing words and pictures to me of what He wanted to do. Working through an interpreter, I repeated what the Lord revealed and began calling people to the front for prayer. First to come was a woman with severe pain in her right elbow. As I obeyed, prayed, and commanded the pain and stiffness to leave, she was healed. The Holy Spirit singled out eight people with chronic lower back pain. Again, all were healed within minutes. As three more women were being healed of foot pain, the demonized woman in the back of the church began screaming at the top of her lungs. I was really distracted, but the congregation seemed unconcerned. I tried to remain cool and give the impression that I had everything under control. As I glanced back at the woman, I suddenly felt compassion for her.

The blood of Jesus is the key

I put the healing service on hold and began to teach. I said that God loves demonized people so much that He sent His Son to set them free. I also preached that all believers have been authorized and empowered to cast out demons. I taught that the blood of Jesus was the source of the power that sets people free of spiritual bondages. The moment I mentioned the blood of Jesus, the demonized lady went absolutely crazy. It took three people to restrain her.

I asked the pastor if it would be all right for the woman to be brought to the front. He signaled the ushers, who brought her forward and tried to set her in a chair. She stiffened and refused to sit normally. She would not look at me, and she continued to scream, spit, and hiss at everyone. In English, I said, "Look at me." When she did, I saw the demon's cold stare glaring at me through hollow eyes. I said, "Be quiet and come out of her!" Immediately, the woman stopped screaming and became completely docile. I did not receive any further instructions from the Holy Spirit so I had the ushers take her back to her seat. I have learned to stop when the Holy Spirit is silent. The woman stopped screaming, and we had no more distractions from her.

She left

The service concluded with more worship. I then began to pray for a long line of those who were in pain or were sick. God began healing people just as He normally does. The demonized woman apparently left quietly as I was praying for the sick. I learned later from an elder that the woman was a member of the church. She had started having strange outbursts in church about a month prior and had become progressively more out of control. He was not sure what had occurred, but suspected that the woman had become involved in some kind of ritualistic sexual activity.

I left with a different attitude about demonized people. It was as if I had been allowed to experience what Jesus did so many times as illustrated in the Gospels. He viewed the demon-possessed in the same category as the brokenhearted, sick, or those in pain. They all needed to be free and well. In Luke 4, Jesus Christ's mission is stated clearly. He wants His followers to continue the same mission.

> The Spirit of the Lord is upon Me, Because He has anointed Me To preach the gospel to the poor; He has sent Me to heal the brokenhearted, To proclaim liberty to the captives And recovery of sight to the blind, To set at liberty those who are oppressed; To proclaim the acceptable year of the Lord.
>
> —LUKE 4:18–19, NKJV

- We are to fulfill the Great Commission by doing the same things Jesus did. We are to preach, heal, set the oppressed free, and give Jesus Christ all the credit.
- We are to set at liberty those who are oppressed of the devil by removing the demons that are oppressing them.

Let's examine the same narratives from the Gospels

Jesus' methods of setting people free of spiritual bondages are clearly observed in the Gospels. In this chapter, we have compiled the same gospel stories into a single composite rendition of the event. Where Matthew, Mark, and Luke tell the same story, we will show it as a single scripture with inserts of chapter and verse where the other Gospel writers might differ slightly or expand the story. Then we will follow up with suggestions for how we might do the same as Jesus did.

Jesus sets the pattern

The following scriptures depict an early event in the ministry of Jesus Christ that reveals the beginning of a series of prayer and ministry patterns. We will closely observe how Jesus set people free from spiritual bondage and then offer suggestions as to how we might employ the same patterns in ministering to people today.

> When evening had come, they brought to Him many who were demon-possessed. And He cast out the spirits with a word, and healed all who were sick, that it might be fulfilled which was

spoken by Isaiah the prophet, saying: "He Himself took our infirmities And bore our sicknesses."

—MATTHEW 8:16–17, NKJV

He laid His hands on every one of them…And demons also came out of many, crying out and saying, "You are the Christ, the Son of God!" And He, rebuking them, did not allow them to speak, for they knew that He was the Christ.

—LUKE 4:40–41, NKJV

These Scriptures reveal the approaches and methods Jesus used in dealing with the demonized. Here are some observations for us to consider:

- The sick or demonized were brought to Jesus. Jesus did not have to go look for that kind of ministry. People knew they would be healed or delivered. Today, people are looking for someone who knows how to set people free.
- When faith is present, we are to minister in the authority granted to us in the name of Jesus Christ.
- Demons often acknowledge the presence of the Holy Spirit upon us before others recognize it. Spirits may respond by crying out and challenging those who operate in spiritual authority.
- Speaking words of authority to spirits that inhabit men and women will cause them to leave. The words that Jesus firmly spoke were simple and to the point. In later verses He said things such as, "Come out of him," or, "Be gone."
- Jesus did not permit demons to speak. Likewise, we should rebuke the spirits and command them not to speak.
- Luke indicated that laying on of hands may be employed when healing the sick or setting people free from spiritual bondages.

Witch doctor set free

In chapter 3 we gave an account of a blind woman from the Lahu tribe of northern Thailand who was healed. News of this miracle traveled quickly through the jungle. Two days later there was quite a stir in the village when a witch doctor came looking for us. The tribal people were amazed when they learned that he wanted help from the God who had healed the blind woman.

Our team members, Steve Darrow from the U.S., and an Australian missionary, began to interview the witch doctor through interpreters. His arm was paralyzed and contorted, and his heart was racing with uncontrollable palpitations. He told them he had heard of the Christian God when he was a youth, but he had forsaken following Him and sought the power of witchcraft instead. He now knew the demons had turned on him and were going to kill him. How marvelous is our God to have us in Thailand at that very time so this man might hear of God's miracle-working power. Our Father's mercy, grace, and compassion are limitless!

Steve and the missionary first took authority over the demons and commanded them to leave the man, which they did. It was amazing to see his arm unfold as the paralysis left his body. Then, instinctively, he raised both arms above his head in surrender and praise to God.

The villagers were utterly amazed

Next, Steve and the missionary led the witch doctor into repenting of his sin and renouncing the witchcraft he had practiced for so many years. He then asked the Lord Jesus Christ to come into his life and become his Savior and Lord. Next, he received the Holy Spirit baptism and began to speak in unknown languages. The villagers were utterly amazed as they watched.

In tribal societies, supernatural activity is a part of their daily lives before people convert to Christianity. However, it is totally fear- and power-based. People are always trying to appease the evil spirits so they will not harm them, their loved ones, or the other villagers. The witch doctors exercise demonic control over these people and keep them in abject fear. When they see the one and only true Creator, the Christian God, taking authority over the witch doctor and evil spirits, they rejoice. Our God not only sets them free but also gives them love, joy, and peace. No wonder Jesus called His message the Good News!

FAITH, AUTHORITY, AND
DISCERNING OF SPIRITS

The Holy Spirit graciously imparts the ability to discern spiritual activity. This ability comes in the form of one of the supernatural gifts of the Holy Spirit called the discerning of spirits, which is described in 1 Corinthians 12:10:

> But the manifestation of the Spirit is given to each one for the profit of all: for to one is given the word of wisdom through the Spirit, to another the word of knowledge through the same Spirit, to another *faith* by the same Spirit, to another gifts of healings by the same Spirit, to another the working of miracles, to another prophecy, to another *discerning of spirits*, to another different kinds of tongues, to another the interpretation of tongues. But one and the same Spirit works all these things, distributing to each one individually as He wills.
> —1 CORINTHIANS 12:7–11, NKJV, EMPHASIS ADDED

- The gifts of discerning of spirits, supernatural faith, and the words of knowledge and wisdom are the tools needed to deal with demons.
- To activate these gifts, we simply ask the Holy Spirit to cause them to manifest when we confront suspicious spiritual activity.

Shooting in the dark

We need the gift of discerning of spirits and/or the gifts of the word of wisdom and knowledge to deal with demons. We define the gift of discerning of spirits as the supernatural perception to distinguish the source of spiritual activity. This gift clearly reveals whether the activity is divine, human, or demonic. The supernatural gifts of the word of knowledge and wisdom will also reveal the same information. Trying to identify and cast out demons without these gifts is like conducting target practice in total darkness. You know the target is out there somewhere, so you keep firing and hoping that you will hit something. These gifts are the spotlight that shows you how to hit the bull's-eye.

Supernatural faith comes with the revelation

The supernatural gift of faith also comes into play when we encounter demons. Upon discerning the presence of an unclean spirit, God imparts supernatural faith that causes us to become fearless in the face of any kind of demonic activity. This kind of faith is imparted to us so we can take charge of the situation and aggressively command the spirits to depart. If we try to proceed in our own faith and understanding, fear may be present. Demons know when we are fearful, and they will take advantage of our fear. To be successful, we need to operate by instructions from the Holy Spirit and in the supernatural faith God gives us.

Jesus gave believers authority to cast out demons

Let us begin our path of becoming equipped to deal with demons. First, we will examine Jesus' teaching regarding the authority He gave every believer to cast out demons. We will also examine why this authority was given in the first place. No one can read the New Testament without seeing that Jesus gave His disciples the clear and indisputable authority to heal the sick and cast out demons.

When we first read the scriptures printed below, we may assume that they applied only to the twelve disciples following Jesus at the time. Our early instruction probably reinforced this assumption. We thought, "He couldn't mean me. Besides, demons are a thing of the past. This surely doesn't apply to us today. Jesus must be describing a spiritual problem unique to simple-minded people of those times."

Not so. When we connect John 14:11–14 with the scriptures below, we clearly see that all believers in Christ have been given the power and authority not only to heal the sick but also to command spirits to depart.

> And when He had called His twelve disciples to Him, He gave them power over unclean spirits, to cast them out, and to heal all kinds of sickness and all kinds of disease.
> —MATTHEW 10:1, NKJV

> He…gave them power and authority over all demons.
> —LUKE 9:1, NKJV

> …and that He might send them out to preach, and to have power to heal sicknesses and to cast out demons.
> —MARK 3:14–15, NKJV

And Jesus came and spoke to them, saying, "All authority has
been given to Me in heaven and on earth. Go therefore and make
disciples of all the nations…teaching them to observe all things
that I have commanded you."

—MATTHEW 28:18–20, NKJV

- Jesus gave His followers power and authority to cast out demonic spirits and to heal all kinds of sickness and disease. This was taught to the first generation of disciples.
- He commanded Christian leaders to teach each successive generation of disciples to observe all things that Jesus told them to do (including casting out demons).
- Jesus gave all believers the power and authority to overcome "all" demons; no categories of demonic spirits are excluded.
- Upon believing this truth and accepting the challenge to go, we become the "sent ones."
- Jesus commissioned His followers to go into the entire world. As we go, we are to make disciples, teach, baptize, heal the sick, and cast out demons.
- There is only one conclusion: We are to obey and go do these things.

What if you do not know how?

That is why we wrote this book. There seems to be a universal lack
of knowledge and understanding regarding how to deal with demons.
This is especially true in the West. Since the turn of the twenty-first
century there has been a plethora of endorsements pertaining to
seeking a "higher spiritual awareness."

Hundreds of books, movies, and television shows unashamedly
promote the existence of extraterrestrials, horrific manifestations of
apparitions rising from the dead, and spirit guides coming to lead us
into a higher consciousness, connecting us to the realm of the neth-
erworld. They all lead to the same place: the outstretched arms of the
one whose only goal is to kill, steal, and destroy lives. Empowered
Christians are the only hope for a world totally and completely

mesmerized with doing whatever feels good and not being accountable to anyone, especially the Lord Jesus Christ. The Bible warns us about this kind of disobedience. This kind of lifestyle eventually leads to spiritual bondage as described in the following scripture:

> Now the works of the flesh are evident, which are: adultery, fornication, uncleanness, lewdness, idolatry, sorcery, hatred, contentions, jealousies, outbursts of wrath, selfish ambitions, dissensions, heresies, envy, murders, drunkenness, revelries, and the like; of which I tell you beforehand, just as I also told you in time past, that those who practice such things will not inherit the kingdom of God.
> —GALATIANS 5:19–21, NKJV

- Any of the above actions, if practiced long enough, may attract demonic spirits. When we accept Christ and truly repent of these things, we are set free and will inherit the kingdom of God.
- If we ever return and practice any of these things, after accepting Christ, we could attract a demonic spirit and fall into spiritual bondage.
- After people come to know the Lord personally and then betray Him, or defy Him by engaging in open disobedience, the enemy has the right to enter them.
- Judas is a good example. As long as Judas was following Jesus, he was protected from the evil one. The moment he openly betrayed Jesus, Satan "entered" him (Luke 22:3) and caused him to commit suicide.

SOME PEOPLE NEED TO BE LOOSED!

When a demonic spirit is given an opening to establish a stronghold in a person's life, the entrance is achieved through deception. It can happen through open disobedience to God's commands and/or choosing to live in the way that is described in Galatians chapter 5. When this happens, a person is susceptible to demonization. If not addressed, the spirit can eventually cause peculiar physical problems. One such problem is identified in the Bible as a "spirit of infirmity." The person may need to be loosed from the spirit that is causing the physical abnormality. Neither the medication nor professional counseling offered by the medical community will heal the person if the condition is caused by a spirit. Only aggressive prayer in the name of Jesus Christ will bring healing. Jesus addresses this particular spirit in John 5:5 and in the scripture below:

> And behold, there was a woman who had a spirit of infirmity eighteen years, and was bent over and could in no way raise herself up. But when Jesus saw her, He called her to Him and said to her, "*Woman, you are loosed from your infirmity.*" And He laid His hands on her, and immediately she was made straight, and glorified God. But the ruler of the synagogue answered with indignation, because Jesus had healed on the Sabbath; and he said to the crowd, "There are six days on which men ought to work; therefore come and be healed on them, and not on the Sabbath day."
>
> The Lord then answered him and said, "Hypocrite! Does not each one of you on the Sabbath loose his ox or donkey from the stall, and lead it away to water it? So ought not this woman, being a daughter of Abraham, whom Satan has bound—think of it—for eighteen years, be loosed from this bond on the Sabbath?" And when He said these things, all His adversaries were put to shame; and all the multitude rejoiced for all the glorious things that were done by Him.
>
> —LUKE 13:11–17, NKJV

- Special note: Spirits can cause various kinds of sickness, disease, pain, or deformities. In this case Satan had caused a severe curvature of the spine. The Bible identifies spirits as having the ability to "bind" people in their physical bodies.
- Not all sickness and disease is caused by spirits. We must rely on the Holy Spirit's revelation gifts to discern between a medical problem and a condition caused by a spirit.

- Jesus saw the woman in the crowd and selected her over everyone else who might have been sick. Remember, Jesus only did what was revealed by the Father.
- Jesus called her to Him, wanting close contact so He could lay hands on her.
- Jesus spoke words of faith and deliverance directly to the woman, saying, "Woman you are (loosed) freed from your sickness."
- She was made erect immediately and began glorifying God.
- Christians have been given the authority to loose people from the spirits that cause physical deformities.
- When we encounter someone who has a similar physical problem, we should pray in the Spirit and remain very sensitive for specific direction from the Holy Spirit.
- When you have a sure word of direction from the Holy Spirit, act immediately. We always have the authority to do it. But, the power is released when we obey the Holy Spirit's instructions.
- We must learn to operate in the Father's timing, direction, and will before we proceed. We will operate in total victory when we immediately respond to what the Holy Spirit wants us to do.
- When the Holy Spirit says, "Release the person from the bondage. It is caused by a spirit of infirmity," then DO IT, just as Jesus did.
- Lay your hands upon them just as Jesus did.
- Speak words of deliverance over them just as Jesus did. You can say the same words Jesus used, "Be loosed from your sickness."
- If you act on instructions from the Holy Spirit, you will witness a miracle.

Plundering the strong man's house

The "strong man" is a reference to a demonic spirit. Spirits appear to be strong if we are ignorant of the authority and power given by Jesus Christ. Jesus has made His followers far superior and much stronger than any demonic spirit. The religious leaders in Jesus' time were totally ignorant of the authority and power He had over demons. They were oblivious to the fact that He was delegating the same authority and power to all of His disciples. This is still true today. Some religious leaders are unknowingly attributing the episodes of the Holy Spirit's successful deliverances to a modern-day version of Beelzebub, which is still the prince of demons (see the following scriptures). We must be very careful to give all the credit to God for loosing people from demon bondage.

> And He was casting out a demon, and it was mute. So it was, when the demon had gone out, that *the mute spoke*; and the multitudes marveled. But some of them said, "He casts out demons by *Beelzebub*, the ruler of the demons." Others, testing Him, sought from Him a sign from heaven. But He, *knowing their thoughts*, said to them: "Every kingdom divided against itself is brought to desolation, and a house divided against a house falls. If Satan also is divided against himself, how will his kingdom stand? Because you say I cast out demons by Beelzebub. And if I cast out demons by Beelzebub, by whom do your sons cast them out? Therefore they will be your judges."
>
> "But if I cast out demons with the finger of God, surely the kingdom of God has come upon you. When a strong man, fully armed, guards his own palace, his goods are in peace. But when a stronger than he comes upon him and overcomes him, he takes from him all his armor in which he trusted, and divides his spoils. He who is not with Me is against Me, and he who does not gather with Me scatters.
>
> —LUKE 11:14–23, NKJV, EMPHASIS ADDED

> How can one enter a strong man's house and plunder his goods, unless he first binds the strong man? And then he will plunder his house.
>
> —MATTHEW 12:29, NKJV

- Jesus was firm and consistent when He identified demonic activity in people. We should do the same. Persistence in allowing the Holy Spirit to reveal the kind of spirit that is manifesting will always result in victory.
- A spirit that causes a person to be mute should be addressed as a "mute spirit." We command the mute spirit to come out and the tongue to be loosed in the name of Jesus Christ. It is the power of the Holy Spirit coming upon the person that brings freedom.
- Be prepared to have "religious" leaders accuse you of being of the devil when you get involved in deliverance. Refuse to argue with them, but do pray for them.
- The "strong man" Jesus referred to is the demon that controls a person's behavior. When you have on the full armor of God and the name of Jesus on your lips, the demon cannot overcome you.
- Be sure to confirm the person's salvation and lead them into the Holy Spirit baptism.
- This is critical so that a person's "house" will be full of God. If not, the house will be "swept and clean" with no armor and without the Holy Spirit guarding the house.
- If you do not fill the house and get rid of the first bondage, more demons will eventually take up residence and the person will be worse off then before (Matthew 12:43-45).
- Note: Being bound works two ways. The principal demon (strong man) cannot plunder our house (mind and body) unless he first binds us with various bondages: rebellion, addictions, disobedience against God, etc. Conversely, we cannot plunder the strong man's house unless we first bind him in the name of Jesus.

THE REALITY OF SPIRITS

Spirits can cause people to be mute

Over the years we have observed many cases where spirits are the source of a person's inability to speak. The person may want to speak, but the spirit has bound them so they believe they cannot. Many came to Jesus with this problem as outlined below.

> As they went out, behold, they brought to Him a man, mute and demon-possessed. And when the demon was cast out, the mute spoke. And the multitudes marveled, saying, "It was never seen like this in Israel!"
>
> —MATTHEW 9:32–33, NKJV

> Then one was brought to Him who was demon-possessed, blind and mute; and He healed him, so that the blind and mute man both spoke and saw. And all the multitudes were amazed.
>
> —MATTHEW 12:22–23, NKJV

- A spirit can cause muteness. We need the gift of discerning of spirits to be absolutely sure.
- Jesus taught us to "cast out" the demon of muteness by firmly speaking to it.
- Bystanders will marvel and be amazed when the person begins to speak. We must be quick to initiate thanksgiving to God for setting the person free.
- Ignore any "religious leaders" who speak negatively about you and your deliverance team. Always respond in love.

The little girl named "No Speak"

One of the many mission teams we took to the hill tribes in northern Thailand consisted of two evangelists, a lady pastor, a CEO of a high-tech company and his daughter, Sonja, and me. Our mission was to teach one week in a Lahu tribal village and one week in a Karen tribal village. Our goal was to equip the Christians to fully understand and operate in the authority given by Jesus Christ. We did it like Jesus did. We taught the

Word, preached the gospel, and healed the sick. During one of the afternoon sessions, Dawn, the daughter of the CEO, felt strongly that a little mute girl she had befriended would be healed if we prayed for her.

The six-year-old had been given the name "No Speak" by the tribe because she had been mute since she was an infant. Her parents gave us permission to pray for her. The Lord led us to have Steve Darrow, the CEO, and the Lahu pastor pray for her. Steve and the pastor laid hands on her and Steve commanded the spirit that had the little girl bound to be gone. Steve prayed, "You mute spirit, I command you to loose this girl in the name of Jesus Christ. I loose her from the curse put on her by this tribe. Be gone, in Jesus' name!" We released her to go play with the other children, but told them to come and tell us when they heard her speak. Later the same day, the children all came running back yelling, "She's speaking, she's speaking!" That evening the children helped her sing the praise songs for the first time in her life. Dawn renamed her "Joy" instead of "No Speak." We serve an awesome God!

Malaria healed

While we were ministering to the Lahu tribe, a Burmese woman came into the village wanting to be healed of malaria. She had walked for many miles over the mountains for she had heard there were miracles happening in the Lahu village. She looked terrible: gaunt, yellowish skin, and so weak she could not stand. The minute she sat down, the Holy Spirit said to me (John), "It's a spirit. An unclean spirit is the source of the symptoms. Cast it out!" Using two interpreters, I immediately commanded the unclean spirit to come out of her. In a matter of minutes her skin became normal, she began to smile, and strength returned to her body. She thanked us and briskly walked away. One of the interpreters was a Thai Foursquare pastor. He was overwhelmed, weeping with joy and amazement. He said, "We hear all these stories from other Christians about Jesus healing people. This time I have seen the glory of God for myself. I have witnessed a miracle with my own eyes. That woman had malaria. I saw Jesus heal her! Praise God!" The following passages describe how Jesus set a boy free from a mute spirit that was causing symptoms similar to epilepsy:

> And when He came to the disciples, He saw a great multitude around them, and scribes disputing with them. Immediately,

when they saw Him, all the people were greatly amazed, and running to Him, greeted Him. And He asked the scribes, "What are you discussing with them?" Then one of the crowd answered and said, "Teacher, I brought You my son, who has a mute spirit. And wherever it seizes him, it throws him down; he foams at the mouth, gnashes his teeth, and becomes rigid. So I spoke to Your disciples, that they should cast it out, but they could not." He answered him and said, "O faithless generation, how long shall I be with you? How long shall I bear with you? Bring him to Me."

Then they brought him to Him. And when he saw Him, immediately the spirit convulsed him, and he fell on the ground and wallowed, foaming at the mouth. So He asked his father, "How long has this been happening to him?" And he said, "From childhood. And often he has thrown him both into the fire and into the water to destroy him. But if You can do anything, have compassion on us and help us." Jesus said to him, "If you can believe, all things are possible to him who believes." Immediately the father of the child cried out and said with tears, "Lord, I believe; help my unbelief!"

When Jesus saw that the people came running together, He rebuked the unclean spirit, saying to it, "Deaf and dumb spirit, I command you, come out of him and enter him no more!" Then the spirit cried out, convulsed him greatly, and came out of him. And he became as one dead, so that many said, "He is dead." But Jesus took him by the hand and lifted him up, and he arose.

And when He had come into the house, His disciples asked Him privately, "Why could we not cast it out?" So He said to them, "This kind can come out by nothing but prayer and fasting."
—MARK 9:14–29, NKJV

…for he is an epileptic and suffers severely; for he often falls into the fire and often into the water…"Because of your unbelief; for assuredly, I say to you, if you have faith as a mustard seed, you will say to this mountain, 'Move from here to there,' and it will move; and nothing will be impossible for you."
—MATTHEW 17:15–20, NKJV

A spirit seizes him, and he suddenly cries out; it convulses him so that he foams at the mouth; and it departs from him with great difficulty, bruising him.
—LUKE 9:37–42, NKJV

- Jesus taught many things about setting people free in this detailed account from the perspectives of Matthew, Mark, and Luke.
- Demons can cause the same symptoms as epilepsy. In this case, the spirit seized the boy and caused him to scream. People may shriek, yell, and get very loud. They may convulse violently as if they are being mauled and thrown to the ground. They may foam at the mouth, grind their teeth and become rigid. Some appear comatose.
- Remember, you can only cast out demons when demons are the source of the problem.
- Jesus said to both the parent and His disciples that unwavering faith is all that is needed to cast out demons.
- He said, "Everything is possible for him who believes!" We should pray and expect the gift of faith to come upon us when we engage in deliverance.
- Fasting and praying will often be necessary for us to successfully operate by revelation and by the gift of faith. Some spirits do not come out easily. Prayer with fasting may be necessary.
- Interview parents: Determine if medication relieves the symptoms. Demons do not respond to medication. Determine exactly what the parents believe God to do. Never go beyond what they authorize.
- Listen for faith: In this case the man said, "But if You can do anything!" Listen for faith to manifest in the family involved. Do not proceed until they expect the deliverance to be successful.
- Engage in the deliverance: Begin by speaking to the spirit behind the physical impairment. Command the spirit to come out. Command the spirit never to return or enter the person again.

- Naming a spirit: We never ask spirits for their names. They always lie. We ask the Spirit of truth, the Holy Spirit, for the principal spirit that has a person bound. If revealed, then we address the spirit by name.
- Continued physical manifestations during the deliverance are only an indication that spirits are responding to the authority of Jesus Christ. Do not focus on the outward manifestations. Listen to the Holy Spirit's instructions.
- When the Holy Spirit says we are done, we are done. We are done not because there are no more outward manifestations. We are done when every member of the team hears the Holy Spirit say, "You are through."
- Have the person who was delivered stay in close accountability with a mature prayer partner.
- Debrief: Use the deliverance as a point of teaching for the team; discuss how to better conduct deliverance in the future.

The demon-possessed boy

While conducting a weeklong healing crusade in Panang, Malaysia, I (John) encountered many people who were either demonized or demon-possessed. The difference is the degree by which the demons have control of the person. Demonized people can function normally in their daily activities. However, in one or more areas of their lives they are unable to control their behavior. Their mental perceptions are skewed. Demon-possessed people have little or no control of their behavior.

A mother brought her demon-possessed boy to the crusade. He was about seven years old and out of control. His mother held him tight in a bear hug in the back of the auditorium until we called for the sick; then she carried him kicking and screaming to the front row. The boy yelled and spit like a wildcat as his mother held him tightly. We had trained 30 healing teams of two people each to minister healing and deliverance. They were full of faith and ready for anything.

A healing team of two ladies stepped up to the boy, bent over, looked him straight in the eyes and said, "You are bound, in the name of Jesus Christ! Come out of him, now!" The boy stiffened out, screamed at the top of his voice, and slumped over exhausted. Minutes later the deliverance was complete. The boy stood, leaned into his mother, and looked around in wonderment. It was as if he were seeing the room and everything going on for the very first time. He was completely set free and behaving normally. The mother was so thankful that she gladly prayed with the ladies and invited Jesus into her life. I took pictures of the incident to remind me of the wonderful power God has given believers to set people free.

The power of the name of Jesus

The next night the place was filled with over 600 people. I was in the back of the auditorium documenting and overseeing the healing teams. Miracles were happening every few minutes. As people were healed and able to get up out of wheelchairs, they walked up on stage and testified to their healings. When twisted or deformed arms, legs, or backs would straighten out, people would be ushered up on stage to testify. Faith and excitement were running high.

I noticed a young man with a puzzled look approaching me. He spoke English so I asked him what he wanted God to do for him. Speaking hesitantly, he said, "I haven't been able to sleep. Could you pray for me?" I asked him if he knew Jesus. The second I said "Jesus," something hit him hard in the chest. I never touched him, but it caused him to stumble backwards and land on the floor. He lay there for 40 minutes. When he got up, he confessed that he had been worshiping the "Goddess of the Sea" and did not know what was happening to him. I told him that Jesus was his only hope. He gladly prayed and asked Jesus to become his Lord. This event demonstrated just how powerful the name of Jesus is in removing demonic strongholds in people's lives.

The Gadarene demoniacs

As we have said before, the difference between being demonized and being totally demon-possessed is the degree to which the demons have control. Demon-possessed people have very little if any control of their behavior. They would be classified in the West as being mentally ill and would most likely be placed in a mental institution. Those who are demonized can function normally in society but may have great difficulty in a specific role or function. That area of their life, if probed or irritated, will cause the person to manifest in strange or aberrant behavior. The following is a case of demon possession.

> Then they came to the other side of the sea, to the country of the Gadarenes. And when He had come out of the boat, immediately there met Him out of the tombs a man with an unclean spirit, who had his dwelling among the tombs; and no one could bind him, not even with chains, because he had often been bound with shackles and chains. And the chains had been pulled apart by him, and the shackles broken in pieces; neither could anyone tame him. And always, night and day, he was in the mountains and in the tombs, crying out and cutting himself with stones.
>
> When he saw Jesus from afar, he ran and worshiped Him. And he cried out with a loud voice and said, "What have I to do with You, Jesus, Son of the Most High God? I implore You by God that You do not torment me." For He said to him, "Come out of the man, unclean spirit!" Then He asked him, "What is your name?" And he answered, saying, "My name is Legion; for we are many." Also he begged Him earnestly that He would not send them out of the country. Now a large herd of swine was feeding there near the mountains. So all the demons begged Him, saying, "Send us to the swine, that we may enter them."
>
> And at once Jesus gave them permission. Then the unclean spirits went out and entered the swine (there were about two thousand); and the herd ran violently down the steep place into the sea, and drowned in the sea. So those who fed the swine fled, and they told it in the city and in the country. And they went out to see what it was that had happened. Then they came to Jesus, and saw the one who had been demon-possessed and had the legion, sitting and clothed and in his right mind. And they were afraid. And those who saw it told them how it happened to him who had been demon-possessed, and about the swine. Then they began to plead with Him to depart from their region.
>
> And when He got into the boat, he who had been demon-possessed begged Him that he might be with Him. However, Jesus did not permit him, but said to him, "Go home to your friends, and tell them what great things the Lord has done for you, and how He has

had compassion on you." And he departed and began to proclaim in Decapolis all that Jesus had done for him; and all marveled.

—MARK 5:1–20

- Jesus taught us to approach a demon-possessed person in love and compassion. We then proceed to set them free.
- Spirits know believers have authority over them and are a threat to their domain. They may speak through a person and demonstrate superhuman strength. Even though human effort may not subdue them, the name of Jesus will bind them and keep them from inflicting physical harm.
- People engaged in martial arts such as Kung Fu and Tai Kwan Do are taught to draw strength from a "master" by focusing on chants that attract demons to help them fight, overpower, and ultimately kill their opponents.
- Demon-possessed people cannot function normally in society.
- Demons do not want to leave the people they inhabit.
- When demons try to negotiate with us, it usually means they know we have power over them. Just cast them out.
- Neighbors acquainted with the demon-possessed will not understand the significance of a person being delivered from demons. They will be afraid of what is happening. They will ask that we go away, especially if the presence of God threatens their way of life and financial livelihood.
- Luke 8:29 says, "For He had commanded the unclean spirit to come out of the man." This implies that the demons did not come out immediately. The demons did not come out until they went into the pigs (Luke 8:33).

- There will be times when we encounter someone with multiple demons. Listen for specific instructions from the Holy Spirit as to the primary spirit that should be addressed.
- Once the person is set free, strongly encourage him or her to give testimony of the deliverance God brought about.

The disciples did what Jesus did

The early disciples continued doing what Jesus had taught them. They were eyewitnesses to His casting out demons. They were to accomplish ministry the way Jesus instructed them. They were simply Holy Spirit-empowered disciples just as we are. They experienced amazing results when they cast out demons just as Jesus had shown them.

Philip casts out unclean spirits

When persecution broke out in Jerusalem, the disciples were dispersed to neighboring towns and countries. They had been taught how to do what Jesus did and were preaching the gospel in the power and anointing of the Holy Spirit. Philip discovered the authority and power given to him by Jesus Christ.

> Therefore those who were scattered went everywhere preaching the word. Then Philip went down to the city of Samaria and preached Christ to them. And the multitudes with one accord heeded the things spoken by Philip, hearing and seeing the miracles which he did. For unclean spirits, crying with a loud voice, came out of many who were possessed; and many who were paralyzed and lame were healed. And there was great joy in that city.
>
> —ACTS 8:4–8, NKJV

- Preaching the Word stirs up unclean spirits. Phillip preached what Jesus said to preach in Mark 16:15-20. Signs followed the proclamation of the gospel.

- People gave attention to what Philip said. They heard that Jesus could set them free from bondages and heal them. There was great rejoicing in that city.
- When spirits come out, they may make a commotion and shout with a loud voice. We are to command them to be quiet.
- When we remove the doubt and unbelief of many in the West, healing and miracles are more likely to manifest.

Paul casts out demons

Paul had been baptized in the Holy Spirit, and he operated in the authority and power given to him by Jesus Christ. He exercised this power in the next passage to cast out a demon inhabiting a slave girl.

Now it happened, as we went to prayer, that a certain slave girl possessed with a spirit of divination met us, who brought her masters much profit by fortune-telling. This girl followed Paul and us, and cried out, saying, "These men are the servants of the Most High God, who proclaim to us the way of salvation." And this she did for many days. But Paul, greatly annoyed, turned and said to the spirit, "I command you in the name of Jesus Christ to come out of her." And he came out that very hour. But when her masters saw that their hope of profit was gone, they seized Paul and Silas and dragged them into the marketplace to the authorities.

—Acts 16:16–19, NKJV

- Paul provided a wonderful example of how to cast out demons.
- Paul made sure he was dealing with a demon. The Holy Spirit evidently confirmed that they were dealing with a "spirit of divination." The demon could tell things about Paul and others that only they knew.
- Paul waited for God's timing to cast out the demon. Paul waited "many days." Finally, the demon-possessed woman was disrupting their meetings, so Paul cast out the demon.

- Paul said, "I command you, in the name of Jesus Christ, to come out of her!" That still works today!

DO NOT MAKE IT DIFFICULT

Novice Christians have a tendency to get loud and emotional when they first get involved in deliverance ministry. If we use the above situation where Paul dealt with the demon in the slave girl, we have a wonderful example of how deliverance should be done.

We should not try to improve on the process or make it more difficult. Be patient and wait for the Holy Spirit's timing. When the Holy Spirit reveals the activities of the demonic spirit and says to cast it out, then command it to come out in the name of Jesus Christ. Be very firm and stay with it until the Holy Spirit says you are done. We do not have to shout and become physical with the person. That demonstrates to the demon that you are resorting to human or fleshly tactics. Rely on the leading of the Holy Spirit, and the person will be set free within a short period of time.

Spirit houses

Many people have asked why there seems to be more demonic activity in third world or developing countries. It is because their people are generally more superstitious. Religions are based in the supernatural power of the enemy. For instance, in Thailand a very significant part of the Buddhist religion is the "spirit house" phenomenon. You can see these in most Thai and some Chinese restaurants in America. Most homes and businesses in Thailand have these beautifully decorated structures for honoring and appeasing spirits. The more successful you are, the larger the spirit house.

You can feel the negative energy

If Christians are sensitive to the spiritual realm, they can actually feel the negative energy coming from the spirit houses. On numerous occasions we have felt the evil presence before we even saw the spirit house. We would sense the negative energy, look around, and, sure enough, there it would be.

People place offerings of flowers, food, even Coca-Cola in spirit houses in order to appease the spirits so they will not harm them. By deliberately inviting the spirits (whom they think may be relatives or friends who have died), people are deceived and give demonic spirits the right to inhabit the premises. Paul admonished Christians not to "be participants with demons":

> Do I mean then that a sacrifice offered to an idol is anything, or that an idol is anything? No, but the sacrifices of pagans are offered to demons, not to God, and I do not want you to be participants with demons. You cannot drink the cup of the Lord and the cup of demons too; you cannot have a part in both the Lord's table and the table of demons.
> —1 CORINTHIANS 10:19–21

- Idols or spirit houses attract demons. People sometimes unknowingly sacrifice to demonic spirits.
- Christians must not open themselves up to spirits by visiting temples or admiring spirit houses or any type of idol, large or small.
- This same negative energy can be discerned in occult or New Age gatherings and in and around their bookstores.

Thai Christians have to contend with pre-Christian relatives who take their idols and witchcraft paraphernalia when they visit from another city. There is a reality to the supernatural dimension, and the Christians have to pray and take authority over the spirits that accompany their relatives into their homes. Otherwise, all sorts of occurrences begin to manifest, and the peace of God that normally permeates their homes is disrupted.

There is concentrated demonic activity in the temples

This may sound farfetched to some of you reading this, but if you would talk with missionaries and Christians living in these countries, you could easily verify this reality. Another area of concentrated demonic activity is in wats, or temples. Again, you can feel the negative energy emanating from these places of worship. The worshipers feel the energy, fear it, and are compelled to try to appease the spirits so they will not be harmed. Christians should not visit these demon-infested sites.

It felt like a wet spider web

On my (John's) first trip to Panang, Malaysia, I traveled with Dr. A. L. Gill, who was especially sensitive to spiritual activity in and around heathen temples. As we drove from the airport to our hotel, I was sitting in the backseat marveling at all the new sights of this "city of a thousand temples." Sitting in the front seat, Dr. Gill watched my reactions in the rearview mirror as we drove close to a very elaborate Hindu temple. Without warning, a horrible feeling came over me as I observed the thousands of demonic gargoyles protruding from its steep roof. I felt something like a cold, damp spider web fall upon me. My reaction caused my friend to smile, laugh, and say, "Looks like your spiritual antenna is doing just fine. Keep it fine-tuned and you'll keep out of trouble." He was referring to the gift of discerning of spirits. I became very thankful as the Holy Spirit continually activated this gift the entire six weeks I spent in Malaysia.

We must allow God to demonstrate His power

Because people in many countries live in the supernatural realm and are enslaved by fear of the demonic spirits, one of the most effective ways to minister to them is in the demonstration of the love and power of God. If we are holding evangelistic meetings for tribal people in northern Thailand and someone goes into a demonic manifestation, falls on the ground and begins slithering like a snake, we better know our authority in Christ. All the eloquent preaching and teaching we learned in seminary will not prevail in that kind of situation. We need to step into the authority given to us by Jesus Christ and allow the Holy Spirit to demonstrate His power through us. Paul knew how to handle situations like that:

> And my speech and my preaching were not with persuasive words of human wisdom, but in demonstration of the Spirit and of power, that your faith should not be in the wisdom of men but in the power of God.
>
> —1 CORINTHIANS 2:4–5, NKJV

- We preach the full gospel message: Jesus Christ, the Son of God as Savior, Healer, Baptizer in the Holy Spirit, and soon-coming King.
- After the preaching of the Word, God is always faithful to heal the sick and set people free from demonic power.

When tribal people *see* and *experience* the power of God and discover that it is greater than any demonic spirit, they accept Jesus Christ as the One and only true God, the Creator! Hallelujah!

Pray over hotel rooms

During my mother's final illness, I (Sonja) did not go with John on one of the mission trips to Thailand. I was staying at a hotel in Vancouver, Washington, near where my mother was convalescing. As a rule, we always pray over our hotel rooms and "sanctify" them through the name and blood of the Lord Jesus Christ.

One night I was tired, and I forgot to pray. In the middle of the night, I awoke with a demonic spirit trying to smother me. I was terrified and could barely get the words out, "In the name of Jesus Christ, I command you to leave!" I repeated the words multiple times, but the spirit would not lift off of me. Finally, I said, "I am covered with the blood of Jesus, and you must depart!" And it did. The bizarre thing about this incident is that I rolled over and went back to sleep! Only the peace of God could explain that.

I thought I was going to die

While staying in a hotel in Mae Sai, Thailand, next to the Myanmar border, I (John) neglected to take authority over any spiritual "residue" that usually lingers in the rooms. About 3:00 a.m., I awoke with a sudden and very acute pain in my abdomen. I stumbled to the bathroom in an effort to rid myself of the pain, but nothing seemed to help. Collapsing back in bed I began to feel extremely weak and began to shiver uncontrollably. Fear hit me as I realized that no hospital was available. I thought I might die.

Then the Holy Spirit interrupted me and said, "Take authority over the spirit!" Immediately I said loudly, "You foul demon. I command you to loose me and get out of here! I take authority over you and forbid you to stay upon me. In the authority of the blood of Jesus Christ, be gone! All spirits in this room are bound. You cannot stay. I command all of you out of here in the name of Jesus Christ!" I did not care if the people in the next room could hear me. This thing was trying to kill me! Within minutes the pain left and the shivering stopped. I rolled over and slept like a baby the rest of the night.

Are demons in America?

We have been exploring demonic bondages in developing countries. Now we turn to America. There has been an increase in demonic activity in the U.S. As Christians, we must face the reality of spiritual entities and the power they hold over certain people. Beginning in the 1960s, we have watched the moral fiber of our nation disintegrate before our very eyes. Entrance points for hordes of demons are prevalent throughout our culture:

- Eastern religious systems
- Occult, witchcraft, and New Age philosophies
- Violence and sex depicted on TV and in movies
- Internet pornography and illicit sexual perversions
- Drug and alcohol abuse

If we are truly to do what Jesus did, we cannot ignore the subject of demonic activity. We need to examine closely the role we need to play to be able to set free those who are being held captive by Satan. Demons are at work worldwide. Jesus commissioned Christians to cast out demons wherever we find them holding people in bondage. The remainder of this chapter brings the issue closer to home, right here in America.

SETTING THE CAPTIVES FREE IN AMERICA

Demonology 101

The following story was my (John's) introduction to the world of spirits. It began in Everett, Washington, during the mid-1970s. My good friend Ken Miracle introduced me to Rev. Jesse Raymond, a man in his seventies who had a reputation for healing the sick, prophesying, and operating in the revelation gifts of the Holy Spirit. Jesse was a frequent speaker in full gospel churches, healing conferences, and the Full Gospel Business Men's Fellowship International (FGBMFI). He conducted Christian counseling in an office in the back of his Lighthouse Christian Bookstore in the north part of town. He invited me to visit his store on my next sales trip to that area.

I dropped in one Friday afternoon and was spellbound by all of his stories about miracles that he had experienced while preaching the gospel. I will never forget what happened next.

Come out

Jesse's afternoon counseling appointment entered the store, and Jesse asked me to watch the store while he counseled the man. The man carried a well-worn Bible, said he was a Spirit-filled believer, and that he wanted help with some "personal concerns." Jesse's office was in the back of the store and had a large glass window between the office and the book displays. I could see everything that was happening, but could barely hear what was being said—that is, until I heard Jesse say "You will have to come out of him, now!"

I looked through the window at Jesse, who seemed relaxed as he leaned back in his big office chair. On the other side of his desk the other man sat, leaning forward with his elbows on his knees; his eyes were red, and he scowled at Jesse, growling, gagging, and coughing. The hair went up on the back of my neck. I did not understand what I was seeing. Fear hit me, and I wanted to get out of there fast!

Then the phone rang. The caller urgently needed to speak to Jesse. I motioned to Jesse to get the phone, and, as he did so, he told me to go into his office and take over for him. I must have looked like a four-year-old seeing the real Frankenstein for the first time. Jesse just smiled and said, "Don't worry. Just speak to the spirit in the name of Jesus! I'll be right back." He pushed me into his office, and I fearfully sat down in his chair.

He just stared at me

Having only the desk between the devil and me was not very comforting. The red-eyed man just stared at me, breathing heavily. I froze. Finally, I managed a weak, "In Jesus' name, you stay where you are.

I command you to sit there!" He just stared at me. I was really getting nervous, and I quietly prayed for the Lord to send Jesse back in a hurry. Then the man uttered a very loud groan and a half growl that petrified me. Finally, Jesse walked in with a small wastebasket, gave it to the man, and said, "Come out you foul, perverse spirit, all the way out. Now! In the name of Jesus Christ!"

The man gagged, convulsed, and coughed into the wastebasket. This happened three or four times. Then he collapsed back into his chair, sighed deeply, wiping his chin, and finally said, "It's gone! It's gone! It's all gone!" He asked Jesse how he knew what the problem was. Jesse said, "The Lord told me when you first walked in here today. He said that you've been deeply into pornography for years and you opened the door to a lying and perverse spirit."

I was stunned. The man who had just been delivered was a charismatic Christian, spoke in tongues, and attended church. I thought Christians could not have demons. I was terribly confused. After the man left, Jesse recommended some books on the subject and invited me back to discuss my findings. I left in amazement. I did not have a clue what to think. I was certain of one thing, however: I had witnessed firsthand the visible grip of spiritual bondage that an entity had on the man. I had also witnessed the awesome power of the name of Jesus that had set the man free from the clutches of a powerful demonic spirit.

CAN A CHRISTIAN HAVE A DEMON?

When the subject of demons comes up, it seems Christians ask the same question: "Can a Christian have a demon?" After more than 30 years of studying this issue, we reached this conclusion: Christians are given the freedom of choice. If they choose to associate with people who participate in evil deeds or choose to disobey God and continue to live a destructive lifestyle of sin and wanton pleasure, they open themselves up to demonic entities. It may take a long time, but eventually they can become demonized. Christians cannot have it both ways. Either we live for God, or we live for ourselves. The choice is ours.

This is shocking

To many it may come as a shock to discover that Christians can have demons. Some argue that Christians cannot have the Holy Spirit and demons at the same time. What they fail to understand is that demons reside in the soul nature (mind, will, and emotions) and in the body, not in the human spirit. When we receive Christ, our spirit nature is made new and becomes alive with the Holy Spirit. However, our mind is not made new. It needs to be renewed day-by-day. People who say they believe in God but have no knowledge of biblical truth are susceptible to the lies of Satan. If we do not know what the Bible says, we remain vulnerable to a "different spirit." Paul warned Christians to be very careful not to be corrupted by a different spirit.

> But I fear, lest somehow, as the serpent deceived Eve by his crafti-ness, so your minds may be corrupted from the simplicity that is in Christ. For if he who comes preaches another Jesus whom we have not preached, or if you receive a *different spirit* which you have not received, or a different gospel which you have not accepted—you may well put up with it!
>
> —2 CORINTHIANS 11:3–4, NKJV

- Those seeking spiritual insight in the wrong place open their minds to spiritual corruption.
- Cults recruit unsuspecting people by preaching "another Jesus" and a different gospel. Jehovah's Witnesses and Mormonism are two from a long list of cults that emanate a "different spirit."
- A "different spirit" is instruction that sounds good or feels good to the soul, but it cloaked with deception that leads away from the gospel.
- We are safe when we strive for mainstream Christian orthodoxy that is consistent with the Word of God.

Now the Spirit expressly says that in latter times some will depart from the faith, giving heed to deceiving spirits and doctrines of demons, speaking lies in hypocrisy, having their own conscience seared with a hot iron, forbidding to marry, and commanding

to abstain from foods which God created to be received with
thanksgiving by those who believe and know the truth.

—1 TIMOTHY 4:1–3, NKJV

- Believers who know the truth of God's Word
  will not be led astray be spiritual legalism,
  deception, or doctrines of demons.
- The gifts of discerning of spirits, words of
  wisdom and knowledge, and a broad understanding of the Bible are the best defense
  against being deceived by cults.

MENTAL ABUSE

We learned in Psychology 101 that the human mind, given the right set
of negative circumstances, can be influenced to the point of becoming
mentally unstable. We believe that trauma from severe physical or
mental abuse can create mind-sets of deception. Witnessing a murder
or other violent crime, or victimization such as beatings, forced sexual
acts, rape, or homosexual attack can make people more vulnerable to
warped belief systems and lies that skew their thinking. If not dealt
with, these mind-sets will remain with a person for life. Accepting
Christ and becoming born again will erase most of these unhealthy
lies from the mind. However, in the case of severe mental abuse
during childhood or adolescence, there can remain a "hook" in the
deep recesses of the mind. If not dealt with through a concerted effort
of aggressive renewal of the mind, the deep-seated lie or fear will be a
magnet for a demonic spirit.

Christians who understand how the enemy works in these areas of
mental abuse and deep wounds in our soul nature should be willing
to reach out in love to those who are bound or who are in opposition
to sound theology. We endeavor to do this according to the following
scripture:

And a servant of the Lord must not quarrel but be gentle to all,
able to teach, patient, in humility correcting those who are in
opposition, if God perhaps will grant them repentance, so that

they may know the truth, and that they may come to their senses and escape the snare of the devil, having been taken captive by him to do his will.

—2 Timothy 2:24–26, nkjv

- Carnal Christians who oppose sound teaching from the Word of God and disobey God may fall into the snare of the devil and be taken captive by him to do his will.
- Genuine repentance is required to reinstate a person who is backslidden and bound by the power of Satan.

Forgiveness and repentance expose the enemy

When a person embraces a lie of the enemy by holding onto unforgiveness, it attracts a lying entity. When the person forgives those who caused the problem, there is an immediate emotional release and spiritual freedom. Similarly, repenting from any participation in a major sinful act that took place either before or after coming to Christ, will result in an emotional deliverance for the individual. In both of these situations, a release from spiritual bondage takes place, and the person is loosed from any influence of a demonic spirit. The person who refuses to repent will be kept in the devil's snare. This will often result in a gradual slide toward demonization.

John's new quest

Along with learning how to heal the sick, I was determined to learn all I could about the unseen realm of spirits. As described in chapter 3, learning how to heal the sick was a long process. Learning about spirits became a parallel learning process. The more I learned about healing, the more the subject of spirits became evident. Divine healing operates in and through the Holy Spirit. Discerning and casting out demons also operates in and through the Holy Spirit. Both are a measurable result of the divine working of a loving God who wants His people to be free. He wants all of us (spirit, soul, and body) to be free to worship Him.

If we pursue a healing ministry, we will eventually face demonic spirits. It just happens. Our purpose here is to extinguish the fear of

the subject of deliverance and to equip believers to effectively deal
with demonic spirits when they surface.

Ignoring demons is dangerous

The most effective weapon our enemy uses is deception. If Satan can
convince Christians to ignore what Scripture tells us about the existence of harmful spirits, then Satan wins. We have heard comments
from various Christian leaders who attempt to discredit those engaged
in deliverance ministry. Likewise, we can testify of the zealous few
engaged in the fanatical excesses that give deliverance ministries a
bad reputation. Pastors and leaders need to wisely inform their congregations of the existence of demons and their potential influence on
Christians. Ignoring the subject allows demonic spirits to set traps for
the uninformed and wreak havoc within the church.

Churches are often where troubled people look for help. We receive
calls from desperate people who cannot find a Bible-based deliverance
ministry in their city. This should not be so! This is why we are committed to establishing Ministry Training Institutes (MTIs) in local
churches where teams of qualified people can be equipped to do deliverance ministry. Skilled lay ministers can relieve the already over-
worked salaried pastoral staff. Many churches use our MTI graduates
as their prayer ministry teams and for hospital visitations. Pastors
know they can trust those in their church who have been given biblical training and hands-on experience through the MTI training.

We don't know how

We believe the hearts of Christian leaders are saying, "We don't
know how! Show us an authentic approach that is biblically based, and
we may consider getting involved." Many biblical accounts show that
Jesus gave His followers the power and authority to loose demonic
strongholds in people's lives. The promises have not passed away. We
strongly advocate that Christian leaders should research the subject
enough to teach a balanced message regarding the existence of spirits
and the influence they may have on Christians. To fail to teach this in
the course of normal Christian discipleship will, by default, keep congregations from learning the truth about spirits. The result will most
often lead to uninformed fears of the whole subject and a perpetua-
tion of the myths about why we should avoid dealing with demons.

If we are to meet the challenge of the spiritual complexities of the twenty-first century, we must equip the saints with knowledge and understanding regarding the strategies of an enemy who is capturing unsuspecting Christians with lies, lust, and lascivious living.

DEMONIC OPPRESSION

We cannot count how many Christians—Spirit-filled Christians— have come to us with demonic oppression. Many times we are able to trace the source to a childhood incident of abuse or victimization by a family member or friend.

Spiritual transference

When sexual abuse occurs, there generally is a spiritual transference from the abuser, who usually has a perverse/unclean spirit. Even though the child or young person is the innocent victim, the transference takes place. In those cases when the precious victim comes to Christ and receives salvation, the person is surely forgiven of all confessed sins. However, until the perverse/unclean spirit has been directly addressed and commanded to leave by the power and authority of Jesus Christ, it continues to have influence in the person's life. In the case of a woman, it can be subtle, such as dressing slightly suggestively. Men will be excessively drawn to her, and she will not know why.

If a man has been victimized, he may turn to homosexuality or be enslaved to progressive levels of pornography. By that, we mean the insatiable appetite of the unclean spirit drives him from one level of perversion to another until he may become involved in child pornography—one of the most vile and perverted forms of sin. We have made an observation that, when a man and woman who have had the above-described experiences come in contact with each other, there is an unnatural magnetic drawing to one another. They cannot explain it, because it is on a spiritual level—the two demonic spirits are being drawn to each other.

Why me?

If the woman has become a Christian, but has not experienced deliverance from this kind of spiritual activity, she will often make comments such as "Why me? I get so sick of guys staring at me and coming on to me—even Christian men who are, supposedly, happily married."

Likewise, the man who has become a Christian but has not been set free from a skewed perspective of his sexuality will have a warped view of women and sex in general. If not dealt with, he can be prone to engage in unnatural sexual activity leading to bisexual or homosexual acts. Achieving a healthy marriage with a satisfying sexual expression becomes a distant dream.

These precious souls need to be set free by the power of the blood of Jesus Christ and the authority He has given us over such evil, tormenting, demonic spirits.

Wrong theology keeps some people bound

Many wonderful Christians believe that demonic spirits cannot torment born-again believers. But the Word and our ministry experience prove that this is a very dangerous position. If you believe that, and if find yourself tormented by a spirit and no matter how much you try to stop a compelling, sinful, destructive behavior, you simply cannot, what do you do? We think that may have been what happened to a very prominent American evangelist and a very well-known pastor of an evangelical megachurch in the Seattle area. If our theology disallows Christians from being delivered from demonic spirits, then those who are enslaved are without hope. We do not believe that those Christians we have described are "possessed." However, they certainly are "oppressed" of the devil and need to be set free.

Catholic priest set free

We were doing a seminar on the Holy Spirit for a charismatic Catholic group, and every Friday night an older priest would stand in the back of the room and listen. We assumed he was simply monitoring our teaching. One evening, he came to the front of the room after the service and approached me (Sonja). We had been teaching about demonization, and he began a conversation about the subject. He related a recurring experience he was having at night when he went to bed. Shortly after he turned the lights out, a dark and foreboding presence would come upon him, almost crushing his chest. He asked me what I thought the source could be. I immediately responded that it sounded demonic and asked if he would like prayer. He said "yes," and John and I discreetly went with him to another room, identified the spirit, prayed a prayer of deliverance, and he was set free. The next week he returned to the meeting with a beautiful smile and a good report. The spirit had not manifested since we prayed! How gracious is our God!

Internet pornography

With the advent of Internet pornography, many men, even Christian men (pastors, priests, and leaders), have become addicted in the privacy of their offices. The progression often goes like this: Out of curiosity, he taps onto a website, and a flood of filth pours out before him. The Holy Spirit immediately convicts him, and he may log off, but the sensual images continue to replay in his mind. Before long, he is back online being seduced deeper and deeper into the cesspool. All the while, the Holy Spirit is talking with him, warning him, grieving over his behavior. It is likely that all the man would have to do to be set free at that time would be to cry out to God. He would need to truly repent (turn from it), tell his wife and tell another man for accountability, and immediately install a foolproof filter on his computer. First John states that that we must confess our sins to experience forgiveness and to be purified from this kind of unrighteous behavior.

> If we claim to be without sin, we deceive ourselves and the truth is not in us. If we confess our sins, he is faithful and just and will forgive us our sins and purify us from all unrighteousness. If we claim we have not sinned, we make him out to be a liar and his word has no place in our lives.
>
> —1 JOHN 1:8–10

---

* Repentance is required to be converted to Christ.
* Repentance is also necessary to stay free.
* Failure to continue repenting from sin gives demons permission to invade our minds.

What happens when a man ignores the Holy Spirit?

If the man ignores the conviction of the Holy Spirit and continues in his sinful behavior, at a certain juncture a perverse/unclean spirit *has a right* to attach itself to the man in that area of his life. At that point the behavior has become compulsive, and the man cannot stop! He is under the influence of that evil spirit and, more often than not, the perverse spirit's companion, the lying spirit, also invades his personality. He is enslaved in sin and must have the power of those spirits broken over his life. Otherwise, it will be a downward spiral that ends in destruction.

What is the mission of the Christian?

Christians need to be educated about spirits and how they work. Jesus expected His followers to accept the challenge He set before them. The first thing all Christians must learn is the mission that Jesus set before us. When we understand where we are commissioned to go and what we are commissioned to do, we can begin to learn how to fulfill the requirements necessary to become a well-balanced and effective minister. We explored the obvious commands of Jesus Christ in chapter 1. In Acts, the first chapter, Jesus commanded His followers not to preach or go into the entire world until they had been baptized in the Holy Spirit. In chapter 3, we concluded that the follower of Christ who is baptized in the Holy Spirit is in a preferred position to operate in the supernatural of God. If we are to heal the sick and cast out demons, then we must be full of the Holy Spirit.

BOOT CAMP DISCIPLESHIP

During the disciples' three-year boot camp of learning from Jesus, they went out simply trusting in His commands and authorization. It worked for them, even though the day of Pentecost was many months away. The Holy Spirit had not yet fully come upon them. How much more can you and I, who are baptized in the Holy Spirit, work miracles in Jesus' name today? This is illustrated in the next passage which tells of Jesus' sending His new recruits to the marketplace and commanding them to do things they had never done before.

> These twelve *Jesus* sent out and *commanded* them, saying: "Do not go into the way of the Gentiles, and do not enter a city of the Samaritans. But go rather to the lost sheep of the house of Israel. And as you go, preach, saying, 'The kingdom of heaven is at hand.' Heal the sick, cleanse the lepers, raise the dead, *cast out demons*. Freely you have received, freely give."
> —MATTHEW 10:5–8, NKJV, EMPHASIS ADDED

He...*gave them power* over unclean spirits...So they went out
and preached that people should repent. And *they cast out many
demons*, and anointed with oil many who were sick, and healed
them.

—MARK 6:7–13, NKJV, EMPHASIS ADDED

- When the Holy Spirit sends us out, we can trust His leading and His power to accomplish what He wants.
- When we preach the full gospel, we will have opportunities to heal the sick and cast out demons.
- When we preach that people should repent of sin, it may cause a "clash of kingdoms" between light and darkness.
- Those held in Satan's bondage might need demons cast out of them. We should be prepared to do this and set them free.

John enters boot camp

During the early years of attending banquets of the FGBMFI, there
were plenty of opportunities to pray for all kinds of sicknesses and
disease. Sometimes there were more people wanting prayer than businessmen available to pray. We had to spread out and work alone. I did
not know the wisdom of Jesus' strategy of ministering with a partner,
"two-by-two." On one occasion a Native American mother pulled her
six-foot-three-inch, 295-pound son to where I was praying. He had
long, dark braids and was dressed in tribal clothing. His mother
wanted him to be prayed for because he thought creatures were trying
to attack him. I laid my hands on him and began praying in tongues.
With my eyes still closed, in my mind I saw a large lobster-type claw
gripping his entire midsection. I opened my eyes and could not see
anything, but with my eyes closed I could still see it. Then I heard the
Holy Spirit say, "He is bound by a spirit."

He growled and bent over

Up until this time, I had never tried to cast out a spirit, but I was
already into the situation and felt the Holy Spirit was helping me.

With all the authority I could muster, I said loudly, "In the name of Jesus, I bind you, you foul spirit!" This young man let out a bloodcurdling growl and bent down, almost touching his knees. Immediately, I knew I was in over my head. I quickly looked around for help. I needed a partner, someone who knew what to do next.

As the young man continued his groaning and growling, I spotted Phil Israelson, got his attention, and waved him over to where I was ministering. Phil had been on a couple of airlifts to Central America, and I remembered his telling of experiences with demonic spirits. I knew he would know what to do. I was operating in the power and authority, but did not have the experience to complete the ministry.

He got up smiling

When Phil came over I told him that the young man had a demon and needed help. Phil smiled at me, turned to the young man, laid hands on his back and firmly took authority over the situation. He prayed, "In the name of Jesus Christ, I command you lying spirit to come out of him!" He did that three times. Suddenly the young man let out a long growl, finishing with a sigh, and fell backwards, hitting the floor with a thud. He lay there for about five minutes and then got up smiling. He and his mother thanked Phil and discussed what the young man needed to do to remain free. Phil led him in a prayer confirming his salvation and then led him into the Holy Spirit baptism.

After they left, I thanked Phil for helping me. I was full of questions, and he gave me some very valuable tips should I find myself facing demonic activity again. It was only a couple of months later that I again confronted a demonized person. That time I knew what to do. The person was set free. It worked just like Phil had taught me. I thank God for ministers who will mentor us in doing things right.

Joy comes when we experience success

There is great satisfaction when you are part of the process of setting people free from spiritual bondages, especially Christians. We just shake our heads with compassion when we see uninformed or immature believers caught in destructive lifestyles. We see the great turmoil, oppression, and agony they are facing. They are desperate, unable to shake themselves loose from what is binding them. They have tried everything, and nothing seems to work. They pray and pray without relief. Though people under the influence of demonic spirits can function well at work and even at home, the bondage keeps them from functioning effectively in a specific area of their personal lives. It is a great privilege to know and understand that, through Christ, the demons are subject to us and must obey our commands to loose these people in the name of Jesus Christ.

The seventy passed the test

The seventy had been with Jesus for quite a while. They had watched how He healed the sick and cast out demons. They were finishing their boot camp discipleship and were being sent forth to try out their new authority and power. It was working!

> Then the seventy returned with joy, saying, "Lord, even the demons are subject to us in Your name." And He said to them, "I saw Satan fall like lightning from heaven. Behold, I give you the *authority* to trample on serpents and scorpions, and over *all* the power of the enemy, and nothing shall by any means hurt you. Nevertheless do not rejoice in this, that *the spirits are subject to you*, but rather rejoice because your names are written in heaven."
> —LUKE 10:17–20, NKJV, EMPHASIS ADDED

- The seventy learned by doing. They practiced what Jesus had taught them, and discovered the awesome authority they had in His name.
- We, too, can do what Jesus said we could do. We have to be bold and step out and exercise our authority in Christ. Though we may read about our authority, until we practice the authority we will never experience it.
- Demons bow to the name of Jesus spoken from our mouths. Jesus said we have authority over all the power of the enemy.
- We are to cast out demons without rejoicing about it. We rejoice that our names are recorded in heaven. We can rejoice all the more when the people we set free live for Jesus and join us in heaven.

We need a personal revelation of this

Luke 10:17–20 is a major revelation. When we get the revelation that this passage means "I have authority," it changes our perception of how we approach the spirit world. Instead of fearing the subject, we embrace our responsibility to appropriate the authority given to us by Jesus Christ and become available to set others free. Some commentators interpret "serpents and scorpions" as referring to all categories of demonic spirits. It is very comforting to know that we have all authority over all serpents, scorpions, and over all the power of our enemy, Satan. All demonic spirits are subject to us. This means they must obey our commands spoken in the name of Jesus. We are to accept this truth, act on it, and use this authority and power whenever demonic spirits surface in people.

We must remain balanced as we rejoice

It is easy to become enthralled with the whole subject of demons. We are not to be focused on the temporal conquering of the enemy and casting him out of people. Jesus said to focus on the destination of eternal salvation with Him. We are to rejoice that our names are written in heaven. Our destiny is to be in glory with the Lord of lords. Our *reason* for setting people free of spiritual bondages is to pave the way for them to also have a place in heaven. Then we both can rejoice!

It is all in the name

Regardless of whether you belong to a denomination or not, your authority and power to cast out demons are totally wrapped up in the name of Jesus Christ. We see this in the following scripture:

> Now John answered Him, saying, "Teacher, we saw someone who does not follow us casting out demons in Your name, and we forbade him because he does not follow us." But Jesus said, "Do not forbid him, for no one who works a miracle in My name can soon afterward speak evil of Me. For he who is not against us is on our side. For whoever gives you a cup of water to drink in My name, because you belong to Christ, assuredly, I say to you, he will by no means lose his reward."
> —Mark 9:38–41, nkjv

- Jesus confirmed that His name is the final authority for the working of miracles. In this context, Jesus included casting out demons along with serving others in any capacity as part of the "works" we are to do.
- If you witness other ministers of another church or denomination casting out demons successfully in the name of Jesus, do not criticize them.
- We must not become proud or promote an air of exclusiveness about how we set people free. Ministry styles and methods are secondary to setting people free from spiritual bondages.
- Always examine the fruit. Are lives being redeemed from bondages of addictions and habitual sin? Are the deliverance teams truly effective? Are people staying free? Are lives being dramatically changed? Is Jesus receiving all the glory?

Training starts by experiencing it

During one of the weekend retreats for FGBMFI in the mid-1970s, I (John) passed through a lounge area where I witnessed what seemed to be an argument brewing among three men. Two men were quoting Scripture to a third man who was not buying what they were selling. The argument stemmed from a disagreement about the Holy Spirit. As a fairly new Christian, I sat down to listen to see what I could learn. Suddenly the third man (whom I will call Joe) turned on the other two, hunched over, and with a frightening growl, screamed, "You will never convince me. I hate all of you!" The other two began to bind the demon and command him to come out of Joe.

Joe dropped to the floor in a crouched position and dared the other two to take him on. He said, "You are lying. I have power over you! Don't come any closer." By that time, other men gathered around the commotion. The two men yelled, "Satan, you are the liar. We bind you, and command you to release this man, in the name of Jesus!" The men grabbed him by the arms in an effort to subdue him and put him in a chair. With amazing superhuman strength, Joe, who could have weighed no more than 150 pounds, quickly threw both men into a pile on the floor.

Joe left without being delivered

Joe snarled at the rest of us, daring anyone to take him on. We all backed away not knowing what to do. Joe quickly turned toward the door, left the building, got in his car, and left the retreat. We were all shaking our heads, discussing what went wrong and why Joe was not delivered of the demon.

We later found out that he had come to the retreat under protest because of the insistence of a Christian co-worker. He was deep into satanic rituals and the martial arts and liked the powers that Satan was granting him. He did not want to be delivered. He liked the demonic powers that allowed him to control others. This early episode again convinced me that the demonic realm was real and that I needed better training to properly deal with spirits.

WHO ARE YOU GOING TO CALL?

When I (John) was the area director for the regional 700 Club Crisis Counseling Center in the Seattle area, I trained over 100 telephone counselors to handle everything from salvation to suicide. It was a wonderfully productive time of training and ministry. Early on, it became apparent that I needed a way to train the counselors how to discern and deal with demonic activity. Many of the counselors had family members and friends that they suspected were demonized, and there was no place to take them for ministry. The churches in our area were ill-prepared to handle people with serious spiritual bondages. After researching the subject, I chose the late Dr. Lester Sumrall's video course, "Demonology and Deliverance." After I had thoroughly trained a dozen people, I organized them into three teams. I then developed an extensive interview process for those people seeking deliverance. It worked very well. The following are some of the things we learned:

1. Only about half of the people who were interviewed truly needed deliverance. Most needed to repent of common habitual sins that held them captive.

2. The half that truly needed deliverance received ministry and were, almost without exception, set free. One exception was a professional man who was set free of several spirits, but refused to complete the deliverance by forgiving his wife and reconciling with her. His spiritual condition today is as bad as or worse than before.

3. Many of the spiritual conditions were a result of unconfessed sin, unforgiveness, and just plain ignorance of biblical principles.

4. Physiological conditions can produce behaviors that are *exactly* like demonic manifestations. It is crucial that the ministers of deliverance operate in the supernatural gifts of discerning of spirits, and/or words of knowledge and wisdom. Otherwise, they will be in danger of trying to exorcise demons that do not exist. Well-meaning, but misinformed ministers have inflicted much damage upon people by trying to cast out demons where there were none. We attempt to eliminate the possibility that a person's condition is physiological. We strongly advise a complete medical examination before inquiring into possible spiritual problems.

5. Take time to properly arrange for an appointment to meet in a comfortable room away from where other people can hear. Though we advise not allowing spirits to shriek or shout, they can surprise us at times.

6. Always conduct deliverance with a team of trusted Christians who are mature and operate in the revelation gifts.

Desperate parents need help

Many young people subject themselves to demonic spirits found in drugs, alcohol, witchcraft, promiscuous sex, and rebellion against any kind of authority. The woman from Canaan had a daughter who was subjected to these kinds of demonic spirits. Jesus showed us what to do in this next passage of Scripture:

Then Jesus went out from there and departed to the region of
Tyre and Sidon. And behold, a woman of Canaan came from that
region and cried out to Him, saying, "Have mercy on me, O Lord,
Son of David! My daughter is severely demon-possessed."

But He answered her not a word. And His disciples came
and urged Him, saying, "Send her away, for she cries out after
us." But He answered and said, "I was not sent except to the lost
sheep of the house of Israel." Then she came and worshiped Him,
saying, "Lord, help me!" But He answered and said, "It is not
good to take the children's bread and throw it to the little dogs."
And she said, "Yes, Lord, yet even the little dogs eat the crumbs
which fall from their masters' table." Then Jesus answered and
said to her, "O woman, great is your faith! Let it be to you as you
desire." And her daughter was healed from that very hour.

—Matthew 15:21–28, nkjv

- When people are willing to submit to Jesus
  Christ, His Word, and the leading of the Holy
  Spirit, they are eligible to be set free and receive the blessings of God.
- When all the conditions of the Holy Spirit
  are met and the ministry is complete, we
  proclaim the same words Jesus used: "Go
  your way; the demon has gone" (Mark 7:29).
  The demons leave because of the authority
  and power granted by Jesus Christ.

They came on Thursday

After training three teams to conduct deliverances at The 700 Club,
we set up appointments for the friends and acquaintances of the team
members. Thursday became known as "demon day." We would only
take one appointment in the morning and one in the afternoon. Those
who had completed the Sumrall video course were allowed to join in
the appointments as part of their training.

The interview process could take up to two hours; we thoroughly
discussed all possible "entrance points" where an entity might have
gained entrance into the person's soul nature. The questions were so
probing and specific that, if the person did have a demon oppressing

him or her, it would manifest during the interview process. If the person was truly experiencing demonic activity, we would make additional appointments until the person was completely free. It would normally take a second, two-hour session to cast out whatever spirits the Holy Spirit identified. Deliverances were always done in a very professional and closely monitored fashion.

The woman in a wheelchair

We were surprised by a demon during one of our Thursday deliverance appointments. We were ministering to a Christian woman who was confined to a wheelchair because of a spinal birth defect. She seemed normal in most respects, but she was slow of speech and had to rely on others to help her with daily routines. During the interview process, we discovered that an unclean spirit had tormented her since puberty. She began to weep uncontrollably as she tried to tell the deliverance team of a horrific experience with a young man who had raped her repeatedly. The Holy Spirit revealed that we were faced with an unclean spirit of lustful perversion that had a stronghold in her mind and body. When we told that spirit to come out of her, the demon screamed so loudly that the offices above and below could hear it. It was the most bloodcurdling scream I had ever heard. We immediately took authority over the spirit and commanded it to be quiet while we ministered to her. The lesson we learned from this event was to immediately do what Jesus did. He said, "Be quiet and come out!" (Mark 1:25). We know why He said that.

Victory was achieved

During that year and a half, I gained several insights regarding how spirits attach to those vulnerable to Satan's deceptions. These became evident during my oversight of the Thursday deliverance sessions. The experiences both Sonja and I have had are invaluable to what we are teaching today. We have absolutely no fear of demons. The Holy Spirit has always been gracious to lead us into total victory when we came face-to-face with powerful demonic forces. The following are some of the more valuable lessons we learned:

1. Focus on Christians that are having severe spiritual problems.

2. Pre-Christians need to repent and accept Jesus Christ as Lord before anything can be done for them.

3. The person needing deliverance should be the one to call for help. If the person is unwilling to come in for an interview, go no further.

4. Never allow the friends of the person to pressure you to act. Take sufficient time to interview and discover what may have caused the person's condition.

5. Get all the facts surrounding the person's history before committing to undertake deliverance.

6. If possible, talk to parents, siblings, close friends, and any Christian that really knows the person. The person should be informed that you are talking to these people.

7. Use terminology such as "personal prayer" instead of "deliverance" to the family or friends of the person receiving ministry.

8. Completely rule out physiological or medical problems, such as a bipolar condition, by insisting on a thorough medical examination before continuing.

9. Deliverance should never be viewed as a "quick fix" to a person's spiritual instability. Deliverance should be considered the first step, allowing a person to fully grasp dependence on the Lord Jesus Christ.

10. Successful deliverance requires follow up. Long-term, personal accountability is required for the person to stay free. The person must commit to avoiding the people or situations that caused the problem in the first place.

11. We suggest a Spirit-filled and very mature prayer partner to meet with the person regularly for about a year or more.

Monkey Temple experience

In America we are seeing a rise of demonic worship, and it produces fear-based results. I (Sonja) had a recent conversation with a

Spirit-filled Christian who attends our church. She had been a New Age devotee before coming to Christ. She related that she would visit a Monkey Temple in the Southwest to seek further enlightenment about the supernatural realm. Her little daughter would begin crying uncontrollably the moment they entered the temple. Finally, this mother was able to find out why her little one was so terrified. She said, "Mommy, can't you see those ugly things flying through the air around the monkey? They hate us and want to kill us." Apparently this child had a perception into the spirit world, and the Lord used it to put a stop to the visits into that demon-infested temple.

Stay out of those temples

Uninformed Christians are easy targets when their curiosity leads them to visit satanic, Buddhist, Hindu, or Islamic temples. We cannot stress enough how dangerous it is to visit such places of concentrated demonic activity. One time, I (Sonja) had a young mother come to me and explain that she had some extremely tormenting and scary spiritual activity going on in her life. I asked her if she could recall when it began. She immediately responded by telling me that it began the very night after she visited the Church of Satan while she was attending university in San Francisco. She and her girlfriends had decided to go out of curiosity—they were not seeking spirituality. That was a tragic mistake! Apparently, some spiritual entity (demonic spirit) attached itself to her. She was constantly tormented with fear and horrible nightmares.

I know who you are, and I hate you

I discerned the presence of spirits and asked the young woman if she truly wanted to be set free. When she said yes, I set up an appointment for the following week. The ministry team was composed of three pastors, the wife of one of the pastors, and me. We went into a prayer room, sat in a circle, and began to pray. The woman immediately lost consciousness and slipped to the floor. She was out like a light. We began to address the spirits, and the most horrible man's voice began to speak through her even though she was not conscious. "I know who you are, and I hate you!" the demon hissed. We commanded it to be quiet. It then began to violently throw the woman around on the floor. It took all three pastors, who were big men, to restrain her.

After about 10 minutes, the spirits were gone. We then called her by name, and she began to regain consciousness. She did not remember a thing, but she knew something wonderful had happened. Her hair was wet with perspiration, and she was exhausted. We led her into a complete understanding of repentance and salvation in the Lord Jesus Christ and the power in His blood that was shed on the cross. She was completely set free that day. Praise God for the power over Satan's minions!

The scary movie

When John was the area director for The 700 Club Crisis Counseling Center in Bellevue, Washington, he had a young family man who was in a place financially that allowed him to volunteer 40 hours a week at the center. He was well-educated and a faithful, Spirit-filled Christian. His family attended Eastside Foursquare Church with us. As we got to know him better, he shared his story with us.

When he was younger, he loved to attend horror movies. He loved the adrenaline rush; the gorier, the better. However, something happened that radically changed his life when he attended the movie, *The Exorcist*. He experienced something that literally scared him to within an inch of his life. He could feel a real presence pressing on his chest. As he tried to shake it off and could not, an ominous fear gripped him and left him terrified! He was sure it would leave him as soon as he left the theater, but it did not.

The fear would almost suffocate him

At night when he turned out the lights to go to sleep, this demonic presence would press in on him. The fear would almost suffocate him, and he would scream out and turn the lights on. He thought he was losing his mind, and he began crying out for understanding. God revealed Himself through a series of situations, and the man accepted the Lord and was eventually set free from the spirit of fear. We share this story as a warning to those innocent people who attend movies such as *The Exorcist*.

Psycho caught me off guard

I (Sonja) remember attending a movie when I was in high school called *Psycho*. I had no idea what it was about, and was completely caught off guard and emotionally unprepared for the shower scene where a woman was stabbed to death. The movie impacted me so strongly that for years I would not take a shower when I was home alone. Now I know that is stupid, but it shows how something like that can impact our emotions for an entire lifetime. I am concerned about the long-term negative effects of some of the movies and TV episodes that children watch. Let us be wise to the ways of the enemy!

SPIRITS VISIT OUR CHURCHES

Precious people who attend our churches may carry entities of shadows from their past that still plague them. They have learned to suppress the stronghold and cope with the feelings it produces because they feel there is no way to get rid of it. As leaders, we must realize that these people need help but they do not know where to get it. They attend church, hoping that God will somehow intervene. When the presence of the Holy Spirit manifests during worship or anointed preaching, deep-seated spirits may come to the surface. We should have a plan in place to deal with the inevitability of such an event.

They manifest at very inconvenient times

Demonic spirits always seem to manifest at inconvenient times. Their mission is to cause confusion and interrupt what the Holy Spirit is doing. They can manifest in classrooms, home meetings, and church services. They appear in the U.S. and in every other country where we minister. People used to think that all the demons were in Africa, but we know they can be found anywhere there are human beings. The following story should give us some insight about how to deal with demons when they manifest in our church services:

> Now there was a man in their synagogue with an unclean spirit. And he cried out, saying, "Let us alone! What have we to do with You, Jesus of Nazareth? Did You come to destroy us? I know who You are—the Holy One of God!" But Jesus rebuked him, saying, "Be quiet, and come out of him!" And when the unclean spirit had convulsed him and cried out with a loud voice, he came out of him. Then they were all amazed, so that they questioned among themselves, saying, "What is this? What new doctrine is this? For with authority He commands even the unclean spirits, and they obey Him."
>
> —MARK 1:23–27, NKJV

The person with an unclean spirit was in a church (synagogue). We may have to contend with demonized people who may visit our services. Jesus taught us how to confront a spirit that is attempting to disrupt a church service. Do the following:

- Quickly and firmly rebuke the spirit that is talking through the person by saying, "I forbid you to speak!" This will normally "bind" the person from causing any more disruption.
- Do not engage in conversation with the person.
- Instruct ushers to tactfully escort the person to a room with closed doors.
- Begin the deliverance with an experienced team. This is when to say, "Come out of him/her."

It happened in our classroom

One time John was teaching at our Ministry Training Institute. This particular lesson was in our advanced curriculum and was dealing with breaking spiritual bondages. The Holy Spirit gave him a word of knowledge that someone in the class was being oppressed by a spirit of fear. He no sooner got the word out of his mouth than a woman in the class began shrieking and crying. The spirit then went into full manifestation. John immediately went to the woman, took authority over the spirit and cast it out of the woman. It so happened that we were videotaping all of our classes at that time, so the entire incident was caught on film!

She was a Christian

The Lord has been gracious over the years to illustrate what we are teaching by real-life examples. We are humbled by His faithfulness to demonstrate His power with signs and wonders following the teaching of the Word. The above incident clearly illustrates how Christians can be oppressed of the devil and need deliverance. The woman had been in our class for over six months. She was saved and had been filled with the Holy Spirit. We knew she had some deep hurts from devastating life experiences, but we had not discerned the spirit of fear that ruled a big part of her life. It was through the supernatural gift of a word of knowledge that the Lord directed her deliverance from this tormenting spirit that had been in her life for years. How gracious is our God!

Spirits want to return

Once people are set free, we must help them stay free. Jesus encourages us to fill the house totally (body, soul, and spirit) with the Spirit of God. People must daily renew their minds with the Word of God and pray in their spiritual languages at every opportunity. They also need to fellowship weekly with healthy, Spirit-filled Christians. This is illustrated in the following scripture:

> When an unclean spirit goes out of a man, he goes through dry places, seeking rest, and finds none. Then he says, "I will return to my house from which I came." And when he comes, he finds it empty, swept, and put in order. Then he goes and takes with him seven other spirits more wicked than himself, and they enter and dwell there; and the last state of that man is worse than the first. So shall it also be with this wicked generation.
>
> —MATTHEW 12:43–45, NKJV

- Dry, waterless places are very difficult to define. It may mean a totally uninhabitable desert-like place. Such a description is given to the fallen city of Babylon as a dwelling place for demons in Revelation 18:2.
- Confirming people's salvation and leading them into the Holy Spirit baptism will ensure they are full of the Holy Spirit.
- If we neglect to do this, people are extremely vulnerable to the same entities that held them in bondage. Demons try to return and bring even more spirits with them.

He began to growl

One Tuesday evening during a home group meeting, we were teaching about the Holy Spirit baptism. Several people had indicated interest the previous week, and had asked us to lead them into the experience. After we had thoroughly taught on the subject, we asked those who wanted to receive the gift of the Holy Spirit and their spiritual language to go to the dining room area. Four women and a man responded. As we began to lay hands on them and pray, the man began growling in a guttural voice. He doubled over as the spirit manifested. I (Sonja) was standing next to him, so I was the first to see what was happening.

Whoops, there is a spirit here

John was on the other side of the room, so I quickly went to him and told him what was happening. He went to the man and quickly discerned it was a lying spirit. It was telling him he was not worthy to receive this gift. As he tried to respond to our teaching, the spirit showed itself. John dealt with the spirit in the mighty name of Jesus Christ, and it left. It was a great teaching time for our group, most of whom had never witnessed a spirit acting out in a person's life.

I am scared of that "demon stuff"

The humorous thing about that evening was that a woman had said to her husband on the way to the meeting that night, "Honey, I hope I am never around when that 'demon stuff' happens. I think it would scare me to death." Afterward, however, she relayed how grateful she was that she was able to observe the whole incident because it dispelled her fears. She said it was the most natural thing she could ever imagine. The evil spirit manifested in an ugly way, but the power of the name of Jesus Christ simply took authority over it and it left. Easy as that! She was amazed.

Leadership couple seeks deliverance

While ministering to leaders in a central California church, we opened a discussion on how unclean spirits can gain footholds in our lives. We mentioned how they have a lifetime to play hide-and-seek until they have established a firm stronghold, causing people to lie and deceive. To our amazement, a leadership couple came to John after the service. The husband told John that he had experienced exactly what we had described, and that he had begun lying to his wife about the sinful behavior. His wife was at her wit's end. John got one of the pastors to minister with him, and they set that young man free from the perverse and lying spirits in the name of Jesus Christ. Then they established accountability in the young man's life; and the last we checked, he was doing great.

As is often the case, John learned that an uncle had molested the man when he was young, and he had a leaning toward pornography, but the total enslavement came when he kept indulging the impulse via the Internet. One day he discovered that he could not stop, even when he understood the horrific ramifications of living in willful sin and possibly losing his precious wife.

Willful sin is dangerous

This story demonstrates what happens in demonic bondage. It can be alcohol, drugs, shoplifting, lying, gossiping, and similar destructive behaviors. It is extremely dangerous for a Christian to continue in willful sin. It has been said of sin that it always takes you further than you wanted to go, keeps you longer than you wanted to stay, costs you more than you wanted to pay, and damages you more than you can ever imagine. It can have eternal consequences.

If you are reading this and you feel what we have described has happened to you, please seek help immediately from a pastor who understands this spiritual dimension and how to exercise God-given authority so that you may be set free. The minister needs to have the supernatural revelation gifts of the Holy Spirit operating in his life if he is to be effective in this type of ministry.

OBSCENE PHONE CALLS AND MENTAL HOSPITALS

One day a dear friend called me (Sonja) and related a heartbreaking story. His father had been fired from a job he loved and, as a consequence, had lost a large part of his retirement benefits. My friend lived in another state and asked me if I would visit his parents, who lived in my city. It was a difficult thing for me to do. I had known this couple since I was in high school and had always had great respect for them.

After greeting the older couple with hugs and tears, I listened carefully as their story unfolded. It was painful for them and me as he answered my respectful, but probing questions. He had indulged in pornographic material for years, but something had happened the previous year that changed his life. He had begun to make obscene telephone calls to women. Before long, the police had traced the calls to him at his workplace. No one wanted to press charges because he was well-liked and respected at his place of employment. He was simply given a verbal warning.

Within a matter of days he made more calls. Of course, he was caught and given a written warning that, should the behavior occur again, his employment would be terminated. All of the ramifications of terminated employment were explained, including retirement plans and health insurance. His company offered to send him to a psychiatrist, but he refused the offer for help. Even when he knew that his telephone was under surveillance, he made more obscene telephone calls. By this time, his wife was weeping uncontrollably, and I was having trouble believing this incredible story.

He continued his story. The police came to his place of employment and arrested him on the spot in front of his coworkers. He was immediately terminated, with the resultant financial loss. There was an article in the local newspaper, and the humiliation and shame were almost more than they could bear.

He said he was "under its spell"

When I asked him why in the world he went ahead and made those final calls even knowing that his telephone was being monitored, he said a very revealing thing:

> I knew in my mind that this would ruin my life, my marriage, my retirement. I also realized it would bring shame on my children, but I could not resist the compulsion to make the calls. It was as if something came upon me at those times, and I was under its spell and I was powerless to resist.

That describes the state of a person under demonic influence. The man was not ready to hear the good news of salvation and deliverance through Jesus Christ, but his wife was, and she rededicated herself to the Lord that night. The man lived many more years under the torment of that evil spirit and did not truly repent and accept the Lord until he was on his deathbed. What a waste to live all those years under Satan's power. Yet God's unbelievable love and mercy were graciously extended.

Generational spirits

We have all heard the expression: "He has a horrible temper just like his father." All families pass on habits, characteristics, and behaviors, but family spirits can also pass from one generation to another if they go undetected.

In the case I just described, the unclean spirit was most likely passed along to his son, our friend. Even though he was a Spirit-filled Christian, he had never dealt with this fascination he had with pornography, primarily magazines and videos. Because he continued in willful disobedience to God, the very same thing happened to him. He was arrested for making obscene telephone calls and fired from his job. Unbelievable as it seems, knowing what happened to his father, he did the same thing. This happened after he became addicted to Internet porn.

I said they should immediately come to our home

After his arrest and subsequent release, his wife called me (Sonja) and I said they should immediately come to our home. They arrived within hours of our phone call. The man was a highly respected person in their community, and this was a devastating blow to him, his wife, family, work associates, and friends. He appeared to be in an emotional meltdown when he arrived. His wife was trying to decide if she was going to initiate divorce proceedings.

We called our associate minister and, after determining that our friend's repentance was deep and genuine, John and our associate—right there in our living room—led him through a complete and thorough deliverance. It was an amazing transformation before their very eyes.

We earnestly prayed for wisdom from on high

All the while, I (Sonja) was with the wife, helping her process the unbelievable pain she was experiencing. She told me of losing respect for her mother-in-law when she did not leave her husband when he was arrested and fired. And she was facing the very same circumstances. We talked about how deliverance works and that restoration was possible. She wanted to believe, but it was difficult to imagine how such a horrific breach could be healed. We earnestly prayed for wisdom from on high.

Totally free

The deliverance was complete and total. The couple did everything we recommended, including getting into a good Spirit-filled church. Now they are totally and completely free and healed. Their marriage is the best it has ever been, and they are serving God with everything they have. What a victory! What a joy! Only our God could perform such a miracle!

A friend ended up in the mental ward

A friend of ours has a bipolar condition, and if he does not take his medication, he becomes delusional. Once he ended up in the psychiatric ward of a local hospital. His family called and asked us to go see him. They told us that he thought the FBI was following him, watching his every move, and getting ready to arrest him. He was paranoid to the point that he was afraid to go to work.

We began talking with him about what he was experiencing. We looked him right in the eyes and told him we knew these things were absolutely real *to him*, but that they were not so. We did not discern any spirits, but sensed it was truly a physical problem that produced the abnormal mental behaviors.

There were no FBI agents chasing him

This man loved and trusted us, but it was hard for him to believe that *his reality* was not true. We reinforced what the doctors and his family had told him, that the medication would put him back in touch with the reality we all were experiencing—there were no FBI agents chasing him. After a few weeks on the medication, he was fine again. He is a brilliant man and does not like the medication because it seems to slow down some of his mental functions. We think that is why people with this and similar conditions quit taking their meds. The appropriate response at this juncture is to pray for healing, which we are doing for our friend. It seems that spirits do not respond to medication, but physical problems do.

The movie, *A Beautiful Mind*, released in 2002, is based on the life of John Nash, the brilliant mathematician. It portrays how he coped with his condition and was awarded the Nobel Prize. We pray that this insightful film will raise our nation's consciousness and understanding of the people who suffer with these conditions.

A BAPTIST GIRL LEARNS ABOUT DEMONS

After I (Sonja) was baptized in the Holy Spirit at age 27, I immediately became a serious student of the Bible. It had become alive and totally relevant. One unlikely subject for a Baptist girl to study was demonization, yet I was fascinated by the New Testament accounts of this supernatural activity. I read everything I could find on the subject. They were mostly accounts by missionaries in developing countries.

They told me I should leave all of that weird stuff alone

One time my pastors stopped by for a quick visit, and they noticed the stack of books I was reading. They told me I should leave all that weird stuff alone. No good would come of it. I was surprised at their adverse reaction to the subject of the supernatural, so I thought I had better listen to them. I put the books aside for a couple of weeks and asked the Lord to lead me in the matter.

The Holy Spirit as "the Teacher" was leading me

My interest in the supernatural not only remained but also dramatically increased. Looking back, I was being led by the Holy Spirit as "the Teacher." It was good that I had listened to the cautions of my pastors because I became extremely critical of everything I read. Could I find correlations in the Bible? If not, I was very suspect of the accounts. By this time I had read the Bible through several times and had learned to use good study aids, including an interlinear Greek-English New Testament. I always leaned toward the more conservative side of theology, and I felt comfortable there.

I was being prepared for a very special assignment

Little did I know that I was being prepared for a very special assignment—one I would not have dreamed of in a million years! My Grammy Hatcher was thrilled at my spiritual growth since I had been baptized in the Holy Spirit. She was my biggest fan and was amazed at how easily I was leading people into the Holy Spirit baptism.

One day Grammy called me and asked if I would be willing to meet with her good friend's son who had just returned to Richland, Washington, after a drug-filled lifestyle in the Seattle area. I could not imagine what I could say to a young man addicted to drugs—I was as straight as could be!

I asked her why she thought I should do this, and she explained that the young man had been walking in downtown Seattle, and he was literally struck down on the sidewalk and could not move. He said he knew that God was telling him he was soon going to be dead if he did not get right with Him. He immediately returned home to a praying mother who arranged for him to meet with her Pentecostal pastor. Apparently, it was not a good experience for either of them, and the mother was desperate for someone to help her son. Thus, the call came from Grammy.

The body art on his arms really caught my eye

I reluctantly agreed to meet with the young man the next Saturday afternoon. Grammy, his mother, and my Saturday morning prayer group were interceding for this appointment. The doorbell rang, and I opened the door to a most unusual sight. The young man who stood there had arms that were covered in fluorescent pink body art. He towered over me, and appeared to be in his early twenties—and he had the emptiest eyes I had ever seen. I am sure he was also sizing me up and thinking what in the world would this obviously super-straight little woman have to say that would be relevant to his life.

The Holy Spirit came upon me in a most unusual way

I asked the young man to have a seat and tell me what was happening in his life. He was understandably nervous and began to relate the sidewalk encounter with God. While he was speaking, the Holy Spirit came upon me in a most unusual way. I was totally immersed in God's agape love for this young man. My heart cried out, "Dear Lord, how many of these lost young people are out there? They are on their way to hell and without hope in a hostile world. No wonder they are medicating themselves with drugs, sex, or who knows what else!"

Somehow, through God's extravagant grace, we connected. I felt the young man's fear and confusion, and he felt God's love emanating from me. All of a sudden he jumped up, startling me, and he said, "Lady, you put out the most far-out vibes I have ever felt! May I come back and bring a couple of friends?"

I later learned that they were big drug dealers

He did return with two friends that I later learned were big drug dealers in our area. Within a couple of weeks the group had grown to around 30, and it was an unbelievable sight. People were having genuine encounters with the living Christ by truly repenting, turning their backs on drugs, and seeking to please their new Lord. One night, kids were sitting on every available space in our living room/ dining room; they all had their Bibles out and were discussing what Jesus meant by a certain passage. I had to laugh, however, as I looked around, because the house was full of smoke. Many churchgoing folks would have thrown up their hands in disgust if they had walked in at that moment. But those kids had come a long way in a matter of weeks, and smoking cigarettes was a pretty minor thing at that point.

My house was staked out

A few weeks after that, one of the former drug dealers asked me if I knew that the police had staked out my house. I was completely surprised and asked him why. He told me to just think about it for a moment. All of a sudden the biggest drug dealers and users in the area were carrying around big black Bibles and congregating in a certain home several times a week. Would you not find that of interest if you were the police? I smacked my forehead with my palm, and marveled at how naive I was. I had been thrust into an entirely new culture.

I have already run narcs into your group

I called the parents of one of the kids and asked if they would go with me to see the chief of police. We made an appointment for the next afternoon. I had never personally met the chief of police, but I knew that he had a good reputation in our town. As we walked into his office, he stood up, walked around his desk, and put out his hand. "Before you say anything," he began, "I want you to know I am a born-again Christian, and I believe what is happening at your home is the only hope for the youth of our community! I know this because I have already run narcs [narcotics agents] into your group, and the reports are most positive. They don't understand all the religious stuff, but they said it is wholesome." I stood there shaking this man's hand with my mouth hanging open. When our group became too large to meet in homes, the police department gave us four hundred dollars to pay the rent on our first meeting place.

My special assignment

I had received a special assignment for which I had been training without even knowing it. Most of the kids we were discipling came from middle- or upper-class homes. They had attended church at some point in their lives, but it had become irrelevant as they grew disillusioned with life in general. They were easy prey for experimenting with drugs and the associated breakdown of all morals. Stealing to support their drug habits became the norm. The ones who had used hallucinogenic drugs were in a pitiful state.

As they came to trust me, they began to relate the horrific experiences they had while "tripping." Most of them were still having flashbacks that came without warning. To my amazement, they were describing demonic encounters just like the ones described by the missionaries. I shared what I had learned in the previous months of study. As they read the New Testament accounts of Jesus taking authority over the evil spirits, they believed that they, too, could be set free, and they were. It was pretty amazing. The first ones set free were setting the others free in a matter of weeks. They simply used the books to show examples of how demons work and then showed them in the Bible that Jesus set people free.

Talk about power-encounters

I know these supernatural deliverances were what made Christianity relevant to them. They had experienced dead religion and wanted no part of it. Talk about power-encounters! They needed them, and they received them! Yes, the Holy Spirit knew exactly what He was doing when He led me to study to show myself approved (2 Timothy 2:15).

About that time an evangelistic couple from Canada came to our area, and several of the young men went to hear them. They came back quite excited because they were dealing with demons, and people were getting healed. My parents were in the middle of all this with me, so I dragged them over to the tent meeting. Sure enough, they were preaching a full gospel message with signs and wonders following.

Some were barefoot

We met with the evangelists after the service and explained what was happening with our group. I asked them if they would consider doing some teaching. By this time I was feeling overwhelmed. None of the churches in our area wanted these hippies to influence their young people. I had taken a group to visit my evangelical church. Some of them were barefoot; one had on overalls, no shirt, no shoes, and a hat that he did not remove during the service. I was so thrilled with what was happening in their lives that their appearances did not matter to me. But the members of my church just did not have that kind of grace. They were happy that they were getting saved, but they wanted them to be someplace else.

Jesus people

The Canadian couple had a few more commitments in the Northwest, and then they agreed to return. We became a church with about 400, and Grammy and my parents were right in the middle of it all. Our worship was fantastic, and the new leaders brought wonderful pastor-teacher friends to minister to these "Jesus people." History shows us that we were a part of a sovereign move of God that began on the West Coast of America among hippie drug users. It is heartening now after more than 40 years to hear from some of the original young people in the group. They are pastors, evangelists, and missionaries, and they have been doing what Jesus did all these years!

Jesus is our hero and supreme example

Setting people free from spiritual bondages is not an easy thing. It can be a confusing, messy ministry. We certainly do not seek it out; however, we deal with it when it becomes necessary in fulfilling the assignments the Lord gives us. Most often in Jesus' ministry, He was walking along to some place when He was interrupted by the need, met it, and went on His way. He is our hero and supreme example!

Only Christians can do it

Only the Christian belief system has the power and authority to cause spirits to obey spoken commands. All other belief systems either worship and appease them or deny their existence. When confronted with spirits, their attempt to deal with the situation results in confusion, fear, and frustration. An example of this is in the following scripture:

> Then some of the itinerant Jewish exorcists took it upon them-
> selves to call the name of the Lord Jesus over those who had
> evil spirits, saying, "We exorcise you by the Jesus whom Paul
> preaches." Also there were seven sons of Sceva, a Jewish chief
> priest, who did so. And the evil spirit answered and said, "Jesus
> I know, and Paul I know; but who are you?" Then the man in
> whom the evil spirit was leaped on them, overpowered them,
> and prevailed against them, so that they fled out of that house
> naked and wounded.
> —Acts 19:13–16, nkjv

- Only Spirit-filled Christians are authorized and empowered by Jesus Christ to cast out demons. The demons know who has the authority and who does not. They will challenge us to find out if we know what we are doing.
- Demons give superhuman power to those they possess. We have nothing to fear when we engage them in the name of Jesus Christ and under the leading of the Holy Spirit.
- Superhuman power is reduced to nothing when the Christian boldly stands in the power of the blood of Christ and commands the spirit to obey in the name of Jesus Christ.

Intercessors are imperative

If you are doing this type of ministry or if you are desiring to, we urge you to ask God to give you believers who will cover you in prayer. We have over 100 faithful intercessors that intercede on our behalf. Their prayers are so powerful that we can actually feel the effects— especially when we are in foreign countries where the spiritual battles are intense. Jesus Christ wants us to function as a body with everyone contributing according to their giftedness. Thank You, Lord, for our intercessors!

IT IS OUR RESPONSIBILITY

Many Christians refer to the above seven sons of Sceva episode as a personal warning not to get involved with demons or deliverance. Not so! This scripture is a warning to pre-Christians. For Christians who know their authority and power, it is an invitation to exercise this authority and set people free!

The people who do not have a relationship with Jesus Christ have an ever-increasing dilemma. They are unknowingly being prevailed upon and seduced by demonic influences. Demons are literally leaping upon them, overpowering them, and causing some to run out of houses naked. Their minds are becoming so poisoned and twisted by drugs, lies, and hopelessness that the demons are causing them to commit suicide. The evening news is replete with children being kidnapped, sexually assaulted, and murdered. Our senses are barraged with reports of murders, rapes, and evil violence. Every part of society is bombarded with horrific images of our youth being swallowed up by demonic powers beyond their control.

Their hope is Christ in us, the hope of glory

We are the only hope for this lost and dying world. If we do not answer our Lord's call to go into our part of the world and set people free and do what He said we could do, then who will? We have the answer! It is Christ in us, the hope of glory. Jesus has given us His name, His authority, and His power to take up where He left off. Our only response is what Isaiah said, "Here am I, send me" (Isaiah 6:8).

LET'S PRACTICE

James 1:22 says to do what we have heard (read).

Consider doing what is recommended in this chapter by referring to the "Let's Practice" in Appendix B, page 263.

Do the Ministry Skill Assignment titled, "Dealing with Demons."

Chapter 7

WHERE DO WE GO FROM HERE?

O NCE WE HAVE discovered all that Jesus Christ has done for us, we are commanded to go tell others and teach them to observe everything He commanded.

> All authority has been given to Me in heaven and on earth. *Go* therefore and make disciples of all the nations, baptizing them in the name of the Father and of the Son and of the Holy Spirit, teaching them to observe all things that I have commanded you; and lo, I am with you always, even to the end of the age. Amen.
> —MATTHEW 28:18–20, NKJV, EMPHASIS ADDED

> *He sent* them to preach the kingdom of God and to heal the sick.
> —LUKE 9:2, NKJV, EMPHASIS ADDED

> *Go,* preach, saying, "The kingdom of heaven is at hand." Heal the sick, cleanse the lepers, raise the dead, and cast out demons. Freely you have received, freely give.
> —MATTHEW 10:7–8, NKJV, EMPHASIS ADDED

GO!

We can do it

With a change of thinking and some training, we can do what Jesus did. Jesus has empowered, authorized, and commanded us to go do what He did. It is more than going to church; it is more than going to a Bible study or prayer meeting. It means going into our part of the world and touching people with the gospel of salvation, empowerment of the Holy Spirit, physical healing, and setting them free from demonic bondages.

True miracles are needed

We totally understand why Christians have been reluctant to answer the Lord's commands to go. Few know they should be doing it, and even fewer have been taught how. It takes a radical change in thinking and hands-on training to change people's lives. Our point is this: Many people around the world will fail to be drawn to Jesus Christ unless they experience an authentic manifestation of God's glory.

> Believe me when I say that I am in the Father and the Father is in me; or at least believe on the evidence of the miracles themselves.
> —JOHN 14:11

- Miracles authenticate our message as being from God.
- The messenger who preaches the gospel of the Lord Jesus Christ, allowing for and expecting signs and wonders to follow, demonstrates that the message is from a life-changing God who is alive and real.

WHERE DO WE BEGIN?

In the previous chapters, we have carefully documented how we came to believe in miracles and to expect God to do them through us. It took 30 years to get to where we are today, but it does not have to take that long for others to get there. We believe it can take about a year, perhaps two at the most. It all depends on how serious a believer is about pursuing God.

We believe the road to doing what Jesus did is very straight and simple. For some it will be easy; for others it requires a change of thinking. It seems that the more sophisticated and highly educated we are, the more difficult the journey. But it does not have to be that way. Jesus advocates becoming like a trusting child in how we believe and apply the gospel to our personal lives.

Beginning to do what Jesus did may require setting aside rigid mindsets that have impaired our vision of who Jesus has made us to be. It does not matter how long people have been Christians. The challenge is how long it takes to get equipped so we can set others free in the name of Jesus. It may seem difficult, but it can be done.

Training should be through the local church

We believe that the logical place for believers to be trained to do what Jesus did is through their local churches. It is not by running off to every conference and revival they hear about. It is the deep longing for the reality of the supernatural that causes people to be constantly on the search for that something they know they are lacking.

Systematic teaching and hands-on experience in a classroom environment is the best way to meet this need. We know from first-hand experience that this model works extremely well. The following Appendix A outlines exactly how pastors are using the *Ambassador Series* and *Doing What Jesus Did* in Ministry Training Institutes in their local churches.

All training must have a hands-on practicum element

In our opinion, whatever training you decide to use must have a hands-on practicum element that exposes people to the supernatural in a safe environment.

By laying a strong scriptural foundation concurrent with the practicum sessions, we avoid non-biblical experiences and excesses. We do this by basing our experiences on the Word. When hungry Christians go to conferences or revivals in other locations, they can easily get caught up in the emotional fervor and fall into copycat behavior rather than authentic, Holy Spirit manifestations.

The power of God

We are contending for the powerful expressions of the Holy Spirit as demonstrated by our Lord Jesus Christ. As we have stated, there are ample Scripture references for us to follow in all of these things. We sometimes see the power of God come upon people in such a mighty way that they cannot stand under it. That is authentic. But to have people line up so they can all fall down is manipulative, contrived behavior. The Holy Spirit does not need our assistance. It is sad when Christians develop the attitude that nothing of value is happening unless they are on the floor.

HERE IS HOW IT COULD WORK

We are not advocating that this type of ministry training replace or alter a church's weekend services. Rather, it would involve something like the following:

1. The senior pastor determines that training his congregation to do what Jesus did is something the Lord is leading him to do.

2. Training classes with practicum are offered on a once-a-week basis.

3. Those completing the classes become or enhance the organized prayer ministry in the church (after-service prayer, hospital visitations, emergency counseling, etc.).

4. Students with identified gifts of discerning of spirits, words of knowledge and wisdom, and faith can be trained and formed into teams to set people free from demonic bondages. This, of course, is under pastoral oversight. Through a structured interview process, this can be a wonderful ministry to church members. Again, this should be done in the context of the local church where proper accountability and follow-up exist.

5. Students who complete the training will have become effective marketplace ministers. They will be doing what Jesus did, and will they be excited!

Weekend services can be "visitor sensitive"

The classroom instruction is at the church, and the trained believers can relieve the pastoral staff of much prayer and personal ministry. But the actual weekend church services are altered very little. We feel they should be "visitor sensitive" in the sense that members and attendees can feel safe to invite their friends, neighbors, relatives, and coworkers. In other words, members will not have to worry about something happening that they cannot explain. People will not risk looking foolish. However, the trained prayer team should always be available for after-service prayer ministry, including prayer for healing, etc.

Mid-week believers' meeting

Mid-week services can be structured as a believers' meeting with the release of the gifts of the Holy Spirit. Leadership should inform those in attendance that the focus is definitely for believers. These meetings can be powerful and life-changing. Prolonged worship allows people to truly enter into the presence of the Lord. Corporate singing in tongues is a tremendously edifying spiritual experience. The key to successful believers' meetings is to have strong platform leadership that is sensitive to the Holy Spirit's leading and will not allow nonsense. When the Holy Spirit is directing, everything will be done decently and in order by edifying, exhorting, and comforting the worshipers. The end result is that the Lord Jesus Christ will be exalted.

Small group growth

Small group leaders who have been given ministry training can encourage the release of the supernatural gifts and ministry to those in attendance at their meetings. From years of personal experience, we know it adds the dynamic that causes growth and excitement in the lives of those involved.

Strategy for the end-time harvest

Our burning desire is to see believers trained to be effective marketplace ministers just like Jesus was. He wants us to lead people into salvation, baptism in the Holy Spirit, and healing. He also wants to set them free from spiritual bondages. Then He wants us to bring them to church and disciple them so they can do the same. That is how the world will be won. That is a fine strategy for the end-time harvest. If you are not already engaged in this awesome and eternal activity, please join us!

So there you have it! It is really pretty simple—properly train believers and show them how to do what Jesus did, and they will!

Appendix A

HOW TO ESTABLISH A MINISTRY TRAINING INSTITUTE

EVERY CHURCH IS A TRAINING CENTER

THE LOCAL CHURCH is the logical place to begin training Christians to become effective "marketplace ministers," that is, effective disciples that know how to share their Christian testimony, lead people to Christ, pray for them to be baptized in the Holy Spirit, and pray for the sick. Advanced training would include how to hear from God, the discerning of spirits, and setting people free from spiritual bondages. Over the last 20 years, we have proven this can be done without making people weird. Ministry Training Institutes (MTIs) are producing biblically based lay ministers who can relieve the salaried staff by assuming most of the prayer ministry, hospital visitations, and other time-consuming areas of ministry.

We learn by doing

It is a major decision for pastors to begin training members to operate in the supernatural. Many pastors want to avoid the recent excesses reminiscent of the Methodist camp meetings at Cane Ridge, Kentucky in 1801. Vinson Synan, author of *The Holiness Pentecostal Tradition*, said, "Their 'Godly hysteria' included such phenomena as falling, jerking, barking like dogs, falling into trances, the 'holy laugh' and 'such wild dances as David performed before the Ark of the Lord.'"[1] The excesses can be avoided when the training is biblical, well thought out, high quality, practical, and totally reproducible. To be effective, the training must include a balance of sound theology while giving multiple opportunities for every student to experience hands-on ministry. Everything should be done under the watchful eyes of mature trainers, who can discern the difference between authentic manifestations of the Holy Spirit and weirdness. Using *Doing What Jesus Did* and the *Ambassador Series* as the curriculum, trainers have everything they need to produce effective, reproducing disciples of Jesus Christ.

THE AMBASSADOR SERIES

Using the authors' *Ambassador Series* and this book, local churches can establish a Ministry Training Institute in any part of the world. It is remarkable that the curriculum works for a meeting place in third world countries as well as megachurches in America and everything in between. We attribute this to the Holy Spirit's influence and anointing that accompany the teaching and hands-on training sessions.

First, select an equipper

We recommend that the senior pastor not be the one who runs the Ministry Training Institute, especially in larger churches. He or she is already too busy. We do recommend that the senior pastor be a part of the MTI teaching team. The person in charge must have a vision for training people to do what Jesus did. Obviously, the instructors must have experience operating in the supernatural. You cannot show someone how to work with the Holy Spirit unless you have done it.

Teachers with experience and a hunger for operating in supernatural ministry obviously make the best trainers. Though hard to find, they exist throughout the body of Christ. Retired or returning missionaries can be a terrific resource. Being trained by leaders in the local church who are operating in the supernatural of God is the quickest and best way to transfer the same anointing to those being trained. This is how we train MTI trainers. The students start doing what their trainers have been doing.

This is how Jesus trained the first disciples. This is how it can be done today. First, they watched Jesus do it. Then, they helped Jesus do it. Next, Jesus watched as they did it. Finally, they did it when Jesus was no longer with them. Today, we call this mentoring.

Second, train the trainers

Leaders with a calling to disciple Christians are encouraged to attend a two-day Teacher Intensive and DWJD Workshop. The train-the-trainer workshop is designed for pastors, teachers, and leaders. On a Friday night and Saturday, leaders are shown how to teach The Ambassador

Series and conduct the six ministry skills from *Doing What Jesus Did.* The leaders are then authorized to order and teach the curriculum. CDs of the six-volume *Ambassador Series* are available as teaching aids for leaders. The CDs are reviewed prior to teaching the lessons and are full of teaching tips and ideas to make the curriculum come alive.

Administrative and practicum guides are made available to leaders so they can put together a successful ministry institute. Any leader, pastor, or teacher who has attended a Teacher Intensive and DWJD Workshop will be fully equipped to oversee or conduct an enduring Ministry Training Institute.

Third, plan for a nine-month institute We recommend a nine-month schedule for an MTI. In the USA, it should be offered concurrent with the school year (September-June) with a graduation immediately following. The three-hour, once-a-week class is offered in an evening format. Leaders wonder if people are willing to make such a long commitment. We have addressed this issue by having them commit to twelve weeks at a time. By the time they have finished the first twelve weeks, you cannot keep them away! We have very little attrition because of the exciting hands-on ministry skill sessions. The graduation is a special time when the graduates receive a formal diploma in practical ministry, along with the laying on of hands and being commissioned as ambassadors for Christ.

MTI is a proven concept

The MTIs worldwide are doing what Jesus did. The classes are structured for maximum effectiveness. MTI trains the trainers how to train others. Effective discipleship must be more than a teacher conducting classes where students take notes. True discipleship is personally working with disciples until they know what the mentor knows and can do what the mentor can do. That is how Jesus did it. MTI functions the same way.

A TYPICAL CLASS SESSION

Worship and teaching

First, strong worship of the Lord helps put everyone into the right frame of mind. Second, the trainers teach two lessons on the many facets of living the abundant life in Christ, obeying God's Word, and doing marketplace ministry. Students receive comprehensive training manuals in which to record personal illustrations so they can reteach the lesson in the future.

Divide into practicum groups

After the teaching sessions, the entire class is divided into groups of ten or less where every student practices the ministry skill from *Doing What Jesus Did*. Every student is scheduled to demonstrate the ministry skills in conjunction with the teaching of the *Ambassador Series*. This is done until every disciple feels confident to attempt the skills in the marketplace. Over the nine months, all six ministry skills are practiced until mastered: leading people to Christ, the Holy Spirit baptism, healing the sick, hearing from God, healing the sick by revelation, and dealing with demons. An optional preaching practicum is offered for those preparing for public ministry.

Everyone receives ministry

The highlight of the weekly gathering is that students will both give and receive one-on-one prayer ministry whenever there is a need. When it is time for a student to demonstrate the assigned ministry skill, it is done within a group of ten or less with a trained leader. Afterward, that student can request personal ministry for current needs. The others are encouraged to respond and pray over the person. The Holy Spirit will often manifest in profound ways, using another student through whom revelation or healing will take place. Everyone gets to minister and receive ministry. Students go home praising God for what they have personally experienced each week. The love quotient and bonding produced in these classes are amazing. It produces true, biblical *koinonia*.

Graduation comes after doing it for real

In order to graduate and receive a diploma in Practical Ministry, student ministers must demonstrate that they can do all six ministry skills. The "final exam" requires that they take what they have learned and "do it for real" in the marketplace. They must make two attempts to lead someone to Christ, two attempts to lead believers into the Holy Spirit baptism, and two attempts to heal the sick. All of the attempts must be done outside of the classroom, in the marketplace.

Confidence is catching

During the last month of training, the testimonies of doing what Jesus did "for real" start coming in. Students give spontaneous reports of healings, deliverances, and various miracles as they attempted to fulfill the marketplace assignments. It always brings a smile to the instructors when they hear exciting testimonies of how the Holy Spirit took over the attempts and turned them into genuine "doing what Jesus did" success stories.

Months before, these students had been ineffective and even fearful of reaching out in the name of Christ. By the time the training is completed, they are going into their part of the world and doing greater things for God than they ever dreamed possible.

HERE IS HOW TO GET STARTED

Trainers must experience the MTI mentoring dynamic. The hands-on practicum is the heart of the training and cannot be learned by reading a book. We have developed the fast-paced DWJD workshops so pastors and leaders can experience how to conduct the ministry skill sessions. Teacher aids are also available for teachers to start an exciting MTI in their church.

Teacher training

We cannot improve on Jesus' strategy for training believers. He put His life into a small group of "trainers" who turned the world upside down. Here is how it is done:

1. MTI will "train the trainers" in regional Teacher Intensives that are open to any active leader involved in pastoring, teaching, evangelizing, or missionary work.

2. The senior pastor of an established church must initiate the inquiry for hosting a Teacher Intensive.

3. Tentative dates, training location, and costs for hosting a regional Teacher Intensive are negotiated and agreed upon with the host church.

4. Other pastors in the region with a vision for ministry training are contacted and invited to participate.

5. Once a final list of participating churches is confirmed, a firm date and training location are established.

6. Updates and other details are available through the website, www.ministrytraining.org.

Teacher Intensive content

The training is conducted on a Friday night and all day Saturday. Leaders learn how to do the following:

1. Teach the *Ambassador Series* and learn how to minister and teach the DWJD ministry skills.

2. Prepare for and conduct a nine-month, church-based MTI.

3. Implement the administrative tasks, including ordering materials, and conducting an MTI graduation.

The word is spreading fast

We started our first Ministry Training Institute in our home church in the fall of 1996; by the end of six years over one hundred training locations were functioning in 17 countries. The need is overwhelming! Christian leaders all over the world are hungering for a way to introduce the supernatural power of God into their churches in a sane and biblical way. Pastors who lacked confidence in doing this kind of ministry are now confidently leading their people into the Holy Spirit baptism, acting on a word of knowledge for healing, and teaching others how to do the same. Genuine excitement has returned to the church as they are doing what Jesus did.

THE CURRICULUM: DOING WHAT JESUS DID

You are holding the key to a successful Ministry Training Institute. This book should be required reading for everyone enrolled in an MTI. Each chapter is dedicated to showing how we can minister in the revelation and power of the Holy Spirit. It will become the handbook for doing the things Jesus said we could do.

THE *AMBASSADOR SERIES*

The *Ambassador Series* is a three-term, 72-lesson discipleship training course authored by John and Sonja Decker and is being used in churches worldwide. These lessons are the academic segment of the curriculum used in all MTIs. There are a total of six volumes.

The *Ambassador Series* is composed of Discipleship One, Two, and Three. Each level consists of 24 lessons, taught in 12 weeks. Six weeks are dedicated to learning each one of the ministry skills. The content of each lesson can be reviewed by visiting our website, www.ministrytraining.org.

Discipleship One
Foundations for Discovery and Disciplines of the Disciple
The ministry skills are leading people to Christ and leading Christians into the Holy Spirit baptism.

Discipleship Two
Bible Basics and The Christian Life
The ministry skills are learning how to heal the sick and hearing from God.

Discipleship Three
Kingdom Living and Equipped for Leadership
The ministry skills are healing the sick by revelation, dealing with demons, and preaching the full gospel (optional).

THE MINISTRY TRAINING INSTITUTE

Discipleship One, Two, and Three can be completed in a nine-month time frame, allowing three hours per week for the ministry training. Two 45-minute lessons and a 45-minute practicum session are conducted each week. A six-month version is available that covers all the lessons and ministry skills. For details, see the following website: www.ministrytraining.org.

Graduation
Both the *Ambassador Series* and the six ministry skills are designed to equip believers to go into their parts of the world and make disciples by doing what Jesus did. Students receive instruction in orthodox

and very practical theology; at least one-third of the time is dedicated to learning the six ministry skills. The course equips disciples with the tools necessary for effective evangelism. Jesus preached, taught, and healed the sick. Graduates of MTIs can do what He did.

A PERSONAL INVITATION

If you have read this far, you undoubtedly know that our (John and Sonja's) passion is to see the body of Christ equipped to do what Jesus did. We are assisting pastors in establishing Ministry Training Institutes in local churches around the globe. Please contact the MTI offices if you are interested in learning how to start a Ministry Training Institute by attending a Teacher Intensive and DWJD Workshop. We schedule them by direct invitation from senior pastors. If you are a pastor and are interested in pursuing ministry training, you are invited to contact the MTI offices. Planning will then begin for training in your region. We would consider it a privilege and an honor to serve pastors of local churches anywhere in the world!

Appendix B

LET'S PRACTICE DOING
WHAT JESUS DID

WE ENCOURAGE THOSE who are followers of Christ to begin putting into practice what He said they could do. The purpose of this book is to help equip believers in Jesus Christ to do what He did. Each chapter presents a different ministry skill that takes some effort to master. When all six ministry skills are mastered, Christians will be very powerful and effective marketplace ministers. We strongly recommend completing the assignments in this final section of Doing What Jesus Did.

> Do not merely listen to the word, and so deceive yourselves. Do what it says.
>
> —JAMES 1:22

First Step: *Decide* to learn the skills *as an individual*, working with another Christian or to learn the skills in *a group* study.

Second Step: *Do it!*

Doing what Jesus did for individuals

* Find another person to read and discuss this book with you. Agree to meet on a regular basis and practice what is presented in each chapter.

* Attempt to complete the ministry skill assignments for each chapter.

* When the assignment refers to a group, apply it to the two of you.

* If you find a portion of the chapter difficult, be honest and admit your feelings. Study the supporting scriptures to see if you can believe what it is telling you to do.

- Keep reading, praying for the Lord's help, and attempting to practice what is recommended.

- Finally, attempt to exercise the ministry skills in the marketplace.

Doing what Jesus did for group study

- Pray for a group leader to assume the responsibility of a *weekly* study group.

- Plan to spend two months or more discussing this book, allowing a minimum of one week in each chapter.

- Each person should obtain a copy of this book and prepare to do the weekly assignment for each chapter in Appendix B.

- One or two people should prepare to fulfill the ministry skill assignment each week. The others should critique how well they shared or demonstrated the ministry skills by offering constructive comments and positive feedback.

- Make time to pray for those who need prayer at the end of each meeting. This is especially important during the study of chapters 4, 5, and 6.

- Always end the study by thanking and praising God for what happened.

- Finally, each person should attempt to exercise the ministry skills in the marketplace and report to the group what happened.

INTRODUCTION

Share What You Believe About Miracles

THE PURPOSE OF this assignment is to prepare believers to share what they believe the Bible says about miracles. This exercise will give an opportunity for Christians who have never shared with others to do so. There is great joy that comes with sharing your beliefs about Christ and what He has done for us. Talking about miracles may seem difficult at first, but it will become easier once we have done it with other Christians. The Holy Spirit is always with us to help us. This introductory assignment will better prepare Christians to gain the confidence to complete the remaining assignments.

How to share what you believe about miracles

- Read the introduction of this book.

- Take time to put in writing your beliefs and conclusions from the pages of the introduction of this book. Make notes regarding what the Scripture references mean to you personally.

- Prepare and share a three-to-five minute talk on what you believe about miracles and what the Bible says about miracles happening today.

- Share about miracles you have witnessed or experienced. Share how they affected your life.

- Ask for feedback and constructive comments that may help you share more effectively in the future.

Preparation

- Make a short outline of what you want to share.

- Organize it according to the points in the introduction of this book.

- Practice your talk, and time yourself.

- Avoid rambling and providing too much detail. Five minutes will go very fast, so keep an eye on your watch.

- Remember that others will also have to do this assignment.

- Use humor if it applies.

- Have fun.

- Relax!

LEADING PEOPLE TO CHRIST

Sharing your story of how you came to Christ

READ CHAPTER 1 and prepare a five-minute story of how you came to know Jesus Christ personally. Use the recommendations in this chapter to help you prepare by using the five discussion points below. Practice your story at home before sharing with the group. Remember to keep it simple by telling what happened as outlined below:

- Tell who you were and the circumstances in your life prior to coming to Christ.
- Tell what caused you to look to God.
- Tell what happened when you surrendered.
- Tell what is happening now.
- End your story with a simple (role-play) invitation for those listening to receive Jesus Christ. Say something like, "He did all this for me, and He will do it for you, too. Would you like to ask Jesus Christ into your life now? I'll help you do it."

When people respond, ask them to pray the following prayer with you:

Jesus Christ, come into my life. I repent of all my sin. Forgive me for what I've said and done that were wrong. I receive You as my Savior and Lord. Thank You for forgiving me. Amen.

After you gain confidence by practicing sharing your story with fellow believers, pray for opportunities to share your story with pre-Christians. The Lord will give you many opportunities.

LEADING CHRISTIANS INTO THE HOLY SPIRIT BAPTISM

Sharing what the experience means to you

THE PURPOSE OF this assignment is to prepare believers to share how God is using them since they were baptized in the Holy Spirit. This assignment will also open opportunities to lead other believers into the Holy Spirit baptism. At the end of sharing, give an invitation (role-play) for those listening to allow you to pray with them to receive the Holy Spirit baptism.

- Read chapter 2 and prepare to share your experiences with the Holy Spirit.

- Prepare a short outline so you can share a five-minute talk on how God is using you since you were baptized in the Holy Spirit.

- Start by sharing the events leading up to your being baptized in the Holy Spirit and how it has made a difference in serving the Lord and ministering to others. Did it help your prayer life? Did it help you witness to others?

- Continue by giving some personal examples of how God has used you to demonstrate His power and how you have helped others since being baptized in the Holy Spirit.

- Finish your talk by encouraging believers to receive the gift of the Holy Spirit. Say:
  The Holy Spirit desires to empower all of us to be better witnesses. I would like to pray with anyone desiring to be baptized in the Holy Spirit. If you want this gift now, I would love to pray with you.

- Pray with those responding:
  Jesus, baptize me in the Holy Spirit. Fill me with Your power so I can be a better witness for You. Thank You, Lord. I have received. Help me now to release my spiritual language. Amen.

- Continue to minister until all release their spiritual languages (role-play).

- Practice your talk and time yourself. The time goes very fast, so keep an eye on your watch.

- Have fun! Remember that others in your group have to do this assignment, too. Relax!

LEARNING HOW TO HEAL THE SICK

Sharing what you believe about divine healing and offering to pray for the sick

READ CHAPTER 3 and prepare to deliver a five-minute message. Include the following:

- What the Bible says about divine healing
- What you believe about divine healing
- Offer of prayer for anyone who needs healing

Prepare to share your message with the people in your group by using the following suggestions:

- Refer to a concordance and select up to five scriptures that promise healing and include them in a short outline.
- Include key phrases in your outline about what you believe about healing; include testimonies you have about healing in your own life.
- End your story with an invitation for listeners to be prayed for at the end of the sharing time. Be prepared to pray for those needing healing.

Praying for the sick: It is recommended that prayer for the sick be offered to all who are not feeling well at the end of each meeting, just after the sharing time. Those who shared should be the ones to pray for the sick.

Reason for this assignment: Jesus said believers in Him would be able to do the things that He did, including healing the sick. This assignment gives new ministers opportunities to express what they believe and to pray for those who need healing. Mark 16:20 says, "The Lord worked with them and confirmed his word by the signs that accompanied it." Let us give the Lord the opportunity to do that.

HEARING FROM GOD

Do what He says

READ CHAPTER 4 and prayerfully prepare your mind and heart prior to meeting together. The day prior to the weekly meeting, each person should read and meditate in three to five chapters from the New Testament with pen and paper in hand. Say to the Holy Spirit, "Please cause me to see, understand, and record the fresh insights You want me to know from Your Word today."

People should pray in their spiritual languages as they meditate in the Bible. They should record anything and everything they are inspired to write during this time with the Lord. This exercise should take thirty minutes to an hour each day. People are to take their notes to the next meeting.

Meet together. Open in prayer, relinquishing control of the meeting to the Holy Spirit. Spend the first part of the meeting sharing what the Holy Spirit revealed during each person's quiet time the past week. All should comment regarding their experiences. Did they hear from the Holy Spirit?

Spend the second part of the meeting praying for people with the most critical needs in their lives:

- Place the people, one at a time, in a chair in the middle of the people gathered.

- Have the person in the chair share the critical need very briefly. Have the person refrain from going into detail.

- Lay hands on the person's shoulder; encourage people to pray in their spiritual languages for a few minutes.

- Encourage each person to participate, allowing the Holy Spirit to spontaneously give answers to the critical need as people pray.

- Limit the number of people with critical prayer needs to no more than two each week. This exercise normally takes a lot of time.

- Conclude in thanksgiving and praise for what God did.

- End on time.

HEALING THE SICK BY REVELATION

READ CHAPTER 5 and prepare to meet together. Continue the weekly quiet time assignment from chapter 4 by having each person read and meditate in several chapters from the New Testament, with pen and paper in hand. Say to the Holy Spirit, "Please cause me to see, understand, and record the fresh insights You want me to know from Your Word today."

People should pray daily in their spiritual languages as they meditate in the Bible, recording everything they are inspired to write during this time. They should attempt to increase the time to an hour each day for this exercise. People should bring their notes to the next meeting. They should ask the Holy Spirit to lead them to a friend who is in pain or is not feeling well, and try to get that person to the next meeting.

Meet together. Open in prayer, relinquishing control of the meeting to the Holy Spirit. Spend the first part of the meeting sharing what the Holy Spirit revealed during each person's quiet time the past week. Each person should participate.

Spend the second part of the meeting praying for those that are not feeling well or are in pain, allowing the Holy Spirit to reveal how He wants to heal them.

- Have the person sit in a chair in the middle of the gathering. The others should come and lay hands on the person. People should start by praying softly in their spiritual languages, *asking the Holy Spirit to reveal how best to pray.*

- Have each person attempt to hear from the Holy Spirit and pray accordingly.

- After all prayer is complete, encourage the person to share what is happening. Allow the person to be honest and give testimony of what happened.

- Invite the next person needing healing to sit in the "hot seat" and continue as before.

- Encourage those who heard from the Holy Spirit to give a short testimony of how it influenced the way they prayed.

- End the meeting in prayer, thanking and praising God for what happened.

DEALING WITH DEMONS

R EAD CHAPTER 6 and prepare for the weekly meeting. The group leader should notify his or her senior pastor of the purpose for the weekly meetings. Continue the same weekly quiet time assignments outlined for chapters 4 and 5.

People should read and meditate daily on a series of chapters from the New Testament, with pen and paper in hand as they pray in tongues. They should pray and ask the Lord to reveal insights from the Word and then record their thoughts. People should take their notes to the next meeting. They should ask the Lord to lead them to a Christian friend who is experiencing severe bondage, spiritual confusion, or attacks from the enemy.

Interview the friend thoroughly to make sure that the person has repented of all sin that may have caused the problem. (This assumes the person wants to be set free.) Call the group leader and schedule the person for the next available meeting. Do not schedule more than two people for each meeting.

The group leader should *notify the senior pastor* of the church where the friend attends, explaining how the group intends to minister; offer to report the results of the ministry. The group leader should also *keep his or her pastor aware of what is happening* in the weekly meetings.

Meet together. Open in prayer, relinquishing control of the meeting to the Holy Spirit. Spend the first part of the meeting sharing what the Holy Spirit revealed during each person's quiet time the past week.

Spend the second part of the meeting ministering to the one or two guests that are experiencing spiritual difficulties, allowing the Holy Spirit to reveal if spirits are involved.

- Have the person sit in a chair in the middle of the gathering, while the others lay hands on him or her. People should start by praying softly in their spiritual languages, asking the Holy Spirit to reveal the source of the person's problem.

- Explain that the *goal is to discern the presence of spirits.* If there is *no confirming evidence* that spirits are the source of the problem, the group leader should not allow the manufacturing of something that is not revealed by the Holy Spirit.

- Minister according to the recommendations in chapter 6 if spirits are the source of the problem.

- Ask the person after all prayer is complete, "What did the Lord do for you tonight?" Allow the person to be honest and give testimony about what happened.

- Invite the next person needing ministry to sit in the "hot seat" for ministry.

- Encourage those who prayed and truly discerned the source of the problem to give a short testimony to how the discernment manifested and how it helped them to minister.

- End the meeting in prayer, thanking and praising God for what happened.

- Notify the senior pastor's office of each guest's home church of what happened.

NOTES

CHAPTER 2
LEADING CHRISTIANS INTO THE HOLY SPIRIT BAPTISM

1. Vinson Synan, *The Holiness Pentecostal Tradition* (Grand Rapids, MI: Wm. B. Eerdmans Publishing Co., 1997).

APPENDIX A:
HOW TO ESTABLISH A MINISTRY TRAINING INSTITUTE

1. Ibid, 12.

ABOUT THE AUTHORS

JOHN AND SONJA DECKER are ordained international teachers and evangelists with the International Church of the Foursquare Gospel. Their book *Doing What Jesus Did* and curriculum *The Ambassador Series* are being used worldwide to equip Christians to do the work of the ministry. To date, they have ministered and taught in over 40 countries. They reside in Bend, Oregon.

CONTACT THE AUTHOR

To contact John and Sonja Decker:

E-mail:
decker@bendbroadband.com

Regular mail:
2602 NW Pilot View Ct. Bend, OR 97701

To schedule a Teacher Intensive and DWJD Workshop:
www.ministrytraining.org

To order additional copies of *Doing What Jesus Did:*

Telephone:
541.593.7774

Online:
www.ministrytraining.org